evidence for GOD

evidence for GOD

50 Arguments for **Faith** from the **Bible**, **History**, **Philosophy**, and **Science**

Edited by

WILLIAM A. DEMBSKI
MICHAEL R. LICONA

a division of Baker Publishing Group
Grand Rapids, Michigan

Published by Baker Books
a division of Baker Publishing Group
P.O. Box 6287, Grand Rapids, MI 49516-6287
www.bakerbooks.com

Printed in the United States of America

Library of Congress Cataloging-in-Publication Data
Evidence for God : 50 arguments for faith from the bible, history, philosophy, and science / edited by William A. Dembski, Michael R. Licona.
p. cm.
Includes bibliographical references.
ISBN 978-0-8010-7260-4 (pbk.)
1. God (Christianity). 2. God—Proof. 3. Apologetics. I. Dembski, William A., 1960– II. Licona, Mike, 1961–
BT103.E95 2010
239—dc22 2010005990

10 11 12 13 14 15 16 7 6 5 4 3 2 1

To all teachers of Christian apologetics
May their numbers multiply

Contents

Introduction

In the spring semester of 2003, Derrick McCarson began his college experience at the University of North Carolina at Chapel Hill. A committed Christian, Derrick enrolled in a course titled "Introduction to the New Testament." On the first day of class, he was surprised to see that nearly five hundred students had enrolled in the same class. The professor, Bart Ehrman, walked in and started abruptly, "I'd like to see a show of hands. How many Bible-believing Christians do we have in the auditorium today? Come on. Don't be bashful." After about a half dozen students raised their hands, Ehrman said, "That's good. It looks like we have a few Christians here today. Welcome to Intro to the New Testament. My goal this semester will be to change everything you Christians think you know about the Bible and about Jesus."

Similar actions have occurred and continue to occur in a number of universities across North America. Students have likewise told us of atheist professors who have informed their Christian students on the first day of class that their goal was for them to give up their faith by the end of the semester.

The ideological war glimpsed here goes beyond the usual political controversies in the U.S. between liberals and conservatives. It even goes beyond the battle between religion and secularism—it is focused against evangelical Christians. A 2007 report by Tobin and Weinberg published by the Institute for Jewish and Community Research reveals that American faculty "overwhelmingly assert[ed] their desire to see Christian influence lessened" while being "far less critical and even supportive of increasing Muslim religious influence in politics." They added that "it is interesting and even perplexing to see a shared inclination among faculty atheists, those faculty with no religion, and those faculty for whom religion holds no importance: They defend the right of Muslims to express their religious beliefs in American politics, while holding openly hostile views of fundamentalist Christians."[1] And for such faculty, any evangelical Christian is an unthinking bigot and therefore a fundamentalist.

The researchers added that "the most troubling finding in the survey" was that American faculty "feel less positively about Evangelicals than about any other religious group." The survey responses showed that evangelical faculty were perceived as few to nonexistent, that Muslims were much more likely to find support when advocating their religious beliefs on the American political scene, and that tolerance, though regarded as a virtue when applied to other religious groups, was regarded as inappropriate when applied to evangelical Christians. According to the researchers, these findings raise "serious concerns about how Evangelical Christian faculty and students are treated or feel they are treated on campus."[2]

This bias against evangelical Christian students might give some a reason to wring their hands. We see it as an opportunity. Indeed, on many college campuses, this can be turned to evangelicals' advantage. After all, Christians are called to defend their faith (1 Pet. 3:15). And in defending the faith, we have the opportunity to share it. Unfortunately, many of our churches have failed to prepare their young people for the task. As a result, many Christians are unaware that philosophy, science, and history all provide abundant evidence that the Christian God exists and that he has powerfully revealed himself to humanity in the person of Jesus of Nazareth.

This book contains fifty articles written by leading scholars and scientists. They give scientific arguments that reveal how the universe and life itself are the products of a Designer of immense intelligence and power. They give philosophical arguments that reveal the goodness, transcendence, and eternity of the Designer. They give historical arguments that reveal how the Designer visited earth in Jesus of Nazareth two thousand years ago. (It's no accident that before embarking on his ministry, Jesus made his living as a designer, specifically, as a carpenter.)

Additional articles in this book address questions such as why an all-good and all-powerful God has allowed evil and suffering and whether Jesus is the only way to God. Still more articles may be found in a number of languages at http://www.4truth.net. This book is not intended as a comprehensive defense of the Christian faith but as a springboard into the exciting and fruitful field of Christian apologetics. Christian students who must deal with iconoclasts like Ehrman will find much in these pages to refresh their souls and satisfy their minds.

Section One

The Question of Philosophy

1

The Cosmological Argument

David Beck

The term "cosmological argument" (hereafter CA) refers to a whole cluster of arguments or patterns of thinking, all of which draw the common conclusion that God is real based on observations that things we see around us cannot exist unless something or someone else makes them exist. Diamonds, dandelions, dromedaries, and davebecks: none of them can exist apart from a whole range of surrounding factors and causes. This argument says that we must think of God as the originating cause, or the initiating source of things and events, because there cannot be an infinite series of things that make the things around us exist.

Arguments like this seem to be present in every culture and religion. Ancient Greek philosophers Plato and Aristotle developed it into clear form. Christian, Jewish, and Islamic traditions all know it. It can be found in African, Buddhist, and Hindu expressions as well.

Within Western traditions, the best known version is the brief statement of Thomas Aquinas found in chapter 15 of the *Summa contra gentiles*. Here he says, "We see things in the world that can exist and can also not exist. Now everything that can exist has a cause. But one cannot go on ad infinitum in causes. . . . Therefore one must posit something the existing of which is necessary."[1]

As I see it, there are three basic steps in this argument.

Step 1: What We Observe and Experience in Our Universe Is Contingent

Note that this is an observation about the things we actually see and know in the real world around us. It is not intended to be about everything in the universe, only what we have actually experienced. The key word in this sentence is "contingent." In this context, this means that something owes its existence to something else; it does not exist by itself. It needs a cause. And everything we know anything about is contingent.

So the universe consists of series and networks of causes, which are in turn connected into whole systems of causes. That is, *a* is caused by *b*, but only as *b* is caused by *c*, and so on. Everything we know exists and functions only as it is caused by other factors in its causal chain. We know of nothing that spontaneously initiates its own causal activity. (Note that nothing here turns on our having to know about everything. Even if something did turn out to spontaneously initiate, it would have no effect on CA.)

Step 2: A Network of Causally Dependent Contingent Things Cannot Be Infinite

The idea here is that regardless of how complex and interconnected it might be the series or system of causally related contingent things cannot be infinite. Thomas uses the illustration of a hand moving a stick, which in turn is moving a ball. Perhaps the most frequently used picture in recent discussions is the train.

Imagine you are seeing for the first time a train moving past you. Baffled, you wonder what is causing the boxcar to move. You come to realize that it is being pulled by another boxcar in front of it, and so on, down the tracks beyond your view.

This picture allows us to visualize the various atheist scenarios, so commonly heard in our society, that attempt to describe how it is that things exist in our universe. "The cosmos is a great circle of life," we are told. But if we were to connect the boxcars all the way around the universe in a circle until the last one hooks up to the first, that will still not explain the motion of even the first boxcar, let alone any of the others. If contingent things cause each other to exist in a circle, there is still nothing to initiate the casual process. The atheist offers perhaps a more promising scenario: "The cosmos is an intricately evolved ecosystem in which everything is related causally to everything else." So boxcars clutter the universe in an unimaginably complex system of railroading such that in some way every boxcar is coupled to every other one and therefore *every* boxcar is pulling that first one. Still, we have no accounting for the motion of that first boxcar. Likewise, the notion of an evolving ecosystem does not account for the existence of any actual thing in our universe.

It is always tempting, of course, to say that it is enough to know that each boxcar is being pulled by the boxcar in front of it. In one sense it is clearly true that boxcar *a* is pulled by boxcar *b*. But *b* can pull *a* only because *c* is pulling *b* at the same time. The pulling action of *b* is transferred from *c*. And so it is also true that *a* is being pulled by *c*. The same is true, of course, about *d*, and about *e*, and so on. In practice, it is enough to know that AIDS is caused by HIV, but it is sometimes important and always possible to keep asking the questions if we really want to understand our reality.

One last option suggests itself. Suppose that there are just infinite boxcars or, as the atheist might say, "The intricacy of the universe is lost in infinite complexity." But infinite boxcars, no matter how complex their arrangement, still leave unexplained why our first boxcar is moving and hence why any of them are. Letting the questions of cause go to infinity fails to explain anything at all.

Step 3: A Network of Causally Dependent Contingent Things Must Be Finite

This last idea simply draws the obvious conclusion from step 2. If the network cannot be infinite, then it must be finite. No other option remains, unless one wanted to argue that nothing actually exists. But that is not a rational option.

Conclusion: There Must Be a First Cause in the Network of Contingent Causes

If the causal sequence is finite then by definition there must be a first cause. This concept of "first cause" obviously contains two ideas. If it is the *first* cause then it neither requires nor has a cause of itself. First is first! So it is fundamentally different from every other cause in the series. It depends on, is limited by, or exists because of absolutely nothing else. It truly initiates causality.

On the other hand, to say of the conclusion that it is the first *cause* is to define its relation to everything else in the network: it is the cause of all of them. It initiates all of the causal activity without negating the fact that each subsequent cause is itself a cause of the following one in the series.

To switch back to our train analogy, the only explanation for the moving boxcars is that somewhere there is a locomotive with the capacity to pull the entire train. The notion of "first cause" is richer than it might at first appear. It is always the case that there are two correct answers to the question of what is causing the existence of something. The immediate cause or causes as well as the first cause are equally correct answers. Both the locomotive and the boxcar in front of boxcar *a*, namely *b*, are the cause of the motion of *b*.

Some Objections

Atheists typically bring four kinds of objections to this argument. The first and certainly the most frequent criticism of CA is the "It's not God" objection. What the conclusion delivers is only a vague and undefined first cause: an initiating source of the universe. This may just be the Big Bang, elementary particles, energy state, or even an original vacuum. In any case, the conclusion does not deliver an infinite creator God who is personal and relational.

In response we could vote that what CA does give us, after all, is a first and uncaused cause. This is already enough to defeat atheistic naturalism, which holds that the universe is a complex causal system existing on its own, purely by chance, without any external source, and consisting of only natural and finite components. The argument demonstrates that there is at least one non-contingent component.

On the other hand, if the objection is that the conclusion is too "small," that God is so much more, then we should just agree. It certainly tells us only a little about God. Those who use this objection often seem to suppose that unless we know *everything* about God then we do not know anything. This is obviously false. We know much about many things without knowing everything about any of them.

A second objection is the "Infinite series are possible" claim. CA depends on a denial of an infinite series of causes. Yet the sequence of cardinal numbers, as we all learned in elementary school, is infinite. Since we can assign a cardinal number to each member of a causal sequence, we then have an infinite sequence of causes.

This objection overlooks the specifics of the network of causes in CA. It has four critical characteristics:

1. It is a system, an interconnected network of causes and effects
2. Each cause is contingent; each one itself needs a cause
3. The dependency in the Aristotelian/Thomistic CA is concurrent not chronological; it refers to concurrent dependency relations (think of the moving train analogy!) within a system of causes
4. The specific relation to which the general CA refers is the causing of *existence* itself

The key point in CA is that there cannot be an infinite series of causes with all four of the above characteristics. This is not to say that there could not be infinite series of other kinds, including some very similar ones, such as chronological sequences of causes in time (such as a series of parent/child relationships). However, there cannot be an infinite series of *contingent* things.

A third typical objection is the "We do not know about the whole universe" contention. We have no way of knowing that everything is contingent. The simplest way to answer this is to admit that it is true. Obviously we do not know about everything in the universe. However, the conclusion holds regardless. What the argument shows is that if there is something that is contingent, then there must be something that is not.

Initially this might seem to leave the possibility of multiple gods. Granted, CA by itself does not eliminate that option. However, as Aquinas learned from Aristotle (and as Parmenides understood much earlier), there can only be a single uncaused or infinite being. A second infinite being would have to be different from the first in some way, but one infinite being cannot be either more or less than another. We all learned early on that infinity minus or plus anything is still infinity. So there can only be one infinite being.

A fourth objection is the "What caused God?" counter. If the universe is a network of causes and effects, then you cannot arbitrarily stop at some point and just call it "God." This, however, simply misses the whole point of the argument. The CA shows that a series of contingents must be finite: it must eventually lead to a non-contingent. It would be nonsense to ask what causes this first uncaused cause. So this objection simply fails to understand the argument.

In conclusion, it is worth pointing out two things. First, this is of course a very brief and overly simplified discussion of an argument with a long and diverse history, about which many books have already been written. This has hardly done it justice. Second, this argument opens up a wealth of additional conclusions that follow from the concept of non-contingency. Together, they round out a much fuller concept of God not apparent in the simple CA itself. Both of these points encourage a fuller study of CA. But what this argument does show is that we cannot make sense of the universe, the reality in which we live, apart from there being a real God.

2

The Moral Argument for God's Existence

Paul Copan

Philosopher John Rist is right: there is "widely admitted to be a crisis in contemporary Western debate about ethical foundations."[1] It seems that, ultimately, the crisis is the result of approaching ethics without reference to God. When morality is severed from its theological roots, secular ethics cannot sustain itself—it withers and dies.

I can only sketch out a brief defense of the connection between God and objective moral values (which I have done more extensively elsewhere).[2] I will argue that if objective moral values exist, then God exists; objective moral values do exist; therefore, God exists. To resolve our ethics crisis, we must recognize the character of a good God (in whose image valuable humans have been made) as the necessary foundation of ethics, human rights, and human dignity.

Objective Moral Values Exist: They Are Properly Basic

Moral values exist whether or not a person or culture believes them ("objective"). Normally functioning human beings take these for granted as basic to their well-being and flourishing.

Humans do not have to find out what is moral by reading the Bible. Such knowledge is available to all people. Romans 2:14–15 says that those without God's special revelation (Scripture, Jesus Christ) can know right from wrong. They have God's general revelation of his basic moral law in their conscience, "Gentiles who do not have the Law [of Moses] do instinctively the things of the Law" (Rom. 2:14 NASB). No wonder. They have been made in the image of God (Gen. 1:26–27). They're constituted to function properly when they live according to God's design. So people (including atheists) whose hearts have not been hardened or self-deceived will have the same sorts of moral instincts as Christians—that rape or adultery or torturing babies for fun is wrong, and kindness is good.

When a person says, "Maybe murder or rape isn't really wrong," he does not need an argument. He is self-deceived. If he really believes this, he needs spiritual or psychological help because he is just not functioning properly. Even relativists who claim that someone's values may be true for one person but not for others are likely the same people who say, "I have rights," or "You ought to be tolerant." But rights and tolerance do not make any sense if relativism is correct. Rather, they entail that objective moral values exist.

Just as we generally trust our sense perceptions as reliable (unless there is good reason to doubt them), we should treat general moral intuitions (aversion to torturing babies for fun, rape, murder) as innocent until proven guilty. Why do we trust our five senses? Most of us find they are regularly reliable. Even if we misperceive things once in a while, we are wise to pay attention to our senses rather than consistently doubt them. Similarly, we have basic moral instincts—for example, a revulsion at taking innocent human life or of raping (the "*Yuck* factor"), or an inward affirmation regarding self-sacrifice for the well-being of our children (the "*Yes* factor"). The burden of proof falls on those denying or questioning basic moral principles. We are wise to pay attention to these basic moral instincts—even if these intuitions need occasional fine-tuning.

Morally sensitive humans can get the basics right regarding morality. In the appendix of C. S. Lewis's book *The Abolition of Man*,[3] he lists various virtues that have been accepted across the ages and civilizations (for example, Greek, Egyptian, Babylonian, Native American, Indian, Hebrew). Stealing and murder are condemned in these law codes while honoring parents and keeping marriage vows are applauded.

Some might argue: Aren't there moral conflicts as well? Some cultures permit polygamy, for instance. Yes, but marriage customs and vows that bind marriages together also prohibit adultery. While *applications* and *expressions* of moral principles may differ from culture to culture, there are basic moral principles that cut across cultural lines. What happens when we encounter (at least on the face of it) conflicting moral principles? We start with morally clear cases and work to the unclear. In light of apparent moral conflict, it would be a faulty jump to conclude that morality is relative. As lexicographer Samuel Johnson put it, "The fact that there is such a thing as twilight does not mean that we cannot distinguish between day and night."

Moral principles are discovered, not invented. Moral reforms (abolishing slavery, advocating women's suffrage, promoting civil rights for blacks) make no sense unless objective moral values exist. Even if creating the atmosphere for reform may take time (even centuries), this does not imply that morality evolves during human history and is just a human invention. Rather, it more readily suggests that moral principles can be discovered and are worth pursuing, even at great cost.

Atheist philosopher Kai Nielsen acknowledges this point: "It is more reasonable to believe such elemental things [wife beating, child abuse] to be evil than to believe any skeptical theory that tells us we cannot know or reasonably believe any of these things to be evil. . . . I firmly believe that this is bedrock and right and that anyone who does not believe it cannot have probed deeply enough into the grounds of his moral beliefs."[4]

God and Objective Morality Are Closely Connected

It is not unusual to hear, "Atheists can be good without God." Atheist Michael Martin argues that theists give the same reasons as atheists for condemning rape: it violates the victim's rights and damages society. What Martin really means is that atheists can be good without believing in God, but they would not be good (have intrinsic worth or moral responsibility) without God (indeed, nothing would exist without him); that is, because humans are made in God's image, they can know what is good even if they do not believe in God. Atheists and theists can affirm the same values, but theists can ground belief in human rights and dignity because we are all made in the image of a supremely valuable being.

Just think about it: Intrinsically valuable, thinking persons do not come from impersonal, nonconscious, unguided, valueless processes over time. A personal, self-aware, purposeful, good God provides the natural and necessary context for the existence of valuable, rights-bearing, morally responsible human persons. That is, personhood and morality are necessarily connected; moral values are rooted in personhood. Without God (a personal being), no persons—and thus no moral values—would exist at all: *no personhood, no moral values*. Only if God exists can moral properties be realized.

Nontheistic Ethical Theories Are Incomplete and Inadequate

Some secularists would suggest that we can have ethical systems that make no reference to God (e.g., Aristotle, Kant). However, while they may make some very positive contributions to ethical discussion (regarding moral virtue/character or universal moral obligations), their systems are still incomplete. They still do not tell us why human beings have intrinsic value, rights, and moral obligations.

What about naturalistic evolutionary ethics, in which we develop an awareness of right or wrong and moral obligation to help us survive and reproduce? Ethical awareness has only biological worth.[5] Such an approach leaves us with the following problems: First, can we even trust our minds if we are nothing more than the products of naturalistic evolution, trying to fight, feed, flee, and reproduce? Charles Darwin had a "horrid doubt" that since the human mind has developed from lower animals, why would anyone trust it? Why trust the convictions of a monkey's mind?[6] The naturalistic evolutionary process is interested in fitness and survival—not in true belief; so not only is objective morality undermined, rational thought is as well. Our beliefs—including moral ones—may help us *survive*, but there is no reason to think they are *true*. Belief in objective morality or human dignity may help us survive, but it may be completely false. The problem with skepticism (including moral skepticism) is that I am assuming a trustworthy reasoning process to arrive at the conclusion that I cannot trust my reasoning! If we trust our rational and moral faculties, we will assume a theistic outlook: being made in the image of a truthful, rational, good Being makes sense of why we trust our senses and moral intuitions.

In addition, we are left with this problem: if human beings are simply the product of naturalistic evolution, then we have no foundation for moral obligation and human dignity. This could easily undermine moral motivation. The sexual predator and cannibal Jeffrey Dahmer acknowledged the seriousness of the matter: "If it all happens naturalistically, what's the need for a God? Can't I set my own rules? Who owns me? I own myself."[7]

To further reinforce the point, a number of atheists and skeptics have noted the God-morality connection. The late atheist philosopher J. L. Mackie said that moral properties are "queer" given naturalism: "If there are objective values, they make the existence of a god more probable than it would have been without them. Thus we have a defensible argument from morality to the existence of a god."[8] Agnostic Paul Draper observes, "A moral world is very probable on theism."[9]

As the Declaration of Independence asserts, humans are "endowed by their Creator with certain unalienable rights." This good Creator is the true foundation of ethics and the ultimate hope of rescuing it from its present crisis.

3

Near Death Experiences

Evidence for an Afterlife?

Gary R. Habermas

Accounts of near death experiences (hereafter NDEs) are by no means restricted to recent times; along with similar phenomena, they have been reported throughout history. Yet they have commanded far more interest in the last few decades. Many readers appear to be enamored of the supernatural sound of the reports themselves: claims of floating above one's dying body, traveling down a dark tunnel, encountering or even being welcomed by a loving being of light, perhaps meeting deceased loved ones, hearing beautiful sounds and seeing wonderful colors, and then afterward losing the fear of death.

What about the Evidence?

For many, these phenomena alone are enough to account for the widespread interest in NDEs. But critics sometimes charge that even similar sightings such as these may indicate nothing more than the presence of common brain chemistry among humans. Perhaps this is simply what happens to the human brain when it nears a state of personal and final extinction.

However, some NDE reports are accompanied by evidential claims. In these cases, the dying persons report data that can often be verified. The closer the individual is to death and the more detailed the evidential report, the more able the experience is to answer subjective claims like those regarding common brain physiology.

For example, in dozens of NDE accounts, the dying person claims that, precisely during their emergency, they actually observed events that were subsequently confirmed. These observations may have occurred in the emergency room when the individual was in no condition to be observing what was going on around them. Sometimes the data are reported from a distance away from the scene and actually may not have been observable from the individual's location even if they had been healthy, with the normal use of their senses.

In more evidential cases, the dying person reported their observations during extended periods of time without any heartbeat. On rare occasions, no brain activity was present in the individual either. Further, blind persons have also given accurate descriptions of their surroundings, even when they had never seen anything either before or since.

One well-documented case involved a little girl who had very nearly drowned, and who did not register a pulse for nineteen minutes. Her emergency room physician, pediatrician Melvin Morse, states that he "stood over Katie's lifeless body in the intensive care unit." An emergency CAT scan indicated that Katie had massive brain swelling, no gag reflex, and was "profoundly comatose." Morse notes that, "When I first saw her, her pupils were fixed and dilated, meaning that irreversible brain damage had most likely occurred." Her breathing was done by an artificial lung machine. She was given very little chance of surviving.

But then, just three days later, Katie unexpectedly made a full recovery. In fact, when she revived, she reproduced an amazing wealth of information regarding the emergency room, specific details of her resuscitation, along with physical descriptions of the two physicians who worked on her. All this occurred while she was completely comatose and most likely without any brain function whatsoever. As Morse recounts, "A child with Katie's symptoms should have the absence of any brain function and therefore should comprehend nothing."

It took her almost an hour to recall all the recent details. However, part of the story made no sense in usual medical terms. Katie related that during her comatose state, she was visited by an angel named Elizabeth, who allowed her to look in on her family at home. Katie correctly reported very specific details concerning what her siblings were doing, even identifying a popular rock song that her sister listened to, watched her father, and then observed as her mom cooked a meal that she correctly identified: roast chicken and rice. She described the clothing and positions of her family members. Later, she shocked her parents by telling them these details that had occurred only a few days before.[1]

How can someone possibly recall such confirmed details in an emergency room as well as at a distance, especially with no known brain activity? Attempts have been made to provide natural explanations of these NDE accounts. Medical factors like oxygen deprivation or temporal lobe seizures have been suggested, as have psychological causes such as hallucinations or faulty memory. However, in addition to the medical and other shortcomings in each case, each of these subjective approaches shares at least one major, common problem: because they deal with internal conditions relative to the individual, they are unable to account for particular observations of the external sort just mentioned, where evidential reports are confirmed. This is especially the case when the evidence occurs a distance away.

For instance, internal brain states cannot explain or produce accurate descriptions of events, particularly highly detailed ones in other areas. Neither can they explain the ability of blind individuals to report their surroundings. The instances where the person's heart and/or brain is not operating increases the inability of the natural explanation to account adequately for the phenomena in question.

NDEs from a Christian Perspective

Do NDEs conflict with biblical beliefs? Actually, near-death phenomena may be reported in the Bible. For example, in Jesus's story of the rich man and Lazarus, we are told that the beggar Lazarus died and was carried by angels into Paradise (Luke 16:22), a brief process that sounds somewhat similar to contemporary reports. Just before being stoned to death, Stephen, a righteous leader in the early church, saw a vision of the glorified Jesus standing at God's right hand (Acts 7:55–56). Paul explains that he had an experience during which he was unsure whether or not he was out of his body, as he visited "the third heaven" (2 Cor. 12:1–5). Some commentators think that the timing of this event coincides with Paul's being stoned and left for dead during his trip to Lystra (Acts 14:19–20). Paul also experienced several other occasions when he was near death's door (2 Cor. 11:23–25).

Admittedly, some tough questions remain in relation to this topic. For instance, non-Christians have described very positive experiences during near death episodes. Rarely do they mention judgment.

However, since these individuals were not biologically (or irreversibly) dead, but near death, we can hardly ascertain their eternal state of existence in the future. Further, when near-death survivors describe what they often take to be their experiences of heaven or hell, they have moved beyond the more mundane reports of events surrounding them on earth. Thus, they are not describing their perception of common, everyday events in their vicinity, as mentioned above, but their personal *interpretations* of another reality altogether.[2] Beyond this, it is crucial to note that in cases where heaven or hell are portrayed, very little *evidence* is ever provided, so verifying their perceptions would be exceptionally difficult. For the record, however, exceptionally negative, even ghastly experiences,[3] including graphic visions of hellfire, have also been reported during NDEs.

What about NDE reports with occultic or satanic content? Undeniably, such aspects are sometimes described, and caution is definitely necessary. But there appears to be nothing inherently occultic about the actual NDEs themselves. These persons simply recount their perceptions during their very difficult times. After all, what do Christians expect to occur immediately after death? Further, many of those who report occultic or satanic phenomena are Christian with no previous occult involvement. Even though these experiences appear to be supernatural, they are not thereby automatically occultic. Besides, if we are correct, similar experiences seem to be reported in Scripture (examples include Luke 16 and 2 Corinthians 12). Therefore, it seems that, as in life as a whole, some experiences are occultic and most others are not.

To be sure, tough questions exist with regard to NDEs; much research still needs to be done. While there appear to be solid rejoinders, it should be remembered that there are many highly evidenced cases too.

The Importance of NDE Studies

Studies of NDEs are valuable for a number of reasons. Initially, as human interest stories, they are absolutely fascinating reading; few accounts make better reading. Beyond that, these accounts purport to address what is arguably the principal mystery of life, that of the nature of death and the possibility of an afterlife.

Alternative attempts to explain NDEs naturalistically have not explained especially the evidential cases. As noted, they are especially unable to account for those observations that are reported at a distance, especially in the absence of heart or brain activity. Arguably, these last cases potentially provide some strong evidence for what may happen near the point of death. Although the argument cannot be restated here, I have developed the case elsewhere that NDEs actually evidence at least the initial moments of afterlife.[4]

It would seem that the sort of data that emerge from NDE research make few distinctions between the competing theistic worldviews and do not decide between them. These theistic options presumably would have few serious problems with these arguments. However, such a conclusion regarding the supernatural or an afterlife, if true, would seemingly create havoc for the tenets of naturalism and its claims that this universe composes all of reality. Since they neither abrogate nor set aside the laws of nature, NDEs are not miraculous events. But these occurrences still argue for a supernatural reality beyond this present reality, thereby presenting serious challenges to naturalism. This may be the chief worldview contribution of NDE research.

We have said that tough questions still remain for NDE research. But it appears that these studies can produce well-evidenced data that may be very valuable in ongoing religious and philosophical discussions.

4

Naturalism

A Worldview

L. Russ Bush III

The word *nature* usually refers to the physical world in its normal condition. If something is "natural," that means it is unmodified by human (intelligent) actions. Many of us love "nature," the unspoiled outdoors, the world of forests and rivers and mountains and meadows.

By adding *ism*, however, we get a related but different meaning. "Naturalism" is the belief that in the final analysis, nature is all that there is, and that "nature" is essentially unmodified by anything other than itself. In other words, nature itself is thought to be the ultimate reality.

Nature is dynamic and active, but according to the worldview known as "naturalism," there is nothing beyond nature that has any causal influence or effect on nature. Either there is no God or God has no effect or influence on nature. Some might suggest that nature itself may be thought of as a creative being. Naturalism claims that life on earth arose from natural substances by natural selection for natural ends. There is no reality that can properly be called *super*natural. Spiritual realities, according to naturalism, are either illusions or they are merely complex or unusual natural realities.

Since the eighteenth century, a materialistic philosophy has been gaining influence in the Western world. Previously, most people in the West believed that the world was a divine creation, but naturalistic thinking gradually challenged that view and sought to replace it, first with naturalistic methods and then with a more comprehensive naturalistic philosophy.

Prior to the rise of naturalism as a prominent worldview (or comprehensive mindset), most Western people believed that God had created the world and was responsible for its form and for its very existence. It was understood that God was upholding all things by the word of his power, for in the beginning God had created all things. Since God was a living being, it was logical to expect life in the world, because life comes from life. Twentieth-century naturalism built itself on the idea that the universe (and everything in it, including life itself) came into being because of a natural quantum fluctuation (or by some other strictly natural means) and developed by natural processes from its original natural state to its present natural state. Life arose from nonlife.

Naturalism affirms no God except the god of impersonal, nonliving, undesigned physical chemistry. A natural process of change is essentially random and/or undirected, but natural processes actually seem to "select" some processes and activities in the sense that "better" or stronger ones survive while others perish. Naturalists believe that this unconscious, nondirected "selection" process along with random genetic fluctuations (i.e., mutations) are the keys that explain the origin of the world of living things as we know it today.

Thus the naturalistic worldview is the overall belief that nature itself is all that there is. God did not design it. Intelligence is a result, not a cause, of the natural world. Nature formed itself by strictly natural processes. This claim has several implications.

On the earth there seems to be a host of different conscious personalities. Naturalism by definition says that personality arose (evolved) from the nonpersonal, from that which was matter and energy only. There is nothing in a naturalistic universe that is essentially personal.

Not only must personality have arisen from the nonpersonal, it also supposedly arose spontaneously, without direction or guidance from any personal source. This would appear to violate the natural law of cause and effect. Energy dissipates. Complexity changes by simplifying. No system spontaneously becomes more complex unless additional energy and order are added from outside the system. A "cause" must either contain the "effect" or at least be sufficiently complex to be capable of producing the less complex "effect." Personality, however, is far more complex than the natural chemical and physical order of things observed in nature. How could this be? The naturalist usually assigns such questions to the intellectual dust bin. Personal beings are here (they and you and I exist), and thus naturalists accept that fact regardless of the significant improbability of highly complex and intelligent and self-aware personality naturally arising from the nonpersonal reality of nonintelligent and nonaware matter.

The same with life! Naturalists admit that there is life. But to maintain their naturalism, they argue that nature spontaneously and without direction or external cause produced life out of nonlife. The lack of evidence for and high improbability of this kind of event does not dissuade these thinkers, because (they say) it only had to happen once. In fact the genetic similarity of all life forms leads naturalists to assume that all life must have come from a single simple cell or collection of chemical processes approximating a working cell. This simple cell must have randomly (and without direction or programming) initiated orderly energy usage and replication processes over the years. The chemical activity and physical changes supposedly led to more complex arrangements that then mutated and began to use energy and replicate in new ways. Over time, all living things supposedly arose from those simple and randomly collected natural chemicals, with those ever more complex processes arising randomly and without intelligent design.

This also means that at some late stage of development, rational mental states arose from utterly nonrational precursors. Rational thinking was and is, for naturalists, simply a complex form of natural chemical interactions. Reason was never intended by the natural, nonintelligent process, for intention is a rational characteristic. So intention or purpose could not exist until reason came into being, but naturalism denies that reason existed in the beginning. Reason evolved only at the end of the process. Prior to the appearance of reason, there could only have been substances characterized by nonreason.

This leads us finally to a very important insight. Reason itself, in the naturalistic worldview, is nothing more than the natural and random result of a particular randomly changing original bit of matter. Reason is not really an independent evaluative process that can critique itself. Reason is only what the chemistry allows through self-arrangement and self-organization, and the shaping of logic and rationality and grammatical language is merely a chance result of an undesigned process that has no necessary relation to truth or meaning. All truth could be merely a pragmatically qualified set of ideas. No intrinsic truth would exist, and yet naturalists claim that naturalism itself is true. But how could that claim avoid the inevitable skeptical conclusion? Nothing can be known for sure to be objectively true, for there is no standard other than the chemical pattern one happens to be using at the time. Why should reason be trusted? How could naturalism be known to be true? The answer is: it can't.

Thus naturalism fails to be able to sustain its own truth claim. In fact, all knowledge becomes mere temporary chemical behaviors in the brain, which is a product of meaningless and random chemical processes. You and I are nothing more than two sets of chemical processes temporarily in this present configuration. Nothing can in the traditional sense be true, for there is no objective standard. The human mind is only a temporary effect of a particular set of chemical processes and thus is not a true observer of fact and reality.

Naturalism claims to be the best and most scientific way to seek truth, but it is an extreme case of circular reasoning that has forgotten its objective roots in the knowledge of the world that stands on divine revelation. ("In the beginning God created the heavens and the earth" [Gen. 1:1 NASB].) Only in theism do we have a personal, living, intelligent cause. Only theism has a sufficient explanation of life in the world. God is a necessary being, but this is exactly what naturalism denies. Thus reason is lost. Truth is lost. Knowledge is lost. Meaning is lost.

Naturalism dies of its own success.

5

Suffering for What?

Bruce A. Little

A casual review of church history or regular attendance at a Christian prayer time will leave no doubt of the fact that Christians suffer. In fact, most if not all who read this will have some firsthand experience of some form of suffering. Of course, it is not only Christians who suffer in this world, as the world is filled with suffering. Nevertheless the subject before us is the matter of why Christians in particular suffer. This is not a question about why God allows Christians to suffer, or why Christians suffer at all. Nor are we looking at the question of Christians suffering when disciplined by the Lord (see Heb. 12:3–17). Each of these questions deserves its own answer, but the inquiry here seeks an answer to a different question. The subject before us looks into the different categories of Christian suffering. This is not about identifying some particular experience of suffering such as battling cancer, but rather considering the broad categories into which particular acts of suffering can be placed. The reason for doing this is to see if some of the promises in the Bible regarding suffering apply only to certain categories of suffering. I will argue that there are three such categories: (1) Christians may suffer when they live righteously for God; (2) often, Christians suffer simply because they are part of the human race living in a fallen world; and (3) Christians might suffer when they behave as evildoers.

The Bible does not hide the fact that Christians suffer because they are Christians. Paul reminds Timothy that those who live godly lives will suffer persecution (see 2 Tim. 3:12). Jesus suffered, and we know that the servant is not greater than his Lord (see John 13:16). Even the great chapter in the Bible recording the lives of those who lived by faith tells not only of their great exploits for God (see Heb. 11:1–34) but also the terrible suffering some endured for their faith (see Heb. 11:35–40). Therefore, it is no great surprise that Christians have gone, and continue to go, through difficult times because of doing the Father's will. Jesus, in his Sermon on the Mount, taught that those are blessed who suffer for his righteousness' sake (see Matt. 5:10). Paul speaks of our consolation when we suffer for Christ (see 2 Cor. 1:3–7). Peter mentions how the trial of our faith is more precious than gold, which perishes (see 1 Pet. 1:6–7). Later, Peter says that if we are reproached for the name of Christ, we are blessed (1 Pet. 3:14). James writes, "My brethren, count it all joy when you fall into various trials, knowing that the testing of your faith produces patience" (see James 1:2–3 NKJV).

All these verses clearly refer to suffering for righteousness' sake. Consequently we should consider the blessings associated with suffering for righteousness' sake to apply only to that category of suffering; that is, the promise of blessing when one suffers for righteousness' sake has no application when Christians suffer for wrongdoing or simply because they live in a fallen world. Most of the texts mentioned above affirm a blessedness but do not indicate what form that blessedness takes. However, as those who walk by faith and not by sight, we take God at his word and leave the work of blessing to him as he sees fit.

Another verse deserving attention regarding this matter of suffering for righteousness' sake is Romans 8:28: "And we know that all things work together for good to those who love God, to those who are the called according to His purpose" (NKJV). This verse may very well be the most frequently quoted in times of difficulty. It is quoted when a Christian has a heart attack; it is quoted when a loved one dies or there is a terrible accident. But does this verse really teach that "all things" in every situation work together for good to them that love God? I will argue that, when taken in the context of the entire chapter, "all things" pertains only to those things that happen as a direct result of our living boldly for Christ.

My investigation begins with the first 17 verses of Romans 8. Clearly, the subject is walking in the Spirit and not according to the flesh. Verse 17 speaks of suffering with Jesus that we may also be glorified with him. At this point, the Apostle launches into a discussion of suffering, which is to be understood from verse 17 as suffering resulting from living for Jesus. He tells us how the suffering in this world is not worthy to be compared to the glory that will be revealed in us in that day (see v. 18). From there Paul speaks about how even creation is waiting for that day (see vv. 19–25). Then he speaks of how the Spirit prays for us when we do not know how to pray for ourselves (see vv. 26–27). The context indicates that it is when we suffer for righteousness' sake and we do not know what to pray that the Spirit prays for us according to the Father's will. Paul goes on to say that we know that God is working "all things" together for good to those who love him. So, even though we may not know how to pray, we can still know that when we suffer for righteousness, God is at work on our behalf. The text goes on to give reasons why we should be assured that God is working for our well-being (see vv. 29–35). He actually names some of the particular kinds of suffering Christians were enduring (see v. 35) and then says that this suffering has resulted from living for the Lord—"For Your sake we are killed all day long" (v. 36 NKJV). The conclusion is that "all things" refers to suffering particular to living righteously and not just any kind of suffering. As the chapter closes, Paul concludes by arguing that we should never shrink back from suffering for righteousness' sake because nothing can separate us "from the love of God which is in Christ Jesus our Lord" (v. 39 NKJV). Therefore, I conclude that Romans 8:28 should only be applied to suffering that comes to us because of righteous living. For all those Christians who live righteously, when persecution comes, they can know that God is at work. They can know that he is working on their behalf, and as a result, they will be blessed. In the midst of the suffering, they can know the comfort, grace, and mercy of the heavenly Father.

The second category is suffering that results simply because Christians live in a fallen world. After the fall, things changed on this planet, and pain and suffering settled in on creation. There are convulsions of nature, as seen in earthquakes, tornadoes, and the like. As part of this world, Christians and non-Christians alike are touched by these things. Moreover, evil people do bad things that have negative consequences of varying scope and intensity, and this often affects Christians. We do not escape the brokenness of this world just because we are Christians. Moreover, when we make poor choices, negative consequences for others and us may follow. Furthermore, Christians and non-Christians suffer heart attacks, fight cancer, and lose children to dreadful diseases. The difference is not that Christians are exempt from the suffering of this world that is horribly out of joint, but rather in how they endure their suffering. As with Paul and his thorn in the flesh, God is able to give sufficient grace to sustain those who suffer. It is often the exhibition of this sustaining grace that gives witness to the world of the reality of the Christian's faith in God. How often the suffering saint lying in a hospital has been a testimony of God's grace. However, this suffering is not for righteousness' sake. Therefore, we should not apply the promises that pertain to suffering for righteousness' sake to such situations. What we should do is seek the face of God fervently in prayer for deliverance as he sees fit and then lean on his grace to sustain us through it all. If it comes in the form of healing, then give God thanks. If it is an abundance of grace, then rejoice in him. If it means restoration in some way, then testify to God's providential work. This applies both to those who suffer directly and those close to them who suffer indirectly. God's grace (whatever form it takes) can be a wonderful occasion to witness to the world. Who knows but that through that testimony some might come to faith in Jesus?

The third category of suffering is that which comes to us because we are involved in wrongdoing. If we continue in sin, the disciplining hand of God will be unpleasant (but profitable) for us (see Heb. 12:6–13). In that case, if we confess our sin and turn from it, then the discipline will work the peaceable fruit of righteousness in our lives. On the other hand, and more to the point, maybe we break the civil laws of the state and suffer as an evildoer (see 1 Pet. 4:15). Peter simply says do not suffer as an evildoer. The reason Paul tells us is clear: civil authorities are God's ministers to bring judgment on those who practice evil (see Rom. 13:1–4). When Christians suffer as evildoers, they should not complain but take their punishment. Here there is no promise that all things are working together for good. They should confess their sin so that they might serve their punishment with a God-fearing attitude and be a testimony of repentance and grace as well as to God's forgiveness. Christians should be witnesses for Jesus where they are and under all conditions whatever their punishment might be. In the event some should come to the Savior, it would still be wrong to quote Romans 8:28 to suggest that the good consequences excuse the bad behavior.

Every time we suffer, it is important to know why we are suffering. Undoubtedly, sometimes it may not be clear to others, but it should be clear to us. Once we have determined why we are suffering, we should respond accordingly. If we are suffering for righteousness' sake, then we may rejoice. If our suffering comes from the brokenness of this world, may we find comfort in the sufficiency of his grace as we bring our prayers to his throne. Should it be that we suffer as an evildoer, then we need to confess and repent of our sin and accept our punishment as an obedient Christian. Let us all be careful about which verses from the Bible we quote in order to encourage others or ourselves when faced with suffering. Different promises for and responsibilities in suffering attend different categories of suffering. May we exercise discernment when applying promises in situations of suffering. The fact is, in all three categories, God can clearly work in our lives as well as in circumstances beyond us. Yet only when we suffer for righteousness' sake should we apply the promise of blessing. In all other suffering we must yield to the grace of God, assured that it is always sufficient.

6

Responding to the Argument from Evil

Three Approaches for the Theist

David Wood

A few weeks ago, my five-year-old son, Lucian, came up with his first argument against the existence of God. He reasoned that, since God can't be seen, God must not exist. Put more formally:

1. If I can't see *x*, *x* doesn't exist.
2. I can't see God.
3. Therefore, God doesn't exist.

The first premise, of course, is false, and it wasn't difficult to show young Luke that seeing isn't the only way to know that something exists. We can, for instance, know that something exists because of its effects. Hence, this argument was easily refuted (and I remain undefeated in debates with five-year-olds). Nevertheless, I doubt my son is going to stop formulating arguments. It's only a matter of time before he presents me with a much stronger case, based on a crucial piece of data that is always before him.

In November of 2007, my son Reid was born. He wasn't moving or breathing. The only sign of life was his heartbeat. He was placed on a respirator, and he was eventually given a tracheostomy. We had to wait several months for a diagnosis, but we finally learned that Reid has myotubular myopathy, a rare genetic disorder that makes his muscles extremely weak—so weak that he can't hold his head up, breathe consistently, swallow when he needs to, or make a sound when he cries.

We teach our sons that God is all-knowing, all-powerful, and completely good. I'm quite certain that, within the next few years, Luke is going to reason as follows:

1. God, by definition, is all-knowing, all-powerful, and completely good.
2. If God is all-knowing, he would know how to prevent children from getting myotubular myopathy.
3. If God is all-powerful, he would have the power to prevent children from getting myotubular myopathy.
4. If God is completely good, he would want to prevent children from getting myotubular myopathy.
5. My brother has myotubular myopathy.
6. Therefore, God doesn't exist.

This argument isn't nearly as easily refuted as the previous argument. How are theists (i.e., people who believe that God exists and acts in our world) to respond?

There are three main approaches we can take when we respond to the argument from evil (hereafter AE). We can point out problems with the argument, we can try to explain suffering, and we can offer additional arguments for theism that outweigh any evidence against theism. Let's take a closer look at these responses.

Problems with the Argument from Evil

Since AE is an argument, the burden of proof is on the proponent to show that the argument is a good one. Thus, the first approach we can take is to point out problems with the argument itself, for example, inconsistencies, unproven assumptions, or ambiguous terms.

Inconsistencies

When atheists present AE, they're usually guilty of a number of inconsistencies. Let's consider one that's quite common. The most popular version of AE goes something like this:

1. If God exists, there wouldn't be any pointless suffering.
2. Since we can't think of reasons for allowing certain instances of suffering, some suffering is probably pointless (e.g., an injured deer experiencing pointless pain as it slowly dies in the woods).
3. Therefore, God probably doesn't exist.

But notice what the atheist is claiming. Since there's *probably* no point to at least some suffering (because we can't think of one), God probably doesn't exist. The atheist is claiming, then, that we shouldn't believe in something that seems improbable. But what happens when atheists are confronted by, say, the design argument? The theist argues, "Look, it's extremely *improbable* that life formed on its own, or that the universe just happened to be finely tuned for life. So life and the world probably have a designer." Here the atheist responds, "Yes, these things may be improbable, but I'm going to believe them anyway." This is a clear inconsistency. When one argument is on the table, we mustn't go against the probabilities; when a different argument is on the table, it's suddenly perfectly acceptable to go against the probabilities.

Based on this inconsistency alone, I would say that even if a theist has no explanation for suffering, he or she is no worse off than the atheist who has no explanation for the origin of the universe or for the complexity of life. If, however, it can be shown that there are other problems with the argument from evil, and if theists can offer reasons for God to allow suffering, theists are on much better ground than atheists.

Ambiguous Terms

Certain words can mean very different things to different people. For instance, if I say to an atheist, "I have *faith* in God," the atheist assumes I mean that my belief in God has nothing to do with evidence. But this isn't what I mean by *faith* at all. When I say that I have faith in God, I mean that I *place my trust* in God based on what I know about him.

Ambiguous terms can cause significant problems when they're used in arguments. Consider a simple word: *good*. Theists say that God is wholly good. But what do we mean by this? As I examine various versions of AE, I find that atheists are using this term quite differently from the way I use it. If we examine atheistic arguments carefully, we find that a "good" being is one who *maximizes pleasure* and *minimizes pain*. Given this definition, we can see why AE seems so persuasive to some:

1. If God existed, he would maximize our pleasure and minimize our pain.
2. Our pleasure is not maximized, and our pain is not minimized.
3. Thus, God doesn't exist.

If the premises of this argument are true, the conclusion follows. But what if we challenge the first premise by rejecting the claim that God's goodness implies giving lots of pleasure? Theists believe that some things are far more important than pleasure or lack of pain. Becoming good people, developing virtues, learning that we're not the center of the universe, seeking God with all our hearts—these are all vastly more important than pleasure or lack of pain. Thus, when theists say that God is wholly good, we're applying the term *good* within a framework of Christian values, where pleasure simply isn't at the top of our priorities.

Unproven Assumptions

When we make an argument, we assume various things. For instance, we assume that our minds are functioning properly, that valid logic preserves truth, and so on. Such things are rarely questioned. Nevertheless, when an assumption is crucial to an argument, and there's no good reason to believe the assumption, the argument is on very shaky ground. Consider the awareness assumption, which is absolutely critical for most versions of AE: If God has reasons for allowing evil, we will be aware of these reasons.

I cannot imagine how a defender of AE could even hope to show that this assumption is true. God's knowledge and wisdom are infinite, while even the smartest of human beings knows practically nothing by comparison. Yet without this assumption, most versions of AE cannot get off the ground.

Explaining Suffering

Given numerous problems with AE (and we've only looked at a few), I don't think that theists are under any obligation to explain suffering. Yet if we can come up with plausible reasons for God to allow suffering, this would increase the overall plausibility of theism.

Theists can account for suffering in two important ways: we can account for suffering *theologically* by appealing to Christian doctrines, and we can account for suffering *philosophically* by appealing to what philosophers call "theodicies."

Christian Doctrine

The most important religious claim to consider when faced with AE is that humanity is in a state of rebellion against God. While an atheist will probably reject such a claim, it's important to keep in mind that AE relies, to a large extent, on how awful humanity is and can become. When atheists offer evidence of suffering, they typically point to the Holocaust, or to the "Rape of Nanking," or to children being horribly victimized. But such events fit quite well with the idea that humanity has turned away from God. To put it differently, the more examples of moral evil an atheist presents in support of his argument, the more evidence he's given that human beings are extremely sinful. And it makes little sense to say, "Human beings are incredibly sinful and are at war with God, but God should give us a world of total pleasure and should rush to our aid whenever something goes wrong."

Theodicies

A theodicy is an attempt to answer the question, What morally sufficient reason could there be for God to allow evil? Let's look at two of the most important types of theodicy.

First, there are free will theodicies, which are based on two central ideas:

1. A world containing free beings is better than a world without free beings, since only free beings can choose the good or genuinely love or be moral in any meaningful sense.
2. True freedom entails that we are also free to choose the bad or not to love or to disobey the moral law.

On this view, moral evil is a *misuse* of moral freedom. Freedom itself, however, is a wonderful gift.

Second, there are soul-building theodicies. As we noted earlier, it's quite common for people to think that, if God exists, his primary goal should be to maximize our pleasure. Such a view doesn't fit well within a Christian framework, for it turns God into a "cosmic thermostat," whose job is to keep the universe just the way we like it. Proponents of soul-building theodicies maintain that God has more important things in mind than pleasure or lack of pain. While it's wonderful to go through times when life is comfortable, it's a simple fact of human experience that we don't grow much during those times. So if becoming mature human beings (or mature Christians) is important, then a world with pain is better than a world without pain.

I don't believe that such theodicies account for all of the evil in our world. Nevertheless, as a theist, I don't believe that our minds are capable of comprehending all of God's reasons for allowing suffering. The fact that we can come up with *some* plausible explanations for suffering (despite our limited knowledge) is itself a serious blow to AE.

Outweighing the Argument from Evil

Since the argument from evil only claims to provide a certain amount of evidence against theism, we must note that, even if we think AE is a good argument, the evidence drawn from it can potentially be outweighed by other evidence. Theists can therefore muster a number of arguments in favor of their position. If these arguments, taken as a whole, provide a stronger case than AE, we must conclude, once again, that AE is not a serious threat to theism. While there are dozens of arguments for the existence of God, we will briefly consider three.

Design Arguments

There are two main versions of the design argument: (1) the argument from fine-tuning, and (2) the argument from biological complexity. Physicists are aware of the fact that the fundamental constants of our universe seem to be finely-tuned for life. If the gravitational force, the weak nuclear force, the strong nuclear force, and the electromagnetic force were altered even slightly, human beings could not exist. Since there's no naturalistic explanation for why these values should be just right for life, the fine-tuning of the cosmos provides strong evidence of a designing intelligence.

A cosmos finely tuned for life, however, doesn't give us life. Additional steps are required to reach living cells, multicellular organisms, complete ecosystems, and especially conscious, self-reflective beings. The complexity of even the most basic living organism (let alone the complexity of more advanced life) is further evidence of a designing intelligence.

Cosmological Arguments

Many arguments for theism attempt to show that the universe must have a cause, or a certain type of cause. One such argument begins as follows:

1. Whatever begins to exist must have a cause.
2. The universe began to exist.
3. Therefore, the universe must have a cause.

The first premise is self-evident; the second can be known scientifically; thus, the conclusion follows. But we can go even further by examining the nature of the cause of the universe. Since the scientific evidence shows that matter and time began to exist when the universe began to exist, the first cause must be immaterial and timeless (both of which are attributes of God). The first cause must also be extraordinarily powerful and free to create. These attributes fit in perfectly with theism; they make no sense in atheism.

The Argument from Morality

Third, consider the following argument.

1. If God does not exist, objective moral values do not exist.
2. Objective moral values exist.
3. Therefore, God exists.

The first premise is certainly true. When we say that there are objective moral values, we're saying that there are moral claims that are true whether or not human beings agree with them. Thus, the claim "rape is immoral" would still be true even if every human being on the planet decided otherwise. But if human beings cannot serve as the ground for objective morality, what can? Only a being that completely transcends humans.

What about the second premise? Interestingly enough, proponents of AE often grant this premise in the course of their argument. By declaring that suffering is evil, atheists have admitted that there is an objective moral standard by which we distinguish good and evil. Amazingly, then, even as atheists make their case against the existence of God, they actually help us prove that God exists!

Assessment

We've looked at three approaches theists can take when we respond to the argument from evil. We must be careful to use such responses at the appropriate time, however. Remember that Job had the best friends in the world, so long as they kept their mouths shut. Job's time of intense suffering was not the appropriate occasion for a deep philosophical and theological analysis of human pain.

Similarly, when my son Luke comes up to me and says (as I know he eventually will), "Why did God allow Reid to get sick?" the appropriate response is not to charge in and say, "Well, let me explain the soul-building theodicy to you." To give specific and confident answers is to pretend that we have certainty of God's reasons for things when we often don't. Human anguish is powerful, sometimes far more powerful than words.

Nevertheless, at appropriate times, we must respond to AE. Atheists claim that their arguments refute theism. Yet they're inconsistent in the application of their principles, and they're smuggling in unproven assumptions and a distorted hierarchy of values. When we combine these problems with the fact that theists can explain a fair amount of suffering (which is all that can be reasonably expected of limited beings) and that we have strong evidence that supports belief in God, it's clear that the only significant argument for atheism fails on multiple levels.

7

God, Suffering, and Santa Claus

An Examination of the Explanatory Power of Theism and Atheism

DAVID WOOD

In the previous chapter, we considered three approaches theists can take when responding to the argument from evil. The present chapter addresses a related issue—the claim that theism should be rejected because it doesn't *explain* or *account for* the presence of suffering in our world.

Since typical formulations of the argument from evil contend that theism offers no reasonable explanation for the evil we observe and experience, the argument is often presented as a challenge to the *explanatory power* of theism. Hypotheses are supposed to account for the facts. If theism doesn't explain a significant fact about our world (the fact that it contains a great deal of suffering), isn't theism an unreasonable hypothesis?

To see the flaw in this claim, we will briefly compare the explanatory power of theism with that of atheism. But first, some thoughts on a more superficial objection to theism are in order, as they will help clarify my central point.

The Santa Objection

As a child, a teenager, and a young adult, I didn't believe in God, angels, demons, ghosts, aliens, the tooth fairy, the Easter bunny, or Santa Claus. Moreover, I placed all of these (nonexistent) beings in roughly the same category—the superstition/ignorance/fiction category. Like many atheists, when asked why I didn't believe in God, I would draw a comparison between believing in God and believing in Santa Claus. I eventually saw the parallel break down.

A child believes that Santa is the explanation for the presents under the Christmas tree. Notice that this explanation does account for the data the child observes. Why, then, do children eventually reject the Santa hypothesis? As they grow older, they realize that there's a simpler explanation for the data: parents put the gifts under the tree. This hypothesis accounts for the same data, yet it does so without appealing to unknown entities. (The idea here is that if there are two possible causes for some effect—one cause that is known to exist and one that is not known to exist—it makes more sense to appeal to the former.)

If the atheist's comparison between God and Santa is to hold, we should find roughly the same pattern of abandoning one hypothesis in favor of a superior hypothesis when we examine the atheist's move from theism to atheism. Let us turn to the "God hypothesis" to test this comparison.

The Explanatory Power of Theism

Suppose we have a set of facts—symbolized as *a*, *b*, *c*, *d*, *e*, *f*, and *g*—and we're seeking an explanation that accounts for these facts. Let us further suppose that hypothesis *x* accounts for facts *a*, *b*, *c*, *d*, *e*, and *f*, but that it's unclear how hypothesis *x* can account for *g*. Here it would be quite easy for a critic of hypothesis *x* to say, "This hypothesis makes no sense in light of *g*; we should therefore reject hypothesis *x*." But is it reasonable to dismiss a hypothesis when it accounts for nearly every fact we're trying to explain?

Atheists maintain that theism is a poor hypothesis because it fails to account for suffering. But surely theism accounts for a number of significant facts about our world. Let's consider just a few. First, theism explains why we have a world at all: God has the power to create, and he exercised this power in creating the world. We know scientifically that the universe had a beginning, and we know philosophically that whatever begins to exist must have a cause. Theism posits a cause powerful enough to create the universe.

Second, theism explains why our world is finely tuned for life. As physicist Paul Davies has noted, "It is hard to resist the impression that the present structure of the universe, apparently so sensitive to minor alterations in the numbers, has been rather carefully thought out."[1]

Third, theism accounts for the origin of life as well as for the diversity and complexity of life we see around us. The more we learn about even the most basic living organisms, the more startled we are at their complexity. Theism accounts for this astounding complexity.

Fourth, theism explains the rise of consciousness. Human beings are so accustomed to thinking, perceiving, contemplating, doubting, affirming, and judging, that we fail to grasp how amazing such abilities are. For many experts, it seems unthinkable that the human mind is nothing but neurons firing. According to neurophysiologist John Eccles, the evidence constrains him "to believe that there is what we might call a supernatural origin of my unique self-conscious mind or my unique selfhood or soul."[2] This view fits in nicely with theism.

Fifth, theism accounts for objective moral values. If morality is simply the byproduct of biological or societal evolution, there's nothing objective about it. If morality doesn't have an absolute foundation, our moral values are relative to culture, situation, and so on. Yet, if we're honest with ourselves, we must admit that people who rape or use others for selfish gain or molest children have crossed a line that is more than cultural. Such absolutes make no sense if man is the measure of all things, but they make perfect sense if God is the absolute moral standard.

Sixth, theism accounts for miracles. Throughout history, and in our own time, people have claimed to have witnessed miracles. Skeptics dismiss these events, but some miracle-claims demand a more serious investigation. For instance, according to all of the historical evidence available to us, Jesus died by crucifixion. We also know, historically, that Jesus's tomb was empty three days later, and that both friends and foes were soon claiming that he had appeared to them, risen from the dead. The only explanation that accounts for these facts without strain (and without appealing to absurd phenomena such as mass hallucinations) is that Jesus rose from the dead. Theism explains how such miracles are possible.

Thus, when atheists say that theism fails to account for suffering, we shouldn't forget that, even if they're right, theism accounts for just about everything else. Beyond this, many theists would challenge the claim that theism can't account for suffering. By appealing to religious doctrines such as the fall of humanity and human depravity, and by appealing to philosophical explanations such as free will theodicies (which claim that God permits moral evil because he values free will) and soul-building theodicies (which claim that a world containing suffering helps us grow morally and spiritually), theists can show that the God hypothesis accounts for at least some (if not all) human suffering.

But can we say the same of atheism?

The Explanatory Impotence of Atheism

Atheism explains, quite literally, nothing. Atheism doesn't explain the existence of our universe or the fact that our universe is finely tuned. It doesn't explain origin and diversity of life. It fails to explain the rise of consciousness or objective moral values or the evidence for miracles; indeed, atheism doesn't even account for the evil that serves as the foundation of the argument from evil, because for something to be truly evil, an objective moral standard is required.

At best, an atheist might say, "Well, *if* we somehow end up with a finely tuned universe and diverse life, suffering won't be surprising on our view, since there's no God to protect us." But we can't ignore the fact that atheism (even if we're generous) explains very little.

Atheists can respond by suggesting that atheism isn't meant to be taken as an explanation for anything. Rather, it's just a denial of theism. But let's return to the Santa objection to see why this response fails.

As we've seen, people who believe in Santa as their explanation for the presents under the tree eventually reject the Santa hypothesis when they realize that there's a far more reasonable explanation of the data. But suppose another person comes along and declares, "Santa didn't put those presents there, and neither did your parents. The presents are just there. Their existence is a brute fact."

The problem with this response is that, by taking away the explanations (Santa and one's parents) that actually account for the data, and by offering no substitute hypothesis to explain the data, we're left with data but no explanation. Indeed, if we had to choose between "Santa put them there" and "No one put them there," I think most of us would find the former explanation superior, since it at least accounts for the presents.

The point here is that if atheists expect theists to take the denial of theism seriously, they must offer a hypothesis at least as powerful as theism. Yet atheism can't explain even the most basic facts about the world. Hence, there is clearly a double standard at the heart of the atheist's thinking. If we're going to reject hypotheses because they fail to explain the data, we must reject atheism long before we reject theism.

Epilogue on Gratitude

We've been analyzing theism and atheism in terms of explanatory power, yet we might just as easily have framed the discussion in terms of gratitude. Children (at least, ideally) are thankful for the presents they receive, and when they're young, they thank Santa. When children eventually reject the Santa hypothesis, they *shift* their gratitude from Santa to their parents.

The real power of the argument from evil is that it can destroy a person's gratitude. If we focus all of our attention on the bad things in our world, we come to see it as a place of nothing but misery, disease, and bloodshed. (I've read many atheistic writings that describe the world in such terms.) When we become, as G. K. Chesterton put it, "Cosmic Pessimists," our gratitude doesn't shift from God to something else. Our gratitude simply dies.

How we view the world, then, can have a massive impact on our religious views. I would say that a person who looks at the world and sees nothing but pain and death has missed out on a truly amazing place. As a blissful young pagan, Chesterton set out to found his own religion. He eventually became a theist and a Christian, a process that had much to do with his sense of gratitude.

> The test of all happiness is gratitude; and I felt grateful, though I hardly knew to whom. Children are grateful when Santa Claus puts in their stockings gifts of toys or sweets. Could I not be grateful to Santa Claus when he put in my stockings the gift of two miraculous legs? We thank people for birthday presents of cigars and slippers. Can I thank no one for the birthday present of birth?[3]

Theists see a universe full of gifts under the Christmas tree. Until atheists offer a reasonable explanation of our marvelous world, it will always seem to theists that atheists have much to be thankful for, and no one to be thankful to.[4]

Section Two

The Question of Science

8

Creator and Sustainer

God's Essential Role in the Universe

Robert Kaita

The year 2005 was the international year of physics. It commemorated the one hundredth anniversary of Albert Einstein's papers that changed the way we see the world. Those papers included evidence for why everything is made up of atoms and an explanation of phenomena on that very small scale in terms of what eventually became quantum mechanics. One of the papers also introduced the world to the special theory of relativity.

Einstein posed a question that scientists, as scientists, still cannot answer. He asked why the universe is comprehensible. We do not know, for example, why there are only a few laws of physics. The same law of gravity can be used to describe how we are held to the earth, but also how immense galaxies are attracted to each other to form clusters.

We know that the universe is very old but that it is not infinitely old. We do not know why it had a moment of origin, which is now commonly called the "big bang." This frivolous name was invented by adherents to a "steady state" universe, and was meant to reflect their contempt for a universe with a beginning. However, astronomers found evidence for the "big bang" by looking at the way distant galaxies were moving away from us. As the theory predicts, those farthest away also had the fastest velocities.

We think that carbon was made inside stars long ago. However, we do not know why enough of it was created in this process, relative to heavier elements, to make life possible on Earth. The carbon is believed to have been released when the stars exploded, and enough eventually coalesced on our planet during its formation to become a part of every living organism.

Some scientists explain all of this by saying that it is just the way it has to be. In other words, if the universe were different, we would not be around to ask why things are the way they are. This "explanation" actually has a formal label. It is the "anthropic cosmological principle," and the first word in the name reflects its emphasis on the existence of human beings as the reason for everything we observe.

Other scientists, like myself, are perfectly comfortable in saying that our universe is all the work of a creator. Everyone would have to agree, however, that a person can hold either position and still be a good scientist. It takes just as much faith to claim that there is no creator behind what I just described as it does to believe that there is one.

Without going to the extreme of the anthropic cosmological principle, many envision a creator who had the very limited role of just "getting the ball rolling." People might be familiar with those who take great pains in setting up a huge number of dominoes, perhaps to get into the *Guinness Book of World Records*. The role of the creator of the universe, in crude analogy, would be to knock down the first domino, and watch the rest fall down.

Somehow, we have a sense that such a picture is not very satisfying. Why would some entity go through the trouble of creating the universe as we know it, and simply sit back and see "how things work out"? But an even more fundamental question for the scientist is this: Does the universe really "work" like a set of dominoes falling, one inexorably after another, without any intervention?

There is a joke that goes like this: How many software engineers does it take to change a lightbulb? The answer is, None. It's a hardware problem. Whether you laugh or groan, the basis of this joke is easy to understand. In our common experience, lightbulbs and every other contrivance of human ingenuity do not last forever.

As an experimental physicist, I sometimes pause to marvel at the miracle of my car starting after I've had a hard day in the lab struggling to make some balky apparatus work. There is no question about the need for an experimenter to take an active role to make experiments succeed. Similarly, everyone knows what happens if the "interventions" specified in a car service schedule are too long neglected. The phrase "driving your car into the ground" has a good empirical basis.

Even leaving equipment on the shelf is no guarantee that it will work when you need it. My research focuses on developing nuclear fusion (which is the process that powers the sun) as a safe and clean energy source. Part of my work involves evacuating chambers that contain the hot, ionized gases, or plasmas, that must be created for fusion reactions to occur. For this purpose, we use high-speed pumps with carefully manufactured bearings. Just letting the bearings sit for a seemingly modest length of time will deform them enough to make the pumps fail.

Given my intimate familiarity with "hardware problems," occasional envy of my colleagues in theoretical physics may not be surprising. Their codes run even after they have been set aside for some time. If they don't, the cause can usually be traced to tangible equipment that can "wear out." The solution for code developers is then to get someone else to fix the hardware. But can they be absolutely certain that this will cure the problem? This bears on a deeper question regarding the physical laws that govern the operation of chips at the heart of modern computers. Why should these laws stay the same from one day to the next? We can imagine hardware wearing out with time, but there is no fundamental reason why the software that runs on them should be as "immutable."

For me, I find the answer at the end of the eighth chapter of Genesis. There God makes the following sacred promise to humanity:

> As long as the earth endures,
> seedtime and harvest,
> cold and heat,
> summer and winter,
> day and night
> will never cease.
>
> Gen. 8:22 (NIV)

There is no a priori reason that season should follow season, so that the seeds we plant will lead to the harvests that are necessary for our survival. Rather, it is God who ensures this regularity "as long as the earth endures."

Of course, not everyone needs the answer Genesis provides for why science will "work" tomorrow. The anthropic cosmological principle could be invoked to "explain" the persistent patterns we see in our universe by asserting that if it were not the case, we could not exist. Such an approach reflects, once again, a focus primarily on ourselves in the here and now. It begs, however, the deeper question of why we are here in the first place, and belies an egocentrism that has existed since the dawn of humanity.

The point is illustrated in the following event, which occurred during the ministry of Jesus Christ two millennia ago. In the seventeenth chapter of the Gospel of Luke, we read the story of Jesus encountering ten men who have leprosy. He tells them to go show themselves to the priests, and they are cured. However, only one comes back and throws himself at the feet of Jesus with thankfulness and praises to God. While the miraculous cure is important in this story, there is an equally significant lesson in the differing reactions of those who were cured.

The miraculous in modern science ultimately has nothing to do with the fact that we now have medical treatments for leprosy, or how many songs you can stuff into an iPod, for that matter. Instead, it is that we can do, and can continue to do, science at all. In that sense, all scientists tacitly believe in this "miracle" to perform their work.

The validity of such an assertion should not be in question. Rather, it is how we react to this reality that is the key issue. The responses of the men Jesus cured thus continue to inform us today. We can focus "anthropically" on ourselves, and run off with blithe disregard of what a blessing our very existence represents. Or we can turn with thankfulness to God, who created us and sustains all of creation.

9

The Pale Blue Dot Revisited

JAY W. RICHARDS AND GUILLERMO GONZALEZ

A recurring theme of the 1994 book *Pale Blue Dot*, by the late astronomer Carl Sagan, is that we are insignificant in the cosmic scheme. In one memorable passage, Sagan pushes this point while reflecting on an image of Earth taken by Voyager 1 in 1990 from some four billion miles away. He writes:

> Because of the reflection of sunlight . . . Earth seems to be sitting in a beam of light, as if there were some special significance to this small world. But it's just an accident of geometry and optics. . . . Our posturings, our imagined self-importance, the delusion that we have some privileged position in the Universe, are challenged by this point of pale light. Our planet is a lonely speck in the great enveloping cosmic dark. In our obscurity, in all this vastness, there is no hint that help will come from elsewhere to save us from ourselves.[1]

You might think that Sagan had an eccentric, melancholy personality. But his sermonette actually expresses an idea, popular among modern scientists, known as the Copernican Principle. Its proponents trace the history of the principle to its namesake, Nicolaus Copernicus (d. 1543). According to the popular story, Copernicus demoted us by showing that ours was a sun-centered universe, with Earth both rotating around its axis and revolving around the sun, like the other planets. He dislodged us from our place of centrality and, therefore, importance. Scientists since Copernicus have only reinforced this initial dethroning. Or so the story goes.

Open virtually any introductory astronomy textbook and you will read some version of this story. It has a single, decisive problem: it's false. Historians of science have protested this description of the development of science for decades, but so far, their protests have not trickled down to the masses or the textbook writers.

The real story is much more subtle. We can only sketch its outline here. The pre-Copernican cosmology was a combination of the physical and metaphysical vision of the Greek philosopher Aristotle (384–322 BC) and the observations and mathematical models of Ptolemy (circa AD 100–175) and other astronomers. The universe they envisioned was a set of nested, concentric spheres that encircled our spherical, terrestrial globe, a model that nicely explained a whole range of astronomical phenomena in the pretelescope era. The crystalline spheres were thought to connect so that the movement of the outer, stellar sphere of the stars moved the inner spheres that housed the planets, sun, and moon. This model gave order to the east-to-west movement of the sun and the moon, the celestial sphere encircling the celestial poles, and the perplexing and somewhat irregular paths of the known planets.

Although it appears naive to modern minds, this pre-Copernican cosmology stood out among other cosmologies because it took account of observations of the heavens in trying to discern the structure of the cosmos. In this sense, it reflected a scientific virtue, namely, openness to observation from the natural world.

The view had in its favor the collaboration of commonsense observation of the apparent movement of the skies, the apparent stability of the earth itself, and a number of plausible arguments. For example, if the earth moved, one would expect a stiff east wind, and that an arrow shot straight in the air would come down west of the archer.

Contrary to popular impression, neither Aristotle nor Ptolemy thought that the earth was a large part of the universe. Aristotle considered it of "no great size" compared to the heavenly spheres, and in Ptolemy's masterwork, the *Almagest*, he says, "The earth has a ratio of a point to the heavens."[2] Both of them reached this conclusion because of observations of Earth's relation to the stars, from which they surmised that the stellar sphere was an enormous distance from the earth. Copernicus, in his *De revolutionibus*, based one of his arguments for the rotation of the earth on this shared assumption, observing: "How astonishing, if within the space of twenty-four hours the vast universe should rotate rather than its least point!"[3]

More importantly, the "center" of the universe was considered no place of honor, any more than we think of the center of the earth as being such. And the earth was certainly not thought to be sitting at the center of heaven. Quite the opposite. The sublunary domain was the mutable, corruptible, base, and heavy portion of the cosmos. Things were thought to fall to Earth because of their heaviness. The earth itself was considered the "center" of the cosmos because of its heaviness. The modernist interpretation of geocentrism, then, has it essentially backward. In our contemporary sense of the words, the earth in pre-Copernican cosmology was the "bottom" of the universe rather than its "center."

In contrast, Aristotelians considered the heavens immutable in their regularity and composition. Whereas the sublunary regions were composed of the four mutable elements of earth, water, air, and fire, the heavens were composed of a "fifth element," called "quintessence," or ether. Heavenly bodies were perfectly spherical, and moved in a circular way befitting their perfection. From this it followed that the laws governing the heavenly realms were quite different from and superior to the laws governing the sublunary regions.

When Christian theology was added to the mix in the Middle Ages, the center or bottom of the universe became, quite literally, *hell*. Dante's *Divine Comedy* immortalized this vision, taking the reader from the earth's surface through the nine circles of hell, which mirror, and hence reverse, the nine celestial spheres above. Man, composed of both earth and spirit, occupied an intermediate state in which he was a sort of micro-cosmos. He could ascend to the heavenly realm or descend to the realm of evil, death, and decay. Other purely spiritual beings populated the wider created reality, and God dwelled "above" the outer "empyrean" sphere as the unmoved mover of everything else.

Metaphysically speaking, reality in the earlier scheme is God-centered, not human-centered. Thus, Augustine argued that God did not create the world "for man" or out of some necessary compulsion, but simply "because he wanted to." It's false, then, to say that the pre-Copernicans gave the earth and human beings the position of highest esteem, while Copernicus relegated us to an insignificant backwater.

So, far from demoting the status of Earth, Copernicus, Galileo, and Kepler saw the new scheme as exalting it. Galileo in particular defended the notion of "earth shine," in which Earth reflected the light and glory of the sun more perfectly than the moon. He thought that the earth's new position removed it from the place of dishonor it occupied in the Aristotelian universe, and placed it in the heavens. In his *Sidereus Nuncius*, Galileo argues:

> Many arguments will be provided to demonstrate a very strong reflection of the sun's light from the earth—this for the benefit of those who assert, principally on the grounds that it has neither motion nor light, that the earth must be excluded from the dance of the stars. For I will prove that the earth does have motion, that it surpasses the moon in brightness, and that it is not the sump where the universe's filth and ephemera collect.[4]

The centrality of Earth in pre-Copernican cosmology meant something entirely different to the pre-Copernicans than it does in the textbook orthodoxy we've all learned. There is no simple inference from central location to high status any more than a modern person would privilege the center of Earth as the ideal terrestial place to be. Geocentrism did not imply anthropocentrism. Dennis Danielson has written an excellent essay laying to rest the mythology surrounding the Copernican Revolution, titled "The Great Copernican Cliché."[5] In it he writes: "The great Copernican cliché is premised upon an uncritical equation of *geo*centrism with *anthro*pocentrism."[6] Denying either or both did not automatically disprove the existence of purpose or design in nature.

The official story gives the false impression that Copernicus started a trend, so that removing the Earth from the "center" of the universe led finally, logically, and inevitably to the scientific establishment of our insignificance. By sleight of hand, it transformed a series of metaphysically ambiguous discoveries into the grand narrative of materialism. None of these historical points answers the wider question of our significance in the scheme of things. But it does us good to remember that materialism does not enjoy the historical and scientific pedigree claimed by its adherents.

10

Oxygen, Water, and Light, Oh My!

The Toxicity of Life's Basic Necessities

Joe W. Francis

Every living creature is made of amazingly small and complex units called cells. Cells viewed under the microscope do not appear to do much, yet they are full of microscale machines involved in tremendously complex reactions. Most of life's processes are so small and transparent that we cannot see them in action with microscopes. But the chemistry of life is constantly in motion in living cells. College-level biochemistry textbooks typically contain over a thousand pages and describe hundreds to thousands of complex reactions that occur simultaneously within these tiny packets of life we call cells.

Despite this immense complexity, living cells are made primarily of four atoms: carbon, hydrogen, oxygen, and nitrogen. Two of these atoms, hydrogen and oxygen, are bonded together to make water, which is the most abundant molecule in living organisms. The oxygen molecule itself plays a critical role in regenerating energy in the cell. In addition, all living creatures need a supply of energy. Energy in most ecosystems ultimately comes from light. For instance, all of the food energy we consume can eventually be traced back to the light energy captured in cells. So it is no surprise that oxygen, water, and light are very abundant on the earth. Living organisms are continually exposed to these very important substances on which life depends. Origin-of-life researchers, who try to determine how life originated by natural means, must incorporate water, oxygen, and light into their formulas for early life. However, curiously enough, all three of these substances are toxic to life. In fact, living cells fight a daily, moment-by-moment battle against the toxicity of oxygen, water, and light. Let us examine the toxicity of each of these substances.

Oxygen interacts with many atoms and molecules. This is evident in metal structures all around us, which tend to "oxidize," or rust, over time. If the oxygen content in our atmosphere were just a few percent higher than its current 21 percent, the potential for devastating forest fires and an unstable explosive atmosphere would increase significantly, making life less likely to thrive on the earth. The toxic effects of elevated oxygen levels can be directly observed in the damaged lungs of human patients who receive oxygen for therapeutic reasons.

Oxygen is toxic to living organisms because when it interacts with living cells the oxygen molecule itself breaks down into toxic intermediates. These intermediates interact with and modify many essential molecules in cells. Consequently, because we live in an oxygen environment, our cells and their contents are constantly being threatened by toxic oxygen intermediates. If this threat is not continually neutralized, life would cease to continue. Cells handle this threat by making a variety of toxic-oxygen-binding enzymes, including a major type called superoxide dismutase (SOD), which binds and deactivates superoxide, the dominant toxic oxygen species. SOD is found within the cell, outside the cell, and in the membranes of the cell. Our body cells are literally surrounded by SOD. In fact, the concentration of SOD in a cell environment can be one hundred thousand times greater than the concentration of toxic superoxide.

Because oxygen appeared very early in the development of life, SOD or a protection mechanism similar to it would be required to appear early in the evolution of life. This is problematic for several reasons. One is that the SOD would need to specifically bind superoxide and not oxygen. Superoxide and oxygen are very similar in size and shape, and if SOD reacted with oxygen and prevented its entry into the cell, this could be life threatening. Cells also possess essential enzymes that specialize in binding to oxygen. Fascinatingly, the enzymes that bind oxygen and those that bind superoxide are similar in that they use the same type of metal atoms to attract and bind oxygen. Thus it appears that, very early in the evolution of life, two complex enzymes with very similar but distinct binding properties would have to appear simultaneously to allow cells to take up oxygen while at the same time protecting cells from the damaging effects of toxic oxygen.

Many origin-of-life scenarios initially exclude molecular oxygen because of its reactivity and toxicity. However, atmospheric oxygen plays a major role in filtering out much of the harmful ultraviolet (UV) light rays from the sun. In the present-day atmosphere, which contains oxygen, some UV light does reach the earth, and it is harmful to living things. UV light alters DNA in cells, ultimately causing mutation, cancer, or cell death. In fact, it is very likely that DNA damage occurs in our cells every time we are exposed to sunlight. It is estimated that in warm-blooded animals over ten thousand alterations in the DNA can take place in each cell every day. However, we seldom notice the damage because our cells possess elaborate DNA repair mechanisms, which can repair the damage caused by UV light and other agents. In humans more than one hundred genes are involved in DNA repair. In fact all organisms, including bacteria, possess complex repair mechanisms to repair DNA damaged by light. Many organisms possess up to four different kinds of DNA repair mechanisms. In bacteria, there is a backup repair mechanism called SOS, which is activated if the cell is overwhelmed with DNA damage. The repair mechanisms are complex and involve many parts to accomplish this repair. Let us consider how the repair of UV light damage is accomplished.

DNA is a double-stranded fiberlike molecule. UV light typically causes the double strand to stick together abnormally in one spot. The repair mechanisms recognize the sticky abnormal spot, cut it out, and resynthesize what was lost. This requires, at a minimum, an enzyme to recognize the sticky spot, a cutting enzyme, and a resynthesis and resealing enzyme. In some organisms a single enzyme can repair the UV light damage, but this single enzyme, called photolyase, requires the assistance of two complex cofactor molecules, and surprisingly must be exposed to a certain wavelength of light to function. Not only do we find elaborate repair mechanisms in all cells, but in plants, algae, and some bacteria very complex systems exist that interact intentionally and very specifically with light. These photosynthesis systems supply carbon and oxygen for most all living things on earth.

A type of photosynthetic bacteria, called cyanobacteria, in the ocean could be responsible for mobilizing about 50 percent of the carbon for living things on earth. Curiously, the photosynthetic machinery of these bacteria can suffer from sunburn; some of the proteins are sunburned so badly they stop functioning. However, researchers have discovered a virus in the ocean that infects these bacteria and repairs the defect. The existence of elegant and essential repair mechanisms that counter the toxic effects of light and oxygen highlights the fact that repair mechanisms would have to be in place early in the evolution of life. In addition, because photosynthesis produces oxygen, cells would have to possess oxygen protection mechanisms before the advent of photosynthesis.

Not only must cells possess repair and protection mechanisms to prevent oxygen and light damage, cells must also be designed to handle the detrimental effects of water. The water molecule possesses many fascinating and unique life-supporting characteristics. Yet water is a tremendously destructive force at the cellular and molecular level. Water is destructive because it can break apart molecules by a process called hydrolysis. During hydrolysis, water molecules force their way into spaces between atoms within molecules, breaking apart or preventing the formation of large molecular structures like proteins. In fact, protein synthesis in cells requires the removal of water, a dehydration reaction. How does this dehydration reaction occur in the water-based environment of the cell? The interior of the cell is thick with molecules, proteins, and enzymes that assist the making of a protein. Origin-of-life researchers do not postulate a similar low-water environment and mechanism to remove water or supply enzyme catalysts during protein synthesis in the dilute watery environment of the early earth. In fact, this problem has led them to conclude that proteins and other large polymers (chain-like molecules) were constructed in dry environments like clay or sand.

Water also destroys cells by inducing uncontrollable swelling. This can be easily observed in red blood cells placed in water: the cells swell and break open rapidly. The cell bursts because water moves freely into cells by diffusion, a process whereby water seeks places that are low in water content. As we have noted, the inside of the typical cell is low in water content compared to its surroundings. Thus all cells on earth face a continual battle against the influx of water.

Cells possess several mechanisms to handle the continual influx of water. Plant and bacteria cells, for example, possess rigid cell-wall structures, which resist cell swelling and breakage. These cell-wall structures can be quite elaborate and, in the case of bacteria, involve an intricate precision-made quilt-like structure made of protein and sugar chains. Animal cells do not possess rigid cell walls but instead constantly pump sodium out of the cell to counter the movement of water into the cell. The pump is a fascinating protein structure called the sodium-potassium pump. The pump sends out three sodium ions in exchange for two potassium ions. The cell membrane contains thousands of these pumps, which constantly work to maintain cell volume against the impending crushing force of water, utilizing up to one third of the energy found in living cells. However, the pump is designed to work in an environment that contains sodium and potassium in certain defined concentrations, for instance, in the human body. Take one of these cells out of this salty, watery environment and place it in a pure water environment and the pump will not be able to prevent the cell from bursting. How then do single-cell organisms that live in fresh water environments survive?

Single-cell pond organisms like paramecium utilize a large bag-like structure called a contractile vacuole, which continually collects and excretes excess water. Water moves into the vacuole because the paramecium actively pumps salts into the vacuole, utilizing proteins similar to the sodium-potassium pump. Thus it appears that paramecia and other single-cell pond organisms resist swelling and bursting by possessing both protein pumps and contractile vacuoles.

One could argue that given enough time one of these protection mechanisms could evolve, but the simultaneous evolution of several elaborate and complex protection mechanisms that are required to protect cells from some of the very basic necessities of life (namely, water, oxygen, and light), certainly complicates the origin-of-life problem. On the other hand, how does this observation fit with creation/design theories? The requirement of life for the simultaneous existence of several complex protection mechanisms certainly is consistent with a creation or design in nature that was premeditated and constructed within a short period of time. However, one could ask why a creator/designer would use toxic agents? Toxicity could be considered to be a byproduct of chemical reactivity. Reactivity is required in a world where things are designed to move and interact. In addition, even the most benign agents can be toxic under certain conditions. We know this from our everyday experience. For instance, many beneficial and required food types can be harmful if ingested in excessive amounts. We also know that potentially toxic and destructive chemicals provide tremendous benefits if they are used within certain parameters. For example, fuel in an engine is a marvelous and tremendous technology that enhances life; however, placed in the wrong part of the engine, it can lead to disaster and destruction.

In conclusion, water, oxygen, and light, three of the most basic necessary requirements for life, can be extremely toxic to living things. But, living organisms possess complex protection mechanisms built into each living cell, which appear to have protected life from its very first appearance on earth.

11

The Origin of Life

Walter Bradley

Introduction

Antony Flew, a British philosophy professor and leading champion of atheism for more than half a century, changed his mind and became a deist at the age of 81. In a telephone interview with ABC News, Flew indicated that a "super-intelligence is the only good explanation for the origin of life and the complexity of nature."[1] Nicholas Wade in the *New York Times* summarized the current state of the affairs regarding the origin of life as follows: "The chemistry of the first life is a nightmare to explain. No one has yet developed a plausible explanation to show how the earliest chemicals of life—thought to be RNA—might have constructed themselves from the inorganic chemicals likely to have been around on early earth. The spontaneous assembly of a small RNA molecule on the primitive earth 'would have been a near miracle' two experts on the subject helpfully declared last year."[2] What is it about the origin of life that has so confounded scientists and persuaded atheists to become deists or theists? Why is the origin of life considered one of the great, unsolved mysteries of science?

The minimal functional requirements for a living system include processing energy, storing information, and replicating. Lila Gatlin captures the essence of the problem by noting that life may be defined operationally as a system that has the ability to store and process information that is essential for its own reproduction.[3] These biological operations are made possible by very complex molecules such as DNA, RNA, and protein. In this essay, I would like to explore the "miracle of the origin of life" by providing an overview of the molecular complexity that is essential to life and by indicating why it is so difficult for unguided natural laws, sometimes characterized as chance and necessity, to ever adequately account for the origin of these remarkable molecules of life.

Information and the Molecules of Life

Protein, RNA, and DNA are all long polymer chains. The *mer* in *polymer* means building block, and *poly* means many. The protein molecule is a polymer typically composed of one hundred to three hundred smaller molecular building blocks (or mers), called amino acids. There are twenty distinct types of amino acid building blocks in protein. These amino acids chemically react to form long polymer chains, which subsequently fold up into three-dimensional structures. It is this distinctive structure that allows various proteins to serve as catalysts, making chemical reactions in living systems go a million times more rapidly.

The sequencing of the twenty different kinds of amino acids is what determines the three-dimensional structure. Only a very, very small fraction of the possible sequences of amino acids give three-dimensional structures that have any biological utility. In fact it has been predicted theoretically and confirmed experimentally that the probability of getting the correct sequence of amino acids for a protein such as cytochrome C is approximately 1 in 1060. How then are proteins ever successfully assembled from amino acids in living cells?

The DNA and RNA molecules are the key to getting the remarkable sequences of amino acids in proteins that provide critical biological functions in living cells. The DNA is encoded with information that can be used to sequence the amino acids in various proteins for a given organism. The m-RNA molecule receives this encoded information from the DNA and then serves as a template to get exactly the right sequencing of amino acids to give over three hundred distinct functional proteins. We may think of the DNA as the "computer brain" for each cell, controlling the sequencing of amino acids in three hundred or more distinctive proteins, which in turn control the necessary chemistry of life in the cell. To make a DNA molecule with the right encoded information for E. coli bacteria would require 4.6 million instructions for the chemist, or the equivalent of eight hundred pages of information. So while this solves the problem of the origin of the necessary information to sequence (or encode) various proteins, it does not solve the mystery of the origin of this huge amount of information but merely transfers it back to the DNA (or possibly RNA in the first living system). The origin of the large amount of information in DNA that is expressed in the amazing molecular complexity essential for life is the central enigma of the origin of life.

Making DNA, RNA, and Protein under Prebiotic Conditions

DNA molecules reproduce themselves (with the help of proteins) and, assisted by RNA, encode the various amino acid sequences in proteins that make possible the efficient uses of energy in living systems. Thus DNA, RNA, and protein provide the necessary functions of life: namely, information storage, replication, and efficient utilization of energy. But how were the first DNA, RNA, and protein molecules produced? Origin-of-life research for more than fifty years has tried to answer this question. What have we learned?

Origin-of-life research began in the 1950s with the attempt to chemically synthesize the basic molecular building blocks for protein and DNA, including various amino acids, bases, and sugars. The early success of Miller and Urey in making these molecular building blocks, ostensibly under early earth conditions, was seriously undercut in the 1980s when it was determined that the early earth's atmosphere was never rich in methane, ammonia, or hydrogen, the chemical gases used in their experiments. One cannot produce more than minuscule yields of amino acids and ribose sugar when one uses a plausible prebiotic chemistry. Today the origin of these essential building blocks of life remains a mystery.

A second problem is that the building blocks on the prebiotic earth would have been surrounded by many other chemical reagents that react with the building blocks much more quickly than they react with each other. Unless such destructive cross-reactions could somehow be avoided, the emergence of DNA, RNA, or protein would be impossible.

A third problem is the assembly of the building blocks into the polymer chains. For example, amino acids can be joined (in chemical reactions) in a variety of ways, but only one type of joining of adjacent amino acid molecules (i.e., chemical bonds called peptides) gives a polymer chain that has the function of a protein. In a similar way, 3–5 phosphodiester linkages are needed, but 2–5 linkages dominate in the polymerization of polynucleotides, which is a primary step in the formation of DNA and RNA.

A fourth challenge results from the fact that amino acids and sugars come in right-handed or left-handed versions (structures that are identical except that they are mirror images). All amino acids chemically react with each version equally rapidly, but living systems have only L amino acids and D sugars. How could we possibly get one hundred or more amino acids that are all Ls from a mixture of equal concentrations of Ls and Ds? This problem has been studied extensively but the explanation remains elusive.

Beyond the problems of producing the building blocks under plausible prebiotic conditions, avoiding fatal cross-chemical reactions, getting the building blocks assembled, and getting only L amino acids or D sugars, the most challenging problem in the origin-of-life scenario is how to get the correct sequencing of amino acids in proteins and the correct sequencing of bases in DNA to give information that can provide biological function. As previously noted, the information encoded on the DNA of E. coli bacteria is the equivalent of eight hundred pages of information. While it is sometimes argued that this can happen with some kind of chemical selection over time, no selection is possible on molecular systems that do not yet have the capacity to replicate with occasional mistakes and provide functions that give selective advantage. Functional DNA, RNA, or protein might be able to incrementally improve with replication mistakes acted on by selection, but this is meaningless in molecules that are not yet sufficiently complex as to provide at least minimal function. It is the molecular version of the old problem of which came first, the chicken or the egg.

Summary

Michael Behe has argued that there are irreducibly complex hurdles that an evolutionary process driven by natural selection cannot overcome—for example, the concurrent development of a multiple-component system that provides no selective advantage until each of the components has developed to a rather advanced level and can function together as a system. The origin of life would seem to be the quiescent example of an irreducibly complex hurdle in the metanarrative of the origin and development of living systems. The necessary information, which expresses itself as molecular complexity, simply cannot be developed by chance and necessity but requires an intelligent cause, an intelligent designer, a Creator God.

12

What Every High School Student Should Know about Science

Michael Newton Keas

Because science is a core feature of modern society, everyone needs a thorough introduction to it. In particular, every high school student should know (1) what science is, (2) the various ways it is practiced, and (3) why it is important. The first topic is philosophical, the second is procedural and historical, and the third motivates students to study science.

What Science Is

What distinguishes science from other endeavors, such as religion, philosophy, or history? This question, as Stephen Meyer has shown, has no conclusive answer, partly because of the amazing variety of ways science is actually practiced.[1] In most cases we simply recognize reputable science when we see it. Students should be challenged to define science and to recognize why this exercise in the philosophy of science is so difficult. In America, about forty state departments of education define science roughly as "investigating the natural world through the use of observation, experimentation, and logical argument."[2] Only Massachusetts and Kansas have proposed restricting science by a definition that only allows unguided natural causes to explain what is observed. Students should know why this restriction is controversial.

The Various Ways Science Is Practiced

Students must appreciate the variety of ways science is practiced, which I call *methodological pluralism*. Laboratory scientists actively manipulate conditions, following the standard experimental method. Astronomers are typically restricted to passively peering into deep space, where celestial objects are beyond their experimental control. Geologists study a single large object (the earth) through methods and natural laws largely borrowed from other scientific disciplines (especially physics and chemistry). Astronomers and geologists sometimes use simulation models to understand large-scale, long-term changes in the objects they study. Many physicists study tiny subatomic particles that present unique investigative challenges. The "scientific method" as presented in the introductory chapter of most science textbooks usually fails to recognize the methodological diversity of actual scientific practice.[3]

Students should also recognize how different beliefs shape scientific practice. This is another form of methodological pluralism. For example, the ancient Babylonians produced the longest sustained scientific research program in human history (twenty centuries). Although their motivation was based on religion and astrology, their resulting mathematical astronomy wielded great predictive power. Many celestial events could be predicted accurately in advance.[4] Students need to appreciate how various religious, antireligious, and nonreligious viewpoints have often motivated empirically successful science. The *National Science Education Standards* affirm this approach: "Scientists are influenced by societal, cultural, and personal beliefs and ways of viewing the world. Science is not *separate from* society but rather science is a *part of* society."[5] Such an approach to science education would include discussion of the influence of naturalism in science. Naturalism in its philosophical form says that nothing beyond nature is real. This amounts to atheism. Naturalism in science has guided many scientists to limit themselves to material causes to explain the natural world. This is also called methodological naturalism. Students should be aware of these social influences on science and be encouraged to critically evaluate them.

Students further need to learn that science is devoted to two fundamentally distinct goals: "how things work" and "how things originated." Each of these aims is achieved through a somewhat different collection of investigative tools. This too is methodological pluralism. The first concern, how things work, encompassed nearly all science until the early nineteenth century, when geology and biology acquired empirically rigorous tools for investigating how things originated. Scientists who investigate "origins" study presently existing things and use this evidence to construct various competing hypotheses of how natural things might have originated. Geologists—in contrast to most ancient philosophers—largely concluded that the earth is not eternal, but had a beginning and changed through unique stages over time.

This view was partly motivated by the Judeo-Christian view of history, with its notion of a unique beginning, unrepeatable development, and end. Real historical development replaced the ancient Greek idea of endless cycles. Both sacred and secular viewpoints provided analogies that guided early attempts to reconstruct the earth's history. For example, early geologists used fossils as markers of the earth's historical record in much the same way as human artifacts, such as coins, were important chronological indicators in archaeology. Fossils were called "nature's coins." Such cultural legacies from the history of science deserve a place in science curricula. The retelling of the early nineteenth-century discovery of the earth's history might help clear up the common misunderstanding that science cannot study past, non-repeatable events occurring in nature. The earth and life sciences since the nineteenth century, and cosmology since the twentieth century, have identified and explained many past events on the basis of currently existing evidence. While not as certain as repeatable laboratory experiments, these results are among the most remarkable achievements of modern science.

Why Science Is Important

Third, we must convince students that science is important. Our understanding of "how things work" helps us to better manage the earth's natural resources and to enhance human health. The scientific debate over the origin of the universe and life deserves special attention in science education because it affects the way we view life and human purpose. The breathtaking intricacy and complexity of even the simplest bacterial cell, with its highly specified molecular machines, should evoke awe among students. Some students may attribute this apparent design to autonomous nature (naturalism). Others may conclude that this points to a designer beyond the realm of nature. Yet others may respond in other ways. The science instructor should help students develop their own opinions in a manner that takes science (and other scholarship) seriously. Without this balance, science education reduces to propaganda.

One way to motivate students to study science and to think critically is to examine case studies of scientific controversy. Through case studies students will gain insight into the standard scientific procedure of inferring the best explanation from among multiple competing hypotheses. Charles Darwin argued, "a fair result can be obtained only by fully stating and balancing the facts and arguments on both sides of each question."[6] In today's climate of public educational policy, this would mean, at a minimum, teaching not just the strengths of Darwin's theory, but also the evidence that challenges it. For example, any complete theory of biological origins must examine fossil evidence. The fossils of the "Cambrian explosion" show virtually all the basic forms of animal life appearing suddenly without clear precursors. It is not merely the geologically sudden appearance that is notable but the observation that major categories (animal phyla) appear before the multiplication of small differences among species. Darwin's theory predicts the opposite: small differences multiplying, and by means of natural selection, later giving rise to major anatomical differences. Students ought to know about this evidential challenge to Darwinism, but few biology textbooks mention it.

Consider another example. Many biology texts tell about the Galapagos finches, whose beaks have varied in shape and size over time. They also recall how some bacteria have acquired resistance to certain antibiotics. Such episodes are presented as conclusive evidence for evolution. And indeed they are, depending on how one defines evolution.[7] Yet few biology textbooks distinguish the different meanings associated with *evolution*—a term that can refer to anything from trivial change to the creation of life by strictly mindless, material forces. Nor do they explain that the processes responsible for cyclical variations in beak size do not explain where birds or biologists came from in the first place. As a host of distinguished biologists (e.g., Stuart Kauffman, Rudolf Raff, and George Miklos) have explained in recent technical papers, small-scale "microevolutionary" change cannot be extrapolated to explain large-scale "macroevolutionary" innovation. Microevolutionary changes (such as variation in beak shape) merely utilize or express existing genetic information; the large-scale macroevolutionary change necessary to assemble new organs or body plans requires the creation of entirely new genetic information. Leading evolutionary biologists know that this distinction poses serious difficulties for modern Darwinism. Students should too.

A "teach the controversy" approach presents biology in a livelier and less dogmatic way. Students will learn science as it is actually practiced. Scientists often debate how to best interpret data, and they even argue over what counts as legitimate "scientific explanation." Controversy is normal within science (not just an intrusion). Students will learn to distinguish better between evidence (factual data) and inference (reasoning to conclusions). Students need these skills as citizens, whether they choose careers in science or other fields. Teaching multiple sides in an "issues approach" to science has, of late, been recognized as a superior educational approach, not just in origins issues but also in other areas. The recent scientific debate over Darwinism and intelligent design theory is of great interest to students who care about the big questions of life. Research based on design theory shows great promise of producing profound results in the near future. To the degree to which it succeeds, the science education community will have increasingly stronger reasons to incorporate this theory into the teaching of science.

Advocates of the Darwin-only approach to education in the life sciences often point to the *National Science Education Standards* (NSES) to bolster their position. The NSES constitute the premier noncompulsory national document that currently guides much reform in science education in the United States.

Ironically, statements in the NSES support the major points in this essay. The NSES call on students to "identify their assumptions, use critical and logical thinking, and consider alternative explanations."[8] If students are simply told to swallow Darwin whole as a "fact," how will this help them to become critical, skeptical, scientific thinkers? Among the content standards for grades nine through twelve is the aim that all students should develop an understanding of biological evolution. We enthusiastically affirm this goal. In fact, we want students to learn more about Darwinism than most Darwin-only advocates wish. The "more" we have in mind includes the weaknesses of Darwin's theory (not just a selective presentation of its strengths). Microevolutionary speciation is well established, and is a tribute to the permanent legacy of Darwin's contribution to human knowledge. Macroevolution is another matter. Experts disagree and students should not be sheltered from this dispute.

The NSES advocate the use of "history to elaborate various aspects of scientific inquiry, the nature of science, and science in different historical and cultural perspectives."[9] In other words, the history of science can be deployed in the science curriculum to help students know what science is, the various ways it is practiced, and why it is important to the rest of human experience.

13

Darwin's Battleship

Status Report on the Leaks This Ship Has Sprung

PHILLIP E. JOHNSON

In the epilogue to the second edition of *Darwin on Trial* (1993), I wrote this:

> Darwinian evolution with its blind watchmaker thesis makes me think of a great battleship on the ocean of reality. Its sides are heavily armored with philosophical barriers to criticism, and its decks are stacked with big rhetorical guns ready to intimidate any would-be attackers. In appearance, it is as impregnable as the Soviet Union seemed to be only a few years ago. But the ship has sprung a leak, and the more perceptive of the ship's officers have begun to sense that all the ship's firepower cannot save it if the leak is not plugged. There will be heroic efforts to save the ship, of course, and some plausible rescuers will invite the officers to take refuge in electronic lifeboats equipped with high-tech gear like autocatalytic sets and computer models of self-organizing systems. The spectacle will be fascinating, and the battle will go on for a long time. But in the end reality will win.[1]

There is always a risk in making a prediction like this. Now it may be worthwhile to take a look back and see how things have progressed. There are several trends that will give us an idea of how things are going.

One thing that clearly has happened is that the intelligent design movement, which resulted from the publishing of *Darwin on Trial*, has become a key player in attacking Darwinism. In 2004 and 2005, rare was the day that did not have a major news story about intelligent design (hereafter ID). As I predicted, the "big rhetorical guns" have been brought out in full force. Science organizations regularly mischaracterize ID, calling it "creationism in a cheap tuxedo." They dream up conspiracies and make false accusations. They try to make sure that no one who is friendly to ID is allowed to publish articles in the peer-reviewed literature and then use the lack of such articles to prove that ID is not science. They try to prevent ID-friendly scientists from attaining research or teaching positions. They enter into the decision-making processes of local school districts to make sure that Darwinism is not allowed to be questioned in any way, bringing in the ACLU if there is any attempt to offer an even-handed approach to the teaching of evolution.

University presidents apparently feel so threatened by students questioning their biology teachers that they make strong statements declaring that ID is "not science." This can sometimes backfire, as students wonder why it is that people in power need to protect evolution from any challenges. Intelligent Design and Evolution Awareness (IDEA) clubs are spreading through the university world, offering forums for students to think through the scientific issues surrounding evolution. The situation has been transformed by the phenomenal growth of home schooling. Home schoolers are becoming more and more educated on this subject and, when they have gone on to college, are able to resist indoctrination and properly evaluate dogmatic statements.

And what about the leak that I recognized back in 1993? Has that been repaired with new scientific evidence? The "leak," as I saw it, was that the Darwinian mechanism of evolution could not explain how the complex living world came about. Many times a year, there is some new headline claiming that a new discovery will prove that Darwin was altogether right. Often it is a new finding that brings into question some earlier assumptions about evolution. Sometimes there are stories about new findings that point to an intelligent designer, although such a direction is never admitted. One such event was the discovery of a plant that repaired detrimental genetic changes, guided by a "template" that was not present in the plant itself or its parents.

In an issue of *Harvard Magazine*, Harvard University's dean of evolutionary science, Edward O. Wilson, described how natural selection does its work not with concrete case studies but with a purely hypothetical example. Accordingly, he wrote about birds with different eye colors and how one color may come to predominate in the population, thus gradually bringing about an evolutionary change. There isn't a hint in this example, however, that the Darwinian or other material mechanisms can explain how life came into being from chemicals or how information-packed complex body plans and organs developed. Wilson provides only general statements about the "beauty" and the "explanatory power" of evolution.

Recently Harvard opened a new major research project especially to study the origin of life. This may be in response to the criticisms of the ID movement. Other recent articles suggest that scientists in the biological establishment are doing research specifically to answer the challenges raised by ID. If this is the case, it should be seen as a good thing by everyone. We in the ID movement are proponents of good science. If our criticisms and questions lead to better research, we are unafraid of the results. In the meantime, our current concern is to keep evolutionary scientists honest about the current state of the evidence and to allow young people to understand why there is a controversy about the subject of evolution.

14

Debunking the Scopes "Monkey Trial" Stereotype

EDWARD SISSON

Whenever a challenge to the truth of Darwinian evolution arises, the scientific establishment and its allies trot out the Scopes monkey trial. It is their position that if the scientific establishment has ratified a science textbook, such as the book from which Scopes taught evolution, the state should not engage in "censoring" the material in that book.

The Scopes monkey trial plays such a prominent role in the debate that I purchased a copy of the transcript; a copy of the textbook from which Scopes taught, *A Civic Biology*; and a copy of the companion lab guide to that textbook. Review of these source materials—very different from the biased picture presented in the book *Inherit the Wind*—was a real eye-opener.

In the Scopes trial, there was never any judgment or verdict that Darwinian evolution is true. The prosecution argued and the judge agreed that the Tennessee statute in question barred the teaching of the Darwinian theory even if it were true, so its truth was not an issue in the case. Nor, notably, was the truth of the theory of Darwinian evolution and the supposed evidence for it ever subjected to cross-examination. Scopes's lawyers presented extensive written statements from seven scientists stating that Darwinian evolution is the correct explanation for the diversity of life on earth. The prosecution sought permission to cross-examine the five pro-Darwinian science experts whose statements had been read in open court, but Clarence Darrow and the other Scopes lawyers objected, and the court refused to allow it.

Nor, ironically, given the popular understanding of the case as a disproof of Christian fundamentalism, was fundamentalism technically an issue in the case. The Tennessee statute did not mandate the teaching of fundamentalism. The statute merely barred the teaching of Darwinian evolution.

But Darrow and the defense team wished to make fundamentalism the issue, and they succeeded. Prosecution lawyer William Jennings Bryan agreed to be questioned by Darrow on his personal interpretation of the Bible (the famous examination shown in a false light in *Inherit the Wind*) only if Darrow agreed to be questioned on the evidence for evolution—and the judge agreed that Bryan could question Darrow after Darrow questioned Bryan. The bargain by Bryan, submitting to examination so that he could examine Darrow, was a last-ditch attempt to place some criticism of Darwinian evolution into the Scopes trial record to counteract the one-sided, unchallenged presentation of the pro-Darwin side.

But Darrow, after his famous examination of Bryan, surprised Bryan by announcing that he had no defense to present and asking the judge to instruct the jury to find Scopes guilty. In substance, Darrow was changing Scopes's plea to guilty, but by using the technical approach of a request for a "directed verdict" against his own client, Darrow avoided a waiver of Scopes's right to appeal. Scopes's effective switch to a plea of guilty closed the evidence and made it impossible for Bryan to call Darrow to the stand to question him on evolution.

Darrow's claim that he had no factual defense to present was patently false. In fact, John Scopes never actually taught evolution; he was sick on the class day evolution was scheduled, so he never delivered the lecture. His failure to actually teach evolution was an excellent defense: in fact Scopes was innocent, and a lawyer who was actually representing Scopes's interests—rather than the ACLU's interest—would have featured that fact prominently. (But the prosecution deserves blame as well; surely the prosecutors, too, knew that Scopes never delivered the lecture.)

Moreover, Darrow could easily have abandoned his defense before his examination of Bryan; the fact that Darrow requested the guilty verdict only after he conducted his examination of Bryan indicates that his intention all along was to use Bryan to challenge Christian fundamentalism and then to escape any challenge to the theory of Darwinian evolution.

The result was that, in the Scopes monkey trial, scientists presented their case for Darwinian evolution without any challenge in the trial to the merits of whether the data they offered really showed that the Darwinian theory was true. Nor was there any review of the scientists' arguments in the appeal. Darrow won the appeal on a technicality—the trial court broke a technical rule in assessing the fine.

is, however, this priceless comment in the appellate concurring opinion essee Supreme Court Justice Chambliss. He noted that Scopes's lawyers prominently featured this statement from Professor Reinke of Vanderbilt University: "The theory of evolution is altogether essential to the teaching of biology. . . . To deny the teacher of biology the use of [evolution] would make his teaching as chaotic as an attempt to teach . . . physics without assuming the existence of the ether."[1]

Well, there is no physics course taught in any high school today that "assum[es] the existence of the ether." The concept was abandoned decades ago. In fact, the progress of physics accelerated with the abandonment of the "ether" concept. The progress of biology might also accelerate with the abandonment of Darwinian evolution.

Darwinian evolution's escape from proper cross-examination is longstanding. Cambridge University astrophysics professor Sir Fred Hoyle, in his book critical of Darwinism, *The Mathematics of Evolution*, wrote that the scientific challenges to Darwinian evolution have "never had a fair hearing" because "the developing system of popular education [from Darwin's day to the present] provided an ideal opportunity for zealots who were sure of themselves to overcome those who were not, for awkward arguments not to be discussed, and for discrepant facts to be suppressed."[2]

Examination of Scopes's textbook, George William Hunter's *A Civic Biology*, demonstrates another important lesson about whether the scientific establishment should receive the great deference it demands from our school boards concerning what should be taught in our schools. *A Civic Biology* and its companion lab book both contain sections on eugenics—introduced by the statement that "the science of being well born is called eugenics."[3] The scientific establishment of the time fully supported this "science" of eugenics. This endorsement by the scientific establishment meant that eugenics was taught in our schools.

Here is what the scientific establishment of that time caused schoolchildren to learn. *A Civic Biology* divides humanity into five races and ranked them in terms of superiority, concluding with "the highest type of all, the Caucasians, represented by the civilized white inhabitants of Europe and America."[4] It also asserts that crime and immorality are inherited and run in families, and that "these families have become parasitic on society. . . . If such people were lower animals, we would probably kill them off. . . . We do have the remedy of separating the sexes in asylums or other places and in various ways preventing intermarriage and the possibilities of perpetuating such a low and degenerate race."[5] The lab book, at Problem 160, asks students to use inheritance charts "to determine some means of bettering, physically and mentally, the human race," and a "Note to Teachers" says that "the child is at the receptive age and is emotionally open to the serious lessons here involved."[6]

Of course, the scientific establishment of today would denounce all of this. Thus the very text book from which Scopes taught—the very book that the scientific establishment of today proclaims Scopes ought to have been able to use in 1925 without any interference by the state—includes material that today the scientific establishment rejects. Eugenics, like the "ether," once thought so essential, has vanished from the curriculum—has "vanished into the ether," one is tempted to say. Yet science continues ever healthier despite the loss of these theories. And science would remain healthy if Darwinian evolution, too, "vanished into the ether."

Thus the important question is whether the rest of the world should wait for the science establishment to catch up before deciding to reject paradigms that have hung on in our textbooks for years, despite manifold and rapidly accumulating flaws.

If we cast ourselves back to 1925 and ask ourselves whether it would have been proper for the state of Tennessee then to have adopted a law that permitted the teaching of eugenics as the scientific establishment demanded but that required challenges to the theory also be taught—would not everyone today applaud the foresight of the state in enacting such a law? Would we not all agree that if such a "science" of eugenics had to be taught in our schools because of the insistence of the scientific establishment, that it would be appropriate also to teach the flaws in that "science"?

The hypothetical example of a state law mandating that doubts about the "science" of eugenics be taught demonstrates that it is appropriate for the people who determine our school curricula not to be slavishly bound to adhere to whatever the scientific establishment espouses at any given time. Instead, the population at large—which is free from the institutional incentives and biases that can and do affect the judgment of members of the scientific establishment—is entirely within its rights to doubt a theory before the scientific establishment might similarly doubt that theory. This kind of approach is well-accepted in other fields where the government significantly affects the lives of the people: for example, while we listen respectfully to military officers who state the need for more weapons, we reserve the final decision for the people's chosen representatives.

Where tens of millions of dollars of funding, and the education of tens of millions of children, are at stake, the recipients of the funds and the purveyors of education deserve respect but should not hold the final say over their own funding and their own jobs. They are not as free from self-interested bias as they flatter themselves to be. Too often, to the parents, the science establishment's claim to be motivated only by the well-being of our children appears tainted by a self-interested desire that our children flatter their teachers' egos by believing everything their teachers believe. Indeed, Darwinians, who claim that all of life is motivated by an irresistible drive for survival, which necessarily means a drive for power, are poorly positioned to claim a special exemption from the very force they say rules life. To the contrary, we are justified in considering that they may be particularly susceptible to the operation of the very theory they advocate so vehemently. In a democracy, the final decisions in these matters must rest with the people who provide the funding and who are the parents who give birth to, raise, and support the children who are in the government's schools. School boards ought to give serious consideration to encouraging the development of suitable curriculum materials by which to present to students the data and analysis that show the weaknesses in Darwinian theory—weaknesses that are sufficiently significant that this teaching may even cause students to doubt that the Darwinian explanation is true.

15

How Darwinism Dumbs Us Down

Evolution and Postmodernism

Nancy Pearcey

At Stanford University in the spring of 2005, I had my first experience of being picketed. Organized by a campus group calling itself Rational Thought, the picketers carried signs protesting the presence of intelligent design (ID) proponents on campus. Several local atheist groups joined the controversy, sparking colorful stories in the local newspapers.

Before me at the podium was Michael Behe, author of *Darwin's Black Box*, speaking on the scientific evidence against evolution. I followed by explaining the cultural and philosophical implications of evolution. As I spoke, astonishingly, some of the protesters softened their hostility and actually began to engage with what I was saying. The gist of my talk was that Darwinism undercuts the very possibility of rational truth—an argument that seemed unsettling to atheist students who had organized a group specifically to promote rational thought!

To understand how Darwinism undercuts the very concept of rationality, we can think back to the late nineteenth century when the theory first arrived on American shores. Almost immediately, it was welcomed by a group of thinkers who began to work out its implications far beyond science. They realized that Darwinism implies a broader philosophy of naturalism (i.e., that nature is all that exists and that natural causes are adequate to explain all phenomena). Thus they began applying a naturalistic worldview across the board—in philosophy, psychology, the law, education, and the arts.

At the foundation of these efforts, however, was a naturalistic approach to knowledge itself (epistemology). The logic went like this: If humans are products of Darwinian natural selection, that obviously includes the human brain—which in turn means all our beliefs and values are products of evolutionary forces. Ideas arise in the human brain by chance, just like Darwin's chance variations in nature, and the ones that stick around to become firm beliefs and convictions are those that give an advantage in the struggle for survival. This view of knowledge came to be called pragmatism (truth is what works) or instrumentalism (ideas are merely tools for survival).

Darwinian Logic

One of the leading pragmatists was John Dewey, who had a greater influence on educational theory in America than anyone else in the twentieth century. Dewey rejected the idea that there is a transcendent element in human nature, typically defined in terms of mind or soul or spirit, capable of knowing a transcendent truth or moral order. Instead he treated humans as mere organisms adapting to challenges in the environment. In his educational theory, learning is just another form of adaptation—a kind of mental natural selection. Ideas evolve as tools for survival, no different from the evolution of the lion's teeth or the eagle's claws.

In a famous essay called "The Influence of Darwin on Philosophy," Dewey said Darwinism leads to a "new logic for application to mind and morals and life."[1] In this new evolutionary logic, ideas are not judged by a transcendent standard of truth but by how they work in getting us what we want. Ideas do not "reflect reality" but only serve human interests.

To emphasize how revolutionary this was, up until this time the dominant theory of knowledge, or epistemology, was based on the biblical doctrine of the image of God. Confidence in the reliability of human knowledge derived from the conviction that finite human reason reflects (to some degree at least) an infinite divine reason. Since the same God who created the universe also created our minds, we can be confident that our mental capacities reflect the structure of the universe. In *The Mind of God and the Works of Man*, Edward Craig shows that even as Western thinkers began to move away from orthodox Christian theology, in their philosophy most of them still retained the conception that our minds reflect an absolute mind as the basis for trust in human cognition.[2]

The pragmatists were among the first, however, to face squarely the implications of naturalistic evolution. If evolutionary forces produced the mind, they said, then all beliefs and convictions are nothing but mental survival strategies, to be judged in terms of their practical success in human conduct. William James liked to say that truth is the "cash value" of an idea: if it pays off, then we call it true.

Pragmatism Today

This Darwinian logic continues to shape American thought more than we might imagine. Take religion. William James was raised in a household with an intense interest in religion. (In the Second Great Awakening his father converted to Christianity, then later converted to Swedenborgianism). As a result, James applied his philosophy of pragmatism to religion: we decide whether God exists depending on whether that belief has positive consequences in our experience. "An idea is 'true' so long as to believe it is profitable to our lives," James once said. Thus, "If theological ideas should do this, if the notion of God, in particular, should prove to do it, how could pragmatism possibly deny God's existence?"[3]

Does this sound familiar? A great many Americans today choose their religion based on what meets their needs, or "affirms" them, or helps them cope more effectively with personal issues, from losing weight to building a better marriage. I was recently chatting with a Christian who is very active in her church; but when the topic turned to a mutual friend who is not a believer, her response was, "Well, whatever works for you." Of course, there is a grave problem with choosing a religion according to "whatever works for you"—namely, that we cannot know whether it is really true or just a projection of our own needs. As Lutheran theologian John Warwick Montgomery puts it, "Truths do not always 'work,' and beliefs that 'work' are by no means always true."[4]

If James's religious pragmatism has become virtually the American approach to spirituality today, then Dewey's pragmatism has become the preferred approach to education. Virtually across the curriculum—from math class to moral education—teachers are trained to be nondirective "facilitators," presenting students with problems and allowing them to work out their own pragmatic strategies for solving them. Of course, good teachers have always taught students to think for themselves. But today's nondirective methodologies go far beyond that. They springboard from a Darwinian epistemology that denies the very existence of any objective or transcendent truth.

Take, for example, "constructivism," a popular trend in education today. Few realize that it is based on the idea that truth is nothing more than a social construction for solving problems. A leading theorist of constructivism, Ernst von Glasersfeld at the University of Georgia, is forthright about its Darwinian roots. "The function of cognition is adaptive in the biological sense," he writes.[5] "This means that 'to know' is not to possess 'true representations' of reality, but rather to possess ways and means of acting and thinking that allow one to attain the goals one happens to have chosen."[6] In short, a Darwinian epistemology implies that ideas are merely tools for meeting human goals.

Postmodern Campuses

These results of pragmatism are quite postmodern, so it comes as no surprise to learn that the prominent postmodernist Richard Rorty calls himself a neo-pragmatist. Rorty argues that postmodernism is simply the logical outcome of pragmatism, and explains why.

According to the traditional, commonsense approach to knowledge, our ideas are true when they represent or correspond to reality. But according to Darwinian epistemology, ideas are nothing but tools that have evolved to help us control and manipulate the environment. As Rorty puts it, our theories "have no more of a representational relation to an intrinsic nature of things than does the anteater's snout or the bowerbird's skill at weaving."[7] Thus we evaluate an idea the same way that natural selection preserves the snout or the weaving instinct—not by asking how well it represents objective reality but only how well it works.

I once presented this progression from Darwinism to postmodern pragmatism at a Christian college, when a man in the audience raised his hand: "I have only one question. These guys who think all our ideas and beliefs evolved . . . do they think their own ideas evolved?" The audience broke into delighted applause, because of course he had captured the key fallacy of the Darwinian approach to knowledge. If all ideas are products of evolution, and thus not really true but only useful for survival, then evolution itself is not true either—and why should the rest of us pay any attention to it?

Indeed, the theory undercuts itself. For if evolution is true, then it is not true, but only useful. This kind of internal contradiction is fatal, for a theory that asserts something and denies it at the same time is simply nonsense. In short, naturalistic evolution is self-refuting.

Clash of Worldviews

The media paints the evolution controversy in terms of science versus religion. But it is much more accurate to say it is worldview versus worldview, philosophy versus philosophy. Making this point levels the playing field and opens the door to serious dialogue.

Interestingly, a few evolutionists do acknowledge the point. Michael Ruse made a famous admission at the 1993 symposium of the American Association for the Advancement of Science. "Evolution as a scientific theory makes a commitment to a kind of naturalism," he said—that is, it is a philosophy, not just facts. He went on: "Evolution, akin to religion, involves making certain a priori or metaphysical assumptions, which at some level cannot be proven empirically."[8] Ruse's colleagues responded with shocked silence and afterward one of them, Arthur Shapiro, wrote a commentary titled, "Did Michael Ruse Give Away the Store?"[9]

But, ironically, in the process, Shapiro himself conceded that "there is an irreducible core of ideological assumptions underlying science." He went on: "Darwinism is a philosophical preference, if by that we mean we choose to discuss the material Universe in terms of material processes accessible by material operations."

It is this worldview dimension that makes the debate over Darwin versus intelligent design so important. Every system of thought starts with a creation account that offers an answer to the fundamental question: Where did everything come from? That crucial starting point shapes everything that follows. Today a naturalistic approach to knowledge is being applied to virtually every field. Some say we're entering an age of "universal Darwinism," where it is no longer just a scientific theory but a comprehensive worldview.

It has become commonplace to say that America is embroiled in a "culture war" over conflicting moral standards. But we must remember that morality is always derivative, stemming from an underlying worldview. The culture war reflects an underlying *cognitive* war over worldviews—and at the core of each worldview is an account of origins.

16

Limits to Evolvability

Ray Bohlin

The Misuse of Artificial Selection

Most people assume that evolution allows almost unlimited biological change. Even so, a few simple observations show that there are indeed limits to biological change. Certainly the ubiquitous presence of convergence suggests that biological change is not limitless since evolution appears to arrive at certain solutions again and again. There appear to be only so many ways that organisms can propel themselves through water, over land, or through the air. The wings of insects, birds, and bats, though not ancestrally related, all show certain design similarities. At the very least, various physical parameters constrain biological change and adaptation. Certainly there are physical constraints. But what about biological constraints?

In arguing for extensive evolutionary change, Darwin relied heavily on the analogy between artificial selection and natural selection. Darwin, a skilled breeder of pigeons, recognized that just about any identifiable trait could be accentuated or diminished through careful breeding (i.e., artificial selection). Darwin then reasoned that a similar form of selection also occurred in nature (i.e., natural selection) and could accomplish the same thing. It would just need more time.

But artificial selection has proven just the opposite. For essentially every trait, although it usually harbors some variability, there has always been a limit. Whether the organisms or selected traits are roses, dogs, pigeons, horses, cattle, protein content in corn, or the sugar content in beets, selection certainly has an effect. But all selected qualities eventually fizzle out. Chickens don't produce cylindrical eggs. We can't produce a plum the size of a pea or a grapefruit. There are limits to how far we can go. Some people grow as tall as seven feet, and some grow no taller than three, but none are over twelve feet or under two. There are limits to change.

But perhaps the most telling argument against the usefulness of artificial selection as a model for natural selection is the actual process of selection. Darwin called it artificial selection. A better term would have been intentional selection. The phrase *artificial selection* makes it sound simple and undirected. Yet every breeder, whether of plants or animals, is always looking for something in particular. The selection process is always designed to a particular end.

If you want a dog that hunts better, you breed your best hunters hoping to accentuate the trait. If you desire roses of a particular color, you choose roses of similar color hoping to arrive at the desired shade. In other words, you plan and manipulate the process. Natural selection can do no such thing. Natural selection, by contrast, operates with no plan and is at the mercy of whatever variations come along. Trying to compare a directed to an undirected process offers no insight into evolution at all.

The Real Power of Natural Selection

It is instructive that we had to wait until the 1950s, almost one hundred years after the publication of Darwin's *Origin of Species*, for a documented case of natural selection, the famous peppered moth (*Biston betularia*). The story begins with the observation that before the industrial revolution, moth collections of Great Britain contained the peppered variety, a light colored, but speckled moth. With the rise of industrial pollution, a dark form, or melanic variety, became more prevalent. As environmental controls were enacted, pollution levels decreased and the peppered variety made a strong comeback.

It seemed that as pollution increased, the lichens on trees died off and the bark became blackened. The previously camouflaged peppered variety was now conspicuous, and the previously conspicuous melanic form was now camouflaged. Birds could more readily see the conspicuous variety, and the two forms changed frequency depending on their surrounding conditions. This was natural selection at work.

There were always problems with this standard story. What did it really show? First, the melanic form was always in the population, just at very low frequencies. So we start with two varieties of the peppered moth, and we still have two forms. The frequencies change but nothing new has been added to the population. Second, we really don't know the genetics of industrial melanism in these moths. We don't have a detailed explanation of how the two forms are generated. And third, in some populations, the frequencies of the two moths changed whether there was a corresponding change in the tree bark or not. The only consistent factor was pollution.[1] The best known example of evolution in action thus reduces to a mere footnote.

Even Darwin's finches from the Galapagos Islands, off the coast of Ecuador, tell us little of large-scale evolution. The thirteen species of finches on the Galapagos Islands show subtle variation in the size and shape of their beaks based on the primary food source of the particular species of finch. While the finches do show change over time in response to environmental factors—hence natural selection—the change is reversible! The size and shape of their beaks will vary slightly depending if the year is wet or dry (varying the size of seeds produced) and revert when the conditions reverse. There is no directional change. It is even possible that the thirteen species are more like six or seven species since hybrids form so readily, especially among the ground finches, and survive quite well. Once again, where is the real evolution?

There are many other documented examples of natural selection operating in the wild. But they all show that whereas limited change is possible, there are also limits to change. No one, as far as I know, questions the reality of natural selection. The real issue is that examples such as the peppered moth and Darwin's finches tell us nothing about evolution.

Mutations Do Not Produce Real Change

While most evolutionists will acknowledge that there are limits to change, they insist that natural selection is not sufficient without a continual source of variation. In the neo-Darwinian synthesis, mutations of all sorts fill that role. These mutations fall into two main categories, mutations to structural genes and mutations to developmental genes. I will define structural genes as those which code for a protein that performs a maintenance, metabolic, support, or specialized function in the cell. Developmental genes influence specific tasks in embryological development and therefore can change the morphology, or actual appearance, of an organism.

Most evolutionary studies have focused on mutations in structural genes. But in order for large scale changes to happen, mutations in developmental genes must be explored.

We'll come back to these developmental mutations a little later.

Most examples that we have of mutations generating supposed evolutionary change involve structural genes. The most common example of these kinds of mutations producing significant evolutionary change involves microbial antibiotic resistance. Since the introduction of penicillin during World War II, the use of antibiotics has mushroomed. Much to everyone's surprise, bacteria have the uncanny ability to become resistant to these antibiotics. This has been trumpeted far and wide as real evidence that nature's struggle for existence results in genetic change, evolution.

But microbial antibiotic resistance comes in many forms that aren't so dramatic. Sometimes the genetic mutation simply allows the antibiotic to be pumped out of the cell faster than normal or taken into the cell more slowly. Other times the antibiotic is deactivated inside the cell by a closely related enzyme already present. In other cases, the molecule inside the cell that is the target of the antibiotic is ever so slightly modified so the antibiotic no longer affects it. All of these mechanisms occur naturally and the mutations simply intensify an ability the cell already has. No new genetic information is added.[2]

The great French evolutionist Pierre-Paul Grassé, when addressing mutations in bacteria, remarked, "What is the use of their unceasing mutations if they do not change? In sum the mutations of bacteria and viruses are merely hereditary fluctuations around a median position; a swing to the right, a swing to the left, but no final evolutionary effect."[3]

So far I have been describing what is commonly called microevolution. Evolutionists have basically assumed that the well-documented processes of microevolution eventually produce macroevolutionary changes given enough time. But this assumption is itself problematic.

Natural Selection Does Not Produce New Body Plans

A fundamental question that now needs to be addressed is how sponges, starfish, cockroaches, butterflies, eels, frogs, woodpeckers, and humans all arose from single-cell beginnings without design, purpose, or plan. All such organisms have very different body plans. How can all these different body plans arise from mutation and natural selection? This is a far bigger and more difficult problem than antibiotic resistance, which only requires small biochemical changes. The question, then, is how morphological change comes about.

The problem of macroevolution therefore requires developmental mutations. Changes must somehow occur in how the organism is built. Structural genes tend to have little effect on the development of a body plan. But the genes that control development, and thus ultimately influence the body plan, tend to find expression quite early in development. But this raises its own problems because the developing embryo is quite sensitive to early developmental mutations. As Wallace Arthur notes, "Those genes that control key early developmental processes are involved in the establishment of the basic body plan. Mutations in these genes will usually be extremely disadvantageous, and it is conceivable that they are always so."[4]

If developmental mutations that can offer actual benefit are so rare, then macroevolution would be expected to be a slow, difficult, and bumpy process.

Darwin indicated as much in the concluding chapter of his *Origin of Species*: "As natural selection acts solely by accumulating slight, successive, favorable variations, it can produce no great or sudden modifications; it can only act in short and slow steps."[5]

Accordingly, not only is the type of mutation a problem, but so is the rate of mutation. Susumo Ohno points out that "it still takes 10 million years to undergo 1% change in DNA base sequences. . . . [The] emergence of nearly all the extant phyla of the Kingdom Animalia within the time span of 6–10 million years can't possibly be explained by mutational divergence of individual gene functions."[6]

Along the way, functional organisms must assume intermediate forms. But even the functionality of these intermediate organisms transforming from one body plan to another has long puzzled even the most dedicated evolutionists. Stephen Jay Gould, the late Harvard paleontologist, asked, "But how can a series of reasonable intermediates be constructed? . . . The dung-mimicking insect is well protected, but can there be any edge in looking only 5 percent like a turd?"[7]

With his usual flair, Gould asks a penetrating question. There do indeed appear to be built-in limits to evolutionary change.

17

Evolutionary Computation

A Perpetual Motion Machine for Design Information?

Robert J. Marks II

Evolutionary computing, modeled after Darwinian evolution, is a useful engineering tool. It can create unexpected, insightful, and clever results. Consequently, an image is often painted of evolutionary computation as a free source of intelligence and information. The design of a program to perform evolutionary computation, however, requires infusion of implicit information concerning the goal of the program. This information fine-tunes the performance of the evolutionary search and is mandatory for a successful search.

Computational Intelligence

Fifty years ago, Ross W. Ashby asked "Can a Mechanical Chess Player Outplay Its Designer?"[1] We know today that it can. A more relevant question is, "Can a computer program generate more information than it is given?" Evolutionary computing, on the surface, seems to be a candidate paradigm. As with all "something for nothing" claims, this is not the case.

Pioneers of evolutionary computing in the 1960s proposed that computer emulation of evolution overcame the difficulty of demonstrating Darwinian evolution in the biology lab. Proof of Darwinian evolution "has from the beginning been handicapped by the fact that no proper test has been found to decide whether such evolution was possible and how it would develop under controlled conditions."[2] "In general, it is usually impossible or impracticable to test hypotheses about evolution in a particular species by the deliberate setting up of controlled experiments with living organisms of that species. We can attempt partially to get round this difficulty by constructing models representing the evolutionary system we wish to study, and use these to test at least the theoretical validity of our ideas."[3]

Engineering Design

Evolutionary computation is used today largely in engineering design and problem solving. Design begins with establishing a goal or design objective. From a favorite list of paradigms, a viable model is chosen. Design consists of identification of parameter values within the chosen model. Design has been defined as "the judicious manipulation of mid-range values" within the confines of a model.[4] Search algorithms do this with the aid of a computer.

Consider the simple example of designing a recipe for boiling an egg. Our questions include the following:

1. Do we place the eggs in cold water and bring to a boil, or place the eggs in boiling water (two choices)?
2. How long do we boil the eggs?
3. Do we remove the pan from the heat and let the water cool, place the eggs on a dish to cool, or immediately place the eggs in cold water (three choices)?

At step 1 there are two choices, and at step 3, three choices. For the duration of boiling in step 2, let's assume there are choices in fifteen second intervals from 30 seconds to three minutes: 0:30, 0:45, 1:00, and so on. That's eleven choices of time intervals. The total number of possible recipes is therefore $2 \times 11 \times 3 = 66$. We have defined a *search space*, but have not yet defined what our design criterion is, namely, what is the optimal recipe? Suppose I taste the egg and rate it from 1 to 100 in terms of taste. This measure, assigned to each of the 66 recipes, is the *fitness* of the recipe. Anything above a 90 will meet the design criterion. The design goal is identification of a recipe that meets the design criterion.

Assume you have never cooked and have absolutely no idea which recipe is best. We apply *Bernoulli's principle of insufficient reason*, which states that, in the absence of any prior knowledge, we must assume that all the recipes have an equal probability of being best. One recipe must be assumed as good as another. To find the optimal recipe, all 66 would need to be tried. One approach to find a decent recipe is trial and error. If trial and error could be done on computer, the tests could be done quickly. Suppose we can emulate the boiling of the egg and the fitness of the result on a computer. Then we could determine the optimal recipe quickly by evaluating all 66 recipes. Looking at all possible solutions is called *exhaustive search*. Unfortunately, search problems scale poorly, and this is not possible for even reasonably sized problems. If we have, instead of 3, 100 variables, and each variable has ten possible outcomes, the number of elements in the search space becomes 10^{100} (i.e., 10 multiplied by itself 100 times), which is a larger number than there are atoms in the universe. Exhaustive search is not possible in such cases.

We can remove Bernoulli's principle of insufficient reason from the search problem only through infusion of information into the search process. The information can be explicit. For the egg example, knowledge of chemistry tells us that placing the boiled eggs in cold water retards the chemical reaction that will ultimately make the eggs smell like sulfur. Assuming a sulfur smell will detract from the fitness, we can eliminate one of the search variables and reduce the search to 44 recipes. Alternately, the information can be implicit. You may know, for example, that of ten famous egg boilers, two place the raw eggs in cold water and eight in boiling water. This information can guide your search of recipes initially to those with a greater chance of meeting the design criterion.

The Need for Implicit Information

Purely theoretical considerations suggest that, given a fast enough computer and sufficient time, a space can be successfully searched to find the optimal solution. But this is the myth of "monkeys at a typewriter." The story, theoretically plausible, says that if enough monkeys pound out random letters long enough, all of the great texts in history—such as *Moby-Dick* (1,170,200 characters), *Grimm's Fairy Tales* (1,435,800 characters), and the King James Bible (3,556,480 letters not including spaces)—will eventually result. The finiteness of the closed universe, however, prohibits this.

Looking for a single solution in a large unstructured search space is dubbed a "needle in a haystack" problem. In moderately large cases, it simply can't be done. Choosing randomly from a 26-letter alphabet, the chances of writing the King James Bible are $26^{3,556,480}$, which equals $3.8 \times 10^{5,032,323}$. This is a number so large it defies description. If all the matter in the universe (10^{58} kilograms) were converted to energy ($E = mc^2$), 10 billion times per second since the big bang (20 billion years) and all this energy were used to generate text at the minimum irreversible bit level (i.e., $\ln(2)\ kT = 2.9\ 10^{-21}$ joules per bit), then about 10^{88} messages as long as the King James Bible could be generated. If we multiply this by the number of atoms in the universe (10^{78} atoms), we have 10^{166} messages, still dwarfed by the required $10^{5,032,323}$.

Let's try a more modest problem: the phrase

IN*THE*BEGINNING*GOD*CREATED

(We could complete the phrase with "the heaven and the earth," but the numbers grow too large.) Here there are 27 possible characters (26 letters and a space) and the string has a length of 28 characters. The odds that this is the phrase written by the monkeys is 27^{28}, which equals 1.20×10^{40} to 1. This number isn't so big that we can't wrap our minds around it. The chance of a monkey typing 28 letters and typing *these specific words* is the same as choosing a single atom from over one trillion tons of iron. Using Avogadro's number, we compute 27^{28} atoms: (1 mole per 6.022×10^{23} atoms) $\times$ (55.845 grams per mole) $\times$ (1 short ton per 907,185 grams) = 1.22×10^{12} short tons.

Quantum computers would help by reduction of the equivalent search size by a square root,[5] but the problem remains beyond the resources of the closed universe. Information must be infused into the search process.

Searching an unstructured space without imposition of structure on the space is computationally prohibitive for even small problems. The need for implicit information imposed by design heuristics has been emphasized by the *no free lunch theorems*,[6] which have shown, "unless you can make prior assumptions about the . . . [problems] you are working on, then no search strategy, no matter how sophisticated, can be expected to perform better than any other."[7] No free lunch theorems "indicate the importance of incorporating problem-specific knowledge into the behavior of the [optimization or search] algorithm."[8]

Sources of Information

A common structure in evolutionary search is an imposed fitness function, wherein the merit of a design for each set of parameters is assigned a number. The bigger the fitness, the better. The optimization problem is to maximize the fitness function. *Penalty functions* are similar, but are to be minimized. In the early days of computing, an engineer colleague of mine described his role in conducting searches as a *penalty function artist*. He took pride in using his domain expertise to craft penalty functions. The structured search model developed by the design engineer must be, in some sense, a *good* model. Exploring through the parameters of a poor model, no matter how thoroughly, will not result in a viable design. In a contrary manner, a cleverly conceived model can result in better solutions in faster time.

Here is a simple example of structure in a search. Instead of choosing each letter at random, let's choose more commonly used letters more frequently. If we choose characters at random, then each character has a chance of 1 in 27, which equals a 3.7 percent chance of being chosen. In English, the letter *e* is used about 10 percent of the time. A blank occurs 20 percent of the time. If we choose letters in accordance to their frequency of occurrence, then the odds of choosing IN*THE*BEGINNING*GOD*CREATED nose dives to *five one millionths* (0.0005 percent) of its original size—from 1.2×10^{40} to 5.35×10^{34}. This is still a large number: the trillion tons of iron has been reduced to 5.5 million tons. If we use the frequency of digraphs, we can reduce it further. (Digraphs are letter pairs that occur frequently; for instance, the digraph *e_*, where _ is a space, is the most common pair of characters in English.) Trigraph frequency will reduce the odds more.

The Fine-Tuning of the Search Space

As more implicit structure is imposed on the search space, the search becomes easier. Even more interesting is that, for moderately long messages, if the target message does not match the search space structuring, the message won't be found.

Let a search space be structured with a disposition to generate a type of message. If a target does not match this predisposition, it will be found with probability zero.

This theorem, long known in information theory in a different context, is a direct consequence of *the law of large numbers*. If, for example, we structure the search space to give an *e* 10 percent of the time, then the number of *e*'s in a message 10,000 characters in length will be very close to 1,000. The curious book *Gadsby*, containing no *e*'s, would be found with a vanishingly small probability.

Structuring the search space also reduces its effective size. The search space consists of all possible sequences. For a structured space, let's dub the set of all probable sequences that are predisposed to the structure the "search space *sub*set." For frequency of occurrence structuring of the alphabet, all of the great novels we seek, except for *Gadsby*, lie in or close to this subset.

The more structure that is added to a search space, the more added information there is. Trigraphs, for example, add more information than digraphs.

As the length of a sequence increases and the added structure information increases, the percent of elements in the search subset goes to zero. This is called the "diminishing subset theorem." Structuring of a search space therefore not only confines solutions to obey the structure of the space; the number of solutions becomes a diminishingly small percentage of the search space as the message length increases.

Final Thoughts

Search spaces require structuring for search algorithms to be viable. This includes evolutionary search for a targeted design goal. The added structure information needs to be implicitly infused into the search space and is used to guide the process to a desired result. The target can be specific, as is the case with a precisely identified phrase; or it can be general, such as meaningful phrases that will pass, say, a spelling and grammar check. In any case, there is yet no perpetual motion machine for the design of information arising from evolutionary computation.

18

Science, Eugenics, and Bioethics

Richard Weikart

In the late nineteenth century, a movement emerged among scientists and physicians that advocated the improvement of human heredity. Francis Galton, a respected British scientist, who founded this movement, named this new field of endeavor *eugenics*. Galton claimed that this field was founded on scientific principles. He first formulated his ideas about eugenics while reading the *Origin of Species*, written by his cousin Charles Darwin. In that book, Darwin argued that hereditary change together with natural selection would produce new species. Because eugenics was based on Darwinian theory, many eugenicists feared that modern institutions, such as medicine and social welfare, were spawning biological degeneration among humans. By softening the struggle for existence, modern society allowed the "inferior" to reproduce. The purpose of eugenics was to reverse this degenerative trend so humans could foster evolutionary progress instead.

The eugenics movement spread rapidly after 1900 throughout the Western world, especially among scientists and physicians. Though eugenics advocates embraced a variety of political positions, it was especially popular among progressives. In Germany the eugenics movement took a major step forward in 1900, when the Krupp Prize competition offered a large monetary award for the best book-length answer to the question: "What do we learn from the principles of biological evolution in regard to domestic political developments and legislation of states?" Wilhelm Schallmayer won the competition with his book *Heredity and Selection* (1903), which forcefully advocated eugenics. The physician Alfred Ploetz organized the German eugenics movement by founding the first eugenics journal in the world in 1904 and the following year establishing the first eugenics society in the world. In the United States, the geneticist Charles Davenport became the key organizer of the eugenics movement by establishing the Eugenics Record Office on Long Island in 1910. He successfully solicited funds for his research from major American business interests, such as the Carnegie Foundation.

By the 1920s the eugenics movement was so well established that many universities in the United States and Europe offered courses on eugenics. Galton had established a professorship at the University of London upon his death in 1911 to promote eugenics. In 1923 the University of Munich established a medical professorship in *racial hygiene* (the German term for eugenics), and in 1927 Germany founded the Kaiser Wilhelm Institute for Anthropology, Human Heredity, and Eugenics. Progressive medical elites in Latin America, Asia, and elsewhere throughout the world imbibed eugenics along with Western medical knowledge.

While some eugenicists focused mainly on the science of human heredity, many simultaneously promoted programs and policies to control human reproduction. By propagating new ideas about sexuality and by pressing for legislation to control reproduction, scientists began promoting a new ethic or new morality. Many early eugenicists based their ethic on evolution, calling eugenics "applied evolution." Whatever promoted evolutionary progress was good, in their view, and anything leading to biological decline was evil. Thus, health and biological vitality became the standards by which they judged all actions and policies. Often, their new morality was in conflict with traditional Christian morality.

Eugenicists did not always agree among themselves about what measures should be taken to control human reproduction. Some stressed positive eugenics (i.e., measures to encourage the "better" humans to reproduce more prolifically.) This could include tax breaks or even subsidies for the upper classes and the intelligentsia to have more children. Embedded in many of these proposals was the assumption that the upper classes and intelligentsia were biologically superior to the masses, especially the working classes. Most eugenicists also supported negative eugenics (i.e., efforts to suppress the reproduction of "inferior" people, usually defined as the congenitally disabled, habitual criminals, and those of allegedly inferior races, such as blacks and American Indians).

Some eugenicists hoped that marriage restrictions or permanent segregation (i.e., incarceration) of those deemed unfit to reproduce would achieve some positive results. However, a new method of controlling reproduction—sterilization—became especially popular among eugenics advocates in the early twentieth century. The United States passed the first compulsory sterilization legislation in the world in 1907, when Indiana decided to force some inmates of its prisons and mental institutions to submit to sterilization. Many other states followed suit, and in 1927 the U.S. Supreme Court declared that compulsory sterilization laws were permissible. By 1940 over thirty-five thousand people had been compulsorily sterilized in the United States. The Nazi regime implemented an even more vigorous sterilization campaign beginning in 1934, which resulted in the forced sterilization of about four hundred thousand people.

Since many eugenicists were racist, they also introduced measures to restrict the reproduction of those deemed to be of inferior racial stock. Some eugenicists in the United States succeeded in getting antimiscegenation laws passed as a way to try to improve human heredity. They also exulted in the passage of the Immigration Act of 1924, which restricted immigration from countries with allegedly inferior biological quality.

Some radical eugenicists even advocated infanticide or involuntary "euthanasia" to get rid of "inferior" persons. In 1870, the famous Darwinian biologist in Germany Ernst Haeckel became one of the first intellectuals in modern Europe to seriously propose that infants with congenital problems be killed. By the early twentieth century, prominent figures such as Jack London, Eugene Debs, Clarence Darrow, Margaret Sanger, H. G. Wells, and Julian Huxley supported the legalization of euthanasia, many of them because they viewed it as a eugenics measure. In its zeal to rid Germany of those considered biologically "inferior," the Nazi regime implemented a program in 1939 (after World War II began) to kill institutionalized persons with congenital illnesses, especially those with mental illnesses, but also the deaf, blind, and others. Altogether the Nazis probably killed about two hundred thousand disabled people by the end of World War II.

The response of the churches to the rise of eugenics varied considerably. Mainline Protestants, especially those with more liberal theology, prided themselves in adapting to modern trends, and in general they eagerly adopted eugenics ideology. The American Eugenics Society received hundreds of entries in the eugenics sermon contests they sponsored in the 1920s. The most vocal and organized opposition to eugenics, especially to sterilization and euthanasia, came from the Catholic Church, though many conservative Protestants also opposed eugenics.

Eugenics, at least as an organized movement, died out in the mid-twentieth century for a variety of reasons. Biological determinism was in decline in the mid-twentieth century, especially in the fields of psychology and anthropology, but in many other fields too. Also, critics of eugenics were able to capitalize on the shoddy quality of some of the science underpinning eugenics. Nazi atrocities brought eugenics into greater disrepute. Finally the call for freedom of reproductive choice that accompanied the Sexual Revolution in the 1960s contradicted the compulsory measures advocated by earlier progressives.

In the past ten to twenty years many dozens of books have appeared on the history of eugenics. This intense interest is probably spawned by fears of a resurgence of eugenics under a different guise. Indeed, new reproductive technologies, such as in vitro fertilization, amniocentesis, and genetic screening, have presented us with new prospects for a more individualized form of eugenics in the late twentieth and early twenty-first centuries. Parents for decades have routinely aborted infants with serious disabilities. More recently it has become possible to select a fertilized egg with specific genetic traits before it is implanted into the mother's womb. Some scientists and physicians are forthrightly arguing that individuals should artificially select the traits of their offspring, though critics warn about the dangers of "designer babies."

Human cloning will likely be a reality in the near future, and with present heated debates over the morality of cloning and stem cell research, the history of eugenics is a cautionary tale. Scientists and physicians in the early twentieth century who supported eugenics often denied the validity of Christian (or any other) ethics on their research and even on their public policy proposals. Eugenics was supposedly an objective, scientific panacea for a myriad of ills, both physical and social. We should take control of our future, eugenics advocates argued, to shape a human destiny free from hereditary illness and crime. Ethical considerations were spurned as detrimental to progress and human health.

Many purveyors of genetic technologies today sound remarkably similar to earlier eugenicists. They claim scientific imprimatur for their views, reject ethical restrictions on their research, make health the highest arbiter of morality, and devalue the lives of the disabled. They promise great advances to help humanity, but they do not consider or understand that by destroying individuals they deem "inferior," they are perpetrating gross injustice.

19

Designed for Discovery

GUILLERMO GONZALEZ AND JAY W. RICHARDS

Read any book on the history of scientific discovery, and you'll find magnificent tales of human ingenuity, persistence, and dumb luck. What you probably won't see is any discussion of the conditions necessary for such feats. A discovery requires a person to do the discovering and a set of circumstances that makes it possible. Without both, nothing gets discovered.

Although scientists don't often discuss it, the degree to which we can "measure" the wider universe from our earthly home—and not just our immediate surroundings—is surprising. Few have considered what science would have been like in, say, a different planetary environment. Still fewer have realized that pursuing that question systematically leads to unanticipated evidence for intelligent design.

Think of the following features of our earthly home: the transparency of Earth's atmosphere in the visual region of the spectrum, shifting crustal plates, a large moon, and our particular location in the Milky Way galaxy. Without each of these assets, we would have a very hard time learning about the universe. It is not idle speculation to ask how our view of the universe would be impaired if, for example, our home world were perpetually covered by thick clouds. After all, our solar system contains several examples of such worlds. Just think of Venus, Jupiter, Saturn, and Saturn's moon Titan. These would be crummy places to do astronomy.

We can make similar comparisons at the galactic level. If we were closer to our galaxy's center or one of its major, and dustier, spiral arms, for instance, the extra dust would impede our view of the distant universe. In fact, we probably would have missed one of the greatest discoveries in the history of astronomy: the faint cosmic microwave background radiation. That discovery was the linchpin in deciding between the two main cosmological theories of the twentieth century. Underlying this debate was one of the most fundamental questions we can ask about the universe: Is it eternal, or did it have a beginning?

The steady state theory posited an eternal universe, while the big bang theory implied a beginning. For a few decades, there was no direct evidence to decide between the two. But big bang theory predicted a remnant radiation left over from the earlier, hotter, and denser period of cosmic history. Steady state theory made no such prediction. As a result, when scientists discovered the cosmic background radiation in 1965, it was the death knell for steady state. But that discovery could not have been made just anywhere. Our special vantage point in the Milky Way galaxy allowed us to choose between these two profoundly different views of origins.

In *The Privileged Planet: How Our Place in the Cosmos Is Designed for Discovery* we discuss these and many comparable examples to show that we inhabit a planet privileged for scientific observation and discovery. But there's more to the story. Not only is Earth a privileged place for discovery, it is also a privileged place for life. It is the connection between life and discovery that we think suggests purpose and not mere chance.

Physicists and cosmologists began realizing decades ago that the values of the constants of physics—features of the universe that are the same everywhere—must be very close to their actual values for life to be possible. As a result, they began talking about the universe being "fine-tuned" for life. And some have even begun to suggest that fine-tuning implies a fine-tuner. Much more recently, astrobiologists began learning that even in our fine-tuned universe, many other "local" things must go just right to get a habitable planetary environment.

If you were a cosmic chef, your recipe for cooking up a habitable planet would have many ingredients. You would need a rocky planet large enough to hold on to a substantial atmosphere and oceans of water and to retain internal heat for billions of years. You would need the right kind of atmosphere. You would need a large moon to stabilize the tilt of the planet's rotation on its axis. You would need the planet to have a nearly circular orbit around a main sequence star similar to our sun. You would need to give that planet the right kind of planetary neighbors within its star system. And you would need to put that system far from the center, edges, and spiral arms of a galaxy like the Milky Way. You would need to cook it during a narrow window of time in the history of the universe. And so on. This is a partial list, but you get the idea.

This evidence is becoming well known among scientists interested in the question of life in the universe. Researchers involved in the Search for Extraterrestrial Intelligence (SETI), for instance, are especially interested in knowing what life needs. That knowledge would allow them to determine their chances of finding another communicating civilization. Unfortunately for SETI researchers, the probabilities do not look promising. Recent evidence favors the so-called Rare Earth Hypothesis (named after a book written by Donald Brownlee and Peter Ward in 2000). The theory posits that planets hosting simple life may be common, but planets with complex life are very rare.

We do not yet know if we are alone in the universe. The universe is a big place with vast resources. Astrobiology research has not yet matured to the point where we can assign precise probabilities to all the factors needed to make a planet habitable. We cannot yet state with certainty whether they exhaust all the available resources. Perhaps the universe is big enough that at least one habitable planet would have emerged by chance. Or perhaps not. In the meantime, it's difficult to make a strong case for intelligent design based merely on the conclusion that habitable planets are rare.

That said, we do think there is evidence for design in the neighborhood. For, as we argue in *The Privileged Planet*, there is a suspicious pattern between the needs of life and the needs of science. The same narrow conditions that make a planet habitable for complex life also make it the best place overall for making a wide range of scientific discoveries. In other words, if we compare our local environment with other, less hospitable environments, we find a striking coincidence: observers find themselves in the best places overall for observing. For instance, the atmosphere that complex life needs is also an atmosphere that is transparent to the most scientifically useful "light." The geology and planetary system that life needs is also the best, overall, for allowing that life to reconstruct events from the past. And the most habitable region of the galaxy, and the most habitable time in cosmic history, are also the best place and time, overall, for doing astronomy and cosmology. If the universe is merely a blind concatenation of atoms colliding with atoms, and nothing else, you wouldn't expect this pattern. You would expect it, on the other hand, if the universe is designed for discovery.

20

Intelligent Design

A Brief Introduction

William A. Dembski

Intelligent design (ID) studies patterns in nature that are best explained as the result of intelligence. Is that radio signal from outer space just random noise or the result of an alien intelligence? Is that chunk of rock just a random chunk of rock or an arrowhead? Is Mount Rushmore the result of wind and erosion or the creative act of an artist? We ask such questions all the time, and we think we can give good answers to them.

Yet, when it comes to biology and cosmology, scientists balk at even raising such questions, much less answering them in favor of design. This is especially true of biology. According to well-known evolutionist Francisco Ayala, Darwin's greatest achievement was to show how the organized complexity of organisms could be attained without a designing intelligence. By contrast, ID purports to find patterns in biological systems that signify intelligence. ID therefore directly challenges Darwinism and other materialistic approaches to the origin and evolution of life.

The idea of design has had a turbulent intellectual history. The main challenge facing it these last two hundred years has been to discover a conceptually powerful formulation of it that will fruitfully advance science. What has kept design outside the scientific mainstream since Darwin proposed his theory of evolution is that it lacked precise methods for distinguishing intelligently caused objects from unintelligently caused ones. For design to be a fruitful scientific concept, scientists need to be sure they can reliably determine whether something is designed.

Johannes Kepler, for instance, thought the craters on the moon were intelligently designed by moon dwellers. We now know that the craters were formed by blind material forces (like meteor impacts). It's this fear of falsely attributing something to design only to have it overturned later that has prevented design from entering science proper. But design theorists argue that they now have formulated precise methods for discriminating designed from undesigned objects. These methods, they contend, enable them to avoid Kepler's mistake and reliably locate design in biological systems.

As a theory of biological origins and development, ID's central claim is that only intelligent causes can adequately explain the complex, information-rich structures of biology and that these causes are empirically detectable. To say intelligent causes are empirically detectable is to say there exist well-defined methods that, based on observable features of the world, can reliably distinguish intelligent causes from undirected material causes. Many special sciences have already developed such methods for drawing this distinction—notably forensic science, cryptography, archaeology, and the Search for Extraterrestrial Intelligence (SETI). Essential to all these methods is the ability to eliminate chance and necessity.

Astronomer Carl Sagan wrote a novel about SETI called *Contact*, which was later made into a movie starring Jodie Foster. After years of receiving apparently meaningless "random" radio signals from outer space, the *Contact* researchers discovered a pattern of beats and pauses that corresponded to the sequence of all the prime numbers from 2 to 101. (Prime numbers are divisible only by themselves and by one.) That got their attention, and they immediately inferred a designing intelligence. When a sequence begins with two beats, then a pause, three beats, then a pause . . . and continues through each prime number all the way to 101 beats, researchers must infer the presence of an extraterrestrial intelligence.

Why is that? Nothing in the laws of physics requires radio signals to take one form or another, so the prime sequence is *contingent* rather than necessary. Also, the prime sequence is a long sequence and therefore *complex*. Note that if the sequence lacked complexity, it could easily have happened by chance. Finally, it was not just complex but also exhibited an independently given pattern, or *specification* (it was not just any old sequence of numbers but a mathematically significant one—the prime numbers).

Intelligence leaves behind a characteristic trademark or signature—what I call "specified complexity."[1] An event exhibits specified complexity if it is contingent and therefore not necessary, if it is complex and therefore not readily reproducible by chance, and if it is specified in the sense of exhibiting an independently given pattern. Note that a merely improbable event is not sufficient to eliminate chance—flip a coin long enough and you'll witness a highly complex or improbable event. Even so, you'll have no reason not to attribute it to chance.

The important thing about specifications is that they be objectively given and not just imposed on events after the fact. For instance, if an archer fires arrows into a wall, and then we paint bull's-eyes around them, we impose a pattern after the fact. On the other hand, if the targets are set up in advance ("specified"), and then the archer hits them accurately, we know it was by design.

In determining whether biological organisms exhibit specified complexity, design theorists focus on identifiable systems, such as individual enzymes, metabolic pathways, molecular machines, and the like. These systems are specified by their independent functional requirements, and they exhibit a high degree of complexity. Of course, once an essential part of an organism exhibits specified complexity, then any design attributable to that part carries over to the organism as a whole. One need not demonstrate that every aspect of the organism was designed; in fact, some aspects will be the result of purely material causes.

The combination of complexity and specification convincingly pointed the radio astronomers in the movie *Contact* to an extraterrestrial intelligence. Within the theory of intelligent design, specified complexity is the characteristic trademark or signature of intelligence. It is a reliable empirical marker of intelligence in the same way that fingerprints are a reliable empirical marker of an individual's presence at the scene of a crime. Design theorists contend that undirected material causes, like natural selection acting on random genetic change, cannot generate specified complexity.

This isn't to say that naturally occurring systems cannot exhibit specified complexity or that material processes cannot serve as a conduit for specified complexity. Naturally occurring systems can exhibit specified complexity, and nature operating by purely material mechanisms without intelligent direction can take preexisting specified complexity and shuffle it around. But that is not the point. The point is whether nature (conceived as a closed system of blind, unbroken material causes) can *generate* specified complexity in the sense of originating it when previously there was none.

Take, for instance, a Rembrandt woodcut. It arose by mechanically impressing an inked woodblock on paper. The Rembrandt woodcut exhibits specified complexity. But the mechanical application of ink to paper via a woodblock does not account for the woodcut's specified complexity. The specified complexity in the woodcut must be referred back to the specified complexity in the woodblock, which in turn must be referred back to the designing activity of Rembrandt himself (in this case deliberately chiseling the woodblock). Specified complexity's causal chains end not with blind material forces but with a designing intelligence.

In *Darwin's Black Box*, biochemist Michael Behe connects specified complexity to biological design with his concept of *irreducible complexity*. Behe defines a system as irreducibly complex if it consists of several interrelated parts for which removing even one part completely destroys the system's function. For Behe, irreducible complexity is a sure indicator of design. One irreducibly complex biochemical system that Behe considers is the bacterial flagellum. The flagellum is an acid-powered rotary motor with a whip-like tail that spins at twenty thousand rpms and whose rotating motion enables a bacterium to navigate through its watery environment.

Behe shows that the intricate machinery in this molecular motor—including a rotor, a stator, O-rings, bushings, and a drive shaft—requires the coordinated interaction of at least thirty complex proteins and that the absence of any one of these proteins would result in the complete loss of motor function. Behe argues that the Darwinian mechanism faces grave obstacles in trying to account for such irreducibly complex systems. In *No Free Lunch*, I show how Behe's notion of irreducible complexity constitutes a special case of specified complexity and that irreducibly complex systems like the bacterial flagellum are therefore designed.

Accordingly, ID is more than simply the latest in a long line of design arguments. The related concepts of irreducible complexity and specified complexity render intelligent causes empirically detectable and make ID a full-fledged scientific theory, distinguishing it from the design arguments of philosophers and theologians, or what has traditionally been called "natural theology."

ID's chief claim is this: the world contains events, objects, and structures that exhaust the explanatory resources of undirected material causes and can be adequately explained by recourse to intelligent causes. Design theorists claim to demonstrate this rigorously. ID therefore takes a long-standing philosophical intuition and cashes it out as a scientific research program. This program depends on advances in probability theory, computer science, molecular biology, the philosophy of science, and the concept of information, to name but a few. Whether this program can turn design into an effective conceptual tool for investigating and understanding the natural world is for now the big question confronting science.

For more on ID, visit the following websites: www.designinference.com (which houses many of my writings on ID), www.ideacenter.org (the Intelligent Design and Evolution Awareness Center—a clearinghouse for college and university students interested in ID), www.arn.org (for purchasing all things ID related), www.iscid.org (the International Society for Complexity, Information, and Design), and www.discovery.org/csc (Discovery Institute's Center for Science and Culture).

21

Intelligent, Optimal, and Divine Design

Richard Spencer

If something has been intelligently designed, people often expect to see structures that are perfectly crafted to perform their individual tasks in the most elegant and efficient way possible (e.g., with no extra components). This expectation is incorrect not only for human design but also for divine design.

In human design, we frequently have to do things in ways that are suboptimal simply because the complexity and magnitude of the overall task preclude spending the time and attention on each detail that would be required to execute an optimal design. A classic example is the microprocessor in a computer. If we tried to optimize every little part of the circuit design, we would never complete the design! This limitation does not, of course, affect divine design.

Nonetheless, a similar limitation does affect divine design. It arises whenever design employs secondary agents. For instance, in designing a microprocessor, we make use of many computer-aided design (CAD) tools. These tools allow us to manage the complexity of the problem by enabling us to work at a higher level of abstraction. So, while an engineer does have to design the individual logic gates that will be used, these gates only get designed once at the lowest levels of abstraction (the transistor level and physical layout). After that, we almost always use tools to connect many gates together to perform higher-level functions (e.g., addition circuits).

When a set of these higher-level functions is available, they are then treated as blocks and are manipulated to perform even higher-level functions, and so on. When the design of a complex system is complete, it is certainly true that one could look at some small piece at the lowest level of abstraction and improve the design. On the other hand, one could also argue that this hierarchical method of computer-aided design is far *more* intelligent than doing it all at the lowest level of abstraction because it enables us to design much more complex functions.

In the same way, but for different reasons, God usually makes use of secondary agents to accomplish his work. Such secondary agents include physical laws since these laws do, at least sometimes, define or help to define structures in nature. For example, there are physical laws and properties of matter that determine the physical structure of certain objects, and once the laws and properties are in place, God does not need to individually create each atom, cell, or higher-level object. Having created physical laws, God is constrained by them unless he specifically chooses to suspend them. As a logical possibility, God is of course free to suspend the physical laws he has instituted. Yet, I don't know a single unequivocal example in which he has done so. This is not to deny miracles. I am simply saying that I don't know of any examples of miraculous structures in nature, and that includes biological structures.

Given that God uses secondary agents to bring about physical structures, we can expect to see certain patterns and processes repeated in many places and used in different ways, even though the design may not be optimal for each *individual* application. In addition, any designer, divine or otherwise, is certainly free (and likely) to reuse structures and to implement similar functions in similar ways, although this will not always be the case. The appearance of similar structures in many different systems, particularly when those structures are not optimal for each situation, is frequently cited as evidence for macroevolution (Stephen Jay Gould's *The Panda's Thumb* makes precisely this point). But it is also exactly what you would expect to see for a system constructed using secondary agents under divine control.

Another reason why even divine designs may appear to be less than optimal is that adaptive systems are inherently wasteful. In order to be able to adapt to different conditions, the system will virtually always have components that are not being used in a given situation. There are many examples of adaptive systems in human engineering, and they are never as efficient a solution as a dedicated system.

Nonetheless, adaptive systems tend to exhibit far more intelligence than dedicated systems because they will work even when the environment changes. A common example is the circuitry used to connect a computer to a network (either wireless or wired). These circuits are virtually all adaptive so that they will work independently of the exact configuration of the network to which they are connecting.

Since biological systems are most definitely adaptive and significantly more complex than anything we design, engineers like me who design adaptive systems expect to see many components that appear to be wasted or left over from some previous use. Although the appearance of such structures is commonly used to argue that evolution is not under any intelligent control, in fact it is a necessary consequence of adaptive systems. Moreover, since adaptive systems are not infinitely malleable (some circuits in a television might be adapted for use in a radio but cannot be adapted for use in a jet engine), this feature of adaptive systems provides evidence for microevolution but not for macroevolution.

A third reason why even divine designs may appear to be less than optimal is that we are rarely in a position to fully understand all of the design objectives and constraints. This point is subtle but significant. I have sometimes thought some part of a circuit or system design was done poorly only to find out later that it was actually quite clever. I simply didn't fully understand the intended purpose or constraints when I first looked at the system.

In an interview in *Science and Spirit* magazine, Francis Collins, director of the National Human Genome Research Institute, said:

> It seems to me we should not make the mistake of assuming that God's perfect will for us is biological perfection, any more than we should assume that God's perfect will for us is the absence of suffering. It is those occasions when things *aren't* perfect that we often learn the most, and when our closeness to God, which is a higher goal even than our own happiness, is most likely to come about. And so perhaps God in a merciful way speaks to us *through* our imperfections, and we shouldn't neglect the significance of that. The underlying assumption that we should all be genetically perfect doesn't necessarily make sense to me.[1]

I wholeheartedly agree with Dr. Collins. While we do not fully comprehend why God allows sin to exist, the Bible gives us many examples of how God uses the painful trials that result from a sinful world to bring us to a greater sense of humility and dependence on him. We must also remember that the world we are observing is *not* the original creation. It is a corrupted version of the creation. I personally think that many, if not all, of the arguments made by the opponents of intelligent design would remain unchanged even if they observed the world prior to the fall. But there is still an unknown factor to deal with since we are not able to observe the original creation at this time.

In summary, the use of secondary agents (including physical laws), the reuse of common design elements, the adaptive nature of biological organisms, and the fact that we don't fully know the purposes of the Creator all indicate that we should not expect to see designs in nature that are, from our limited vantage, optimal.[2]

22

Molecular Biology's New Paradigm

Nanoengineering Inside the Cell

Bill Wilberforce

Imagine a barcode reader that, instead of decoding black and white stripes, would print out the list of parts in any complicated machine. Point it at an alarm clock and its tickertape would start whizzing, "Two bells, eighteen gears, one spring . . ." Point it at a laptop and the tickertape would stretch for miles.

This cool device would be the envy of all your friends, and a handy tool for manufacturers seeking to reverse engineer their competitors' products. But this reader would be even more useful if it could read out parts that would otherwise be undetectable—for example, if a machine had such small parts that even the most powerful microscope couldn't identify them.

As you might have guessed, this fancy barcode reader is a metaphor for the revolution that the world has experienced in molecular biology over the past fifty years. With commercially available kits, which require less mixing than a cake baked from scratch, a relatively inexperienced graduate student can start to inventory the parts in his or her favorite living organism. And with more powerful automated tools, a complete list of parts from any creature can be obtained.

What is the nature of these parts that are found in living systems? Primarily, they are chains of amino acids called proteins (a subset of which are called enzymes). There are twenty types of amino acids that can be strung together to make every protein on the planet. The ordering sequence of the amino acids determines the type of protein. This is analogous to our alphabet of twenty-six letters being able to form every English sentence on the planet, where the sequence of the letters uniquely determines which sentence is formed.

How, you might wonder, do commercial kits and automated tools detect these proteins, whose amino acid sequences are invisible to our most advanced microscopes? The answer is by reading the "barcode" of deoxyribonucleic acid, or DNA. DNA is the inventory list of parts carried within every cell of every organism in the world. There is a direct correlation between a three-letter "word" of DNA and each of the twenty amino acids. For example, if you find a string of one thousand such words in the DNA (for a total of three thousand DNA letters), that organism will have a protein part that is one thousand amino acids long. More importantly, the exact nature of that protein can be known by the order of the DNA letters.

The mechanism by which these tools read DNA is beyond the scope of this essay, but the important point is that these tools of molecular biology have revolutionized the way we understand living systems. Before these tools existed, scientists thought cells were rather simple, just a blob of protoplasm (i.e., a chemical soup), surrounded by a thin membrane. But after pointing these new tools at various forms of life, scientists have realized that there are a lot more parts "under the hood" than they had originally expected. (For details, see the postscript below.)

Just to get a taste of what some of these parts do, let us look at one particular protein, namely, kinesin heavy chain. This medium-sized protein, formed from a pair of identical chains (each with about one thousand amino acids), normally operates with a smaller partner protein called kinesin light chain, which is also made from a pair of identical chains.

As protein machines go, the pairs of kinesin light and heavy chains, which constitute what is known as conventional kinesin, are a pretty simple system. The heavy chains have two parts. One half of the molecule can use a molecular fuel called adenosine triphosphate, or ATP. This fuel powers a process by which the heavy chain binds and releases from another protein: tubulin. As its name suggests, tubulin can form tubes—microtubules, to be exact—which form part of the skeleton of each cell. Ultimately, the binding and releasing of the heavy chains from these microtubules allows the kinesin system to march from one end of the cell to the other, taking hundreds of steps per second.

The purpose of this high-speed marching is revealed in the other half of the heavy chain molecule. This half is a long tail, to which the two kinesin light chains, as well as various types of cellular cargo, attach. In essence, by marching through the cell, kinesin carries packages of material that would normally move far too slowly by random mixing.

Nerve cells present a particularly striking example of how important kinesin transport is for proper cellular functions. Our longest cells, which stretch from our lower back to our toes, are found in the sciatic nerve. Much of what is needed to keep the ends of these nerve cells alive comes directly from the blood in our toes. But some things must come all the way from the beginning of the cells in our lower back. If we had to wait for these things to randomly diffuse their way down to the end of our toes, we would have to wait for years! Instead, we rely on the active transport of kinesin to supply the ends of our nerve cells with the necessary components.

Kinesin is just one protein among thousands that all work together in each organism. The rich diversity of these protein machines has only been made known recently, as a result of the revolutionary tools of molecular biology. This diversity and the complexity of each individual protein machine underscore a new paradigm in biology: the inner workings of cells are feats of high-tech nanoengineering.

Biologists most often identify the high-tech nanoengineer as Nature herself, and the implications of intelligent activity are quickly brushed aside. But, as Lehigh University biochemist Michael Behe has publicly stated in regard to this situation, "If it looks like a duck, walks like a duck and quacks like a duck, it probably is a duck." Behe's "inducktive" reasoning is quite sound. In any other field, things that look like they have been carefully engineered are presumed to be engineered.

The fly in this "inducktive" ointment is the fact that the only engineer that could have produced these protein machines appears to be God, or "someone with the same skill-set"—as Jon Stewart of *The Daily Show* has said. So, instead of embracing the implications of their new paradigm, biologists (for the most part) ignore or denounce them, not wanting their field to destroy the separation between church and state that they feel is so essential for fruitful scientific progress. But at this point, the right question to ask is, Will further applications of molecular biology's revolutionary tools vindicate these denunciations, or will they continue to highlight the complex engineering of living systems?

From everything we have learned thus far, the answer seems to be the latter. Though it is possible that the tools of molecular biology will uncover some self-engineering mechanism (akin to self-organization, but which produces complex machines instead of repeating fractal patterns), this scenario seems unlikely. For starters, the trend has been toward the unveiling of more and more complicated systems, not mechanisms that show how they are produced. Furthermore, laws of information production, developed to address questions arising in our computer-driven information age, weigh heavily against such a mechanism.

What seems therefore to be the likely outcome of molecular biology's fantastic revolution is a growing awareness that living things, including us, are best explained as objects of intelligent nanoengineering. This awareness will no doubt follow the normal course that new ideas follow. First, it will be ignored. Then it will be ridiculed. Next it will be grudgingly tolerated. Finally, it will be said, "Well, we knew that all along!"

Postscript: Ballpark figures given for the number of genes in higher organisms represent an interesting exception to this tendency to underestimate the number of parts. For example, before the Human Genome Project, it was thought, based on results from simpler organisms, that we had about one hundred thousand genes.[1] Now that number is thought to be around twenty thousand,[2] about the same as for the simplest worm![3]

In this case, the overestimation was due to a brute-force extrapolation from simpler organisms, based on the naive assumption that our greater complexity was due to a greater number of genes. Ultimately, this error has shown us that the parts list we obtain from reading genes in DNA is only the tip of the iceberg. The nanoengineering of organisms extends far beyond mere protein parts and includes intricate networks of feedback signals and three-dimensional protein arrays.

23

Panning God

Darwinism's Defective Argument against Bad Design

Jonathan Witt

The metaphor of cosmos as "watch" (a timepiece) captured the imagination of Enlightenment thinkers, confronted as they were with fresh insights into the laws governing motion both near and far. Despite the advance of science since the Enlightenment, the metaphor of the cosmos as a watch persists. Indeed, we now know that the physical constants of nature are finely tuned to an almost unimaginable degree, so that, for instance, even slight changes in the force of gravity or electromagnetism would render the universe incapable of permitting life. In a crucial sense, then, the universe is watch-like, its physical constants resembling a precision instrument.

But trouble comes when metaphors are reified. The metaphor of cosmos as watch is an illuminating image. Even so, all metaphors break down if pressed far enough, and this one breaks down pretty quickly.

Think of the morally compromised gods of Mount Olympus meddling in the affairs of their various mortal offspring, or of Plato's "the One" (what he also called "the Good" or "Father of that Captain and Cause"), or the holy God of the Bible, father and shepherd and husband of his people. With none of these conceptions of the deity is the world construed primarily as a precision instrument meant to function so perfectly its Maker need never pay it any mind. Whenever the Deity is construed as a personality, and not merely as a nonsentient organizing first principle, he is depicted as interested in the world itself, as a Creator who delights in the work of his hands.

In an interview with the *Philadelphia Inquirer*, biologist and leading Darwinist Kenneth Miller said, "The God of the intelligent-design movement is way too small. . . . In their view, he designed everything in the world and yet he repeatedly intervenes and violates the laws of his own creation. Their god is like a kid who is not a very good mechanic and has to keep lifting the hood and tinkering with the engine."[1] Miller is a Roman Catholic, but notice how blithely he equates the Designer's ongoing involvement in creation with incompetence. Why? What if the Creator prefers to stay involved? What if he doesn't intend to wind up the watch of the cosmos and simply leave it to wind out everything from supernovas to sunflowers? What if he wishes to get his hands dirty making mud daubers?

What if the Designer is more like a spirited dramatist than a fastidious watchmaker? Would we say to Shakespeare, "You keep writing and rewriting your plays! You have the unhappy imperfection of wanting to stage your creations with live actors, and even worse, of directing them! You repeatedly violate the laws of drama and poetry with your detestable and irrepressible urge to create something new—absolutely unable to leave well enough alone! Shame!"

Certainly we could try to discuss the order of nature without considering the Designer's attitude toward his creation (that is, whether he is more a watchmaker, bridegroom, or dramatist). But the Darwinists have already smuggled this issue into the debate by assuming that, if there were a Designer, he could only be a detached and hyper-tidy engineer. Having smuggled the assumption in, they then regard as beneath consideration any evidence of a Designer who (as they put it) "meddles in his creation."

Similarly, they dismiss the notion that an omnipotent and omniscient Designer might fashion a creature that, considered narrowly, would seem to fall short of an ideal design. Here they not only make a theological claim but ignore key questions at once practical and aesthetic: How do concerns about ecological balance impinge on a critique of animal structures? Or more poetically, how does each creature play a part in the overall drama of life? They fault the Designer, for instance, for not giving pandas opposable thumbs. An omniscient and omnipotent Designer would already have known about the superior opposable thumb, they argue, and would have been sure to give it to them. Since he did not, he obviously does not exist or at least is not directly involved in designing thumbs.

The irony is that the panda's remarkably sturdy thumbs work beautifully for peeling bamboo. Must the cosmic Designer's primary concern for pandas be that they are the most dexterous bears divinely imaginable? From a purely practical standpoint, might opposable-thumbed über-pandas wreak havoc on their ecosystem? From a purely aesthetic standpoint, might not those charming pandas up in their bamboo trees with their unopposing but quite workable thumbs be just the sort of humorous supporting character this great cosmic drama needs to lighten things up a bit? If Shakespeare could introduce a comical gravedigger into the tragedy of *Hamlet*, why cannot God introduce whimsy into his work?

Pandas as comic relief? To spurn the notion as patently ridiculous, as beneath consideration, is merely to expose one's utilitarian presuppositions. Why, after all, should the Designer's world read like a dreary high school science textbook, its style humorless, homogenous, and suffocating under the dead weight of a supposedly detached, passive voice? Why should the Designer's world not entertain, amuse, and fascinate, as well as "work"? Why, in short, should we not expect it to have the richness of variety and tone we find in a work of art like *Hamlet*?

The bad-design versus good-design discussion is often framed by an engineer's perspective, not an artist's or mystic's. When I noted this to philosopher Jay Richards a few years ago, he responded in a letter: "After all, why do we assume that God created the universe to be a watch, in which a self-winding mechanism makes it 'better'? Maybe the universe is like a piano, or a novel with the author as a character, or a garden for other beings with whom God wants to interact. It is amazing how a simple image can highjack a discussion for a century and a half."

For evolutionists like Stephen Jay Gould and Richard Dawkins, reductionist thinking paves the way to all sorts of unwarranted conclusions. Gould preaches against the atomistic view that "wholes should be understood by decomposition into 'basic' units"; but then Gould himself practices such thinking. He and many other biologists assume not only that nature is a kind of watch but that each individual design is its own watch, its own machine, meant to be judged in relative isolation. They evaluate the panda's thumb by how well it works as a thumb, not by how well it fits into the whole life of the panda, including its place in its own environment. At the aesthetic level, this assumes that the panda's maker could not have been thinking (as artists do) of the whole work. It is the same mistake Darwinists make again and again.

For instance, in *The Blind Watchmaker*, Richard Dawkins ignores the larger demands of vision in his critique of the mammalian eye, zeroing in on the eye's so-called backward wiring:

> Each photocell is, in effect, wired in backwards, with its wire sticking out on the side nearest the light. . . . This means that the light, instead of being granted an unrestricted passage to the photocells, has to pass through a forest of connecting wires, presumably suffering at least some attenuation and distortion (actually probably not much but, still, it is the *principle* of the thing that would offend any tidy-minded engineer!).[2]

His analysis collapses under two mistakes. First, geneticist Michael Denton has clearly demonstrated that the backward wiring of the mammalian eye actually confers a distinct advantage by dramatically increasing the flow of oxygen to the eye. Dawkins the reductionist misses this because he analyzes organs in isolation when it suits his purpose.

Then there is Dawkins's obsession with neatness, his assumption that any proper Creator would idolize tidiness over all. But do we really want to substitute the exuberantly imaginative, even whimsical Designer of our actual universe for a cosmic efficiency freak? Such a deity might serve nicely as the national god of the Nazis, matching Hitler stroke for stroke: Hitler in his disdain for humanity's sprawling diversity; the tidy cosmic engineer in his distaste for an ecosystem choked and sullied by a grotesque menagerie of strange and supposedly substandard organs and organisms. Out with that great big prodigal Gothic cathedral we call the world; in with a modern and minimalist blueprint for a new and neater cosmos.

Interestingly the god of the English canon, William Shakespeare, has received much the same criticism from the tidier eighteenth century neoclassical critics. This actor-turned-playwright lacked classical restraint, the argument went. Lewis Theobald perhaps initiated the century's long criticism of Hamlet's coarse speech when, in 1726, he commented on a particularly bawdy line spoken by Hamlet to Ophelia: "If ever the poet deserved whipping for low and indecent ribaldry, it was for this passage."[3] Never mind that Hamlet's comment was not gratuitous but, instead, crucial to both plot and character development.

Around the same time, Charles Gildon regarded Shakespeare's general habit of mingling the low with the high, the comic with the tragic as a "wholly monstrous, unnatural mixture."[4] With only a little more restraint, Edward Taylor (not to be confused with the American metaphysical poet of the same name) lamented, "How inattentive to propriety and order, how deficient in grouping, how fond of exposing disgusting as well as beautiful figures!" How often he compels the audience "to grovel in dirt and ordure."[5]

As modern critic Herbert Spencer Robinson noted in his work on English Shakespearian criticism, even the admiration of the more sympathetic neoclassical critics was always "modified and tempered . . . by regrets that Shakespeare had elected, either through ignorance or by design, to embrace a method that discarded all classical rules."[6]

What do we make of such criticism today? Most find it damagingly narrow. Few wish to substitute for the works of the "myriad minded" Shakespeare the relatively impoverished fare left over after unsympathetic neoclassical critics tidied him up.

The relevance of the comparison should be clear. The criticism of Shakespeare is akin to the Darwinist's overly tidy treatment of vision or the panda's thumb. In each case the critic analyzes the work narrowly, ignoring the larger context, be it ecological, aesthetic, or otherwise. Proponents of this line of argument value a hyper-constricted and abstract elegance over other and often more vital criteria like variety, imaginative exuberance, freedom, even moral complexity. In their attempt to master everything, they deny anything that exceeds their grasp. They lose the meaningful whole. If that is lucidity, it is also madness.

Now the Darwinist might complain, "What is all this artistic, aesthetic balderdash? We are scientists, not poets or starry-eyed mystics. Leave the artists to their pattern-making and let us get back to our hard-nosed, empirical science." Fine, but if they wish to avoid an argument about aesthetic principles, they should not assume within their arguments aesthetic principles that are at best highly debatable, and at worst contrary to the canons of art.

24

The Role of Agency in Science

ANGUS MENUGE

Agents

Human beings habitually understand themselves as *agents*. An agent is an individual with reasons for its behavior. Agents have goals (things they desire) and produce behavior that they believe will achieve those goals. Thus, for example, Hans, a native of Wisconsin, positions his stepladder under the roof because he believes his gutters are clogged and desires to save them from ice damage. So much is part of the intuitive self-understanding called *folk psychology*.

Scientific Materialism

The very idea of agency is problematic for scientific materialism, according to which everything that happens can be explained by the undirected behavior of matter. An event can occur as the result of a lawful regularity or because of chance or because of a combination of law and chance, but if matter is all there is and matter has no goals, then the appearance of goal-directed behavior is difficult for the scientific materialist to explain. Some materialists, like Paul and Patricia Churchland, think that agency is incompatible with materialism and must be eliminated in favor of the materialistic category of neurophysiology. This strategy is *eliminative materialism*. Other materialists, like Daniel Dennett, Fred Dretske, and Jerry Fodor, see agency as crucial to our self-understanding as rational beings but hope to show that it can naturally arise from materialistic categories. This strategy is called *naturalism of the mental.*

Eliminative Materialism

According to the Churchlands, folk psychology, with its talk of goals and purposes, beliefs and desires, is simply the last vestige of a prescientific worldview already largely displaced by the advances of scientific materialism. The laws of physics make no mention of the "goals" of heavenly bodies. Darwin, it is claimed, removed the need to speak of an intelligent designer of living organisms. The last frontier to be conquered is the human mind.

For the Churchlands, there are no such things as beliefs and desires. Beliefs and desires have to go because they imply *intentionality*: Unlike material entities, beliefs and desires include thoughts *about* something with *propositional content*, such as the belief that gasoline prices have risen or the desire that gas prices will fall. Thoughts can be true or false, they may lack a real object (e.g., beliefs about leprechauns), and they may jointly provide a reason for an action, such as buying a hybrid automobile. By contrast, material events either happen or do not happen (but cannot be true or false); they can only stand in causal relations with other material events (so they cannot point to nonexistent objects), and though they may cause a behavior, they do not give an agent's reason for doing it.

The Churchlands maintain that advances in the brain sciences show the way forward. Here cognition is reduced to transformations of neural activation patterns. These patterns look nothing like propositional content, nor is there anything analogous to an agent's reason for acting. From this perspective, folk psychology appears redundant. However, there are a number of important reasons to reject eliminative materialism.

First, there is the abstraction problem. Neural activation patterns may explain specific bodily movements, but they do not capture the abstract specification of human actions. Consider the action of greeting. One may greet someone with spoken words, a smile, a wave, a handshake, a hug and/or kiss, a card, an electronic message, or an airborne banner. Since each of these methods involves physically different behaviors, each requires a different set of neural activation patterns to explain it. But this fails to capture what all of the behaviors have in common, the fact that they are all actions of greeting. By contrast, folk psychology can appeal to a common desire or intention to greet. The categories of folk psychology are at the right level to account for actions, and not merely specific movements.

Second, there is the subjectivity problem. The transitions of neural activations are completely impersonal and in no way involve a point of view. But there is no doubt that there are subjects, individuals with distinct points of view. This has always been recognized by folk psychology since it seeks to provide *personal* reasons for an agent's actions. Jack does not (ultimately) open the fridge because Jill believes it contains a beer. Note that it will not help the eliminativist to claim that points of view are illusory since only something with a point of view can be subject to an illusion.

Third, there is the robustness problem. The eliminativist argues that folk psychology is silent about abnormal psychology, so it is probably a false theory, ripe for displacement. But when folk psychology goes, so will its ontology of beliefs and desires. However, as a normative discipline, folk psychology is no more refuted by abnormal psychology than classical logic is refuted by fallacious reasoning. And, even if folk psychology were shown false, that would not discredit its ontology of beliefs and desires. At one time, folk physics supposed that weights were intrinsic, constant properties of bodies. The discovery that weight is a relation that varies with gravitation showed that the folk conception of weight needed reform. But no one concluded that weights do not exist. Given the entrenched status of the concepts of belief and desire in our self-understanding as rational beings, it seems much more likely that empirical failures in folk psychology would provoke a reformed conception, rather than elimination, of its ontology.

Last, there is the coherence problem. Paul Churchland has never provided a coherent explanation of what it would mean to abandon folk psychology. He cannot describe it as rejecting folk psychology and accepting a neural replacement because the whole idea of rational rejection and acceptance is part of folk psychology. More fundamentally, eliminativism undermines the rationality of science because it removes anything that could count as reasons for the scientist's actions. If there are no intentional states, then scientists do not literally design their experiments, analyze their data, infer conclusions, and devise alternative theories. And then there is no reason to say that scientific practice is rational. Although scientific materialists claim that science provides the reasons to be a materialist, materialism undermines the very idea of having a reason for anything. Any worldview capable of defending the rationality of science must be one that allows scientists to have identifiable reasons. Since intelligent design allows intelligent and goal-directed causes as part of nature, it is in the right position to do this.

Naturalism of the Mental

Even among materialists, eliminativism is unpopular. Most materialists believe in naturalism of the mental: intentionality and other problematic mental categories are real but can be shown to be compatible with materialism. There are two main problems for this project: (1) there is good reason to think agency cannot be understood in purely materialistic terms; (2) if human agency is simply declared part of nature, then the naturalist has abandoned materialism by allowing the existence of directed causation and in that case can no longer exclude the possibility of nonhuman (and possibly divine) agency active in nature.

The Failure of Naturalism

Early on, naturalists proposed the Identity Theory, according to which types of mental states could be identified with types of brain states. Thus, perhaps all pain states are C-fibers firing. The theory fell because empirical study of the brain revealed important structural differences between the brains of creatures who feel pain. There is no interesting neural similarity between all and only creatures who feel pain. However, there are characteristic physical causes of pain and characteristic responses to pain among diverse creatures. So functionalism suggested that pain and all other mental states are states with the functional role of mediating characteristic causes and effects. Since the same causal role can be physically realized in different ways (just as a mousetrap can be built in many ways), the objection to identity theory was avoided.

But functionalism has numerous troubles of its own. Most fundamental is the problem of giving an illuminating materialistic account of functions. Functions can be understood either nonteleologically, as formal mappings between elements, or teleologically, as contributing to a system's goals.

In the nonteleological case, crucial features of the mental are not explained. Impersonal mappings give no account of the subjective experience of being in a mental state such as pain. The functionalist theory could hold perfectly for a creature that displayed the right behavior but did not feel pain. Functionalism might be satisfied in a world of zombies. Further, the mappings between physical elements do not exhibit intentionality (they are not about anything). For example, a computer could map questions about baseball to their correct answers using a large database. It would then fulfill a functionalist account of "understanding" baseball, even though the computer has no concept of "baseball" as such, outputting the answers merely by matching the form of uninterpreted elements to their constituent parts. And finally, impersonal mappings do not explain an agent's personal reasons for action.

On the other hand, if functions are viewed teleologically, then naturalism may account for the mind, but only by allowing that directed causation is part of nature. But this directly contradicts materialism. Thus either functionalism is unable to naturalize important features of the mental, or it does so by abandoning materialism.

As an ingenious alternative, Dennett proposes that intentionality can be fully explained by "Mother Nature," or natural selection. Dennett thinks that Mother Nature has a low-level "intentionality" in that it makes "choices" that better serve organisms. But there is no good reason to accept this. Natural selection has no reasons for its "choices," and it has no goals, only selecting on the basis of past performance. As I have argued in detail elsewhere,[1] Dennett equivocates between an authentically materialist Mother Nature, which offers no explanation of intentionality, and a mythological Mother Nature, who possesses intelligent characteristics incompatible with materialism.

The Legitimacy of Intelligent Design as Science

The second problem for naturalism is that if there is even one case (the human one) in which the evidence shows that agency is an irreducible feature of reality, then materialism is false, and agency is a legitimate causal category for scientific explanation. But then the question of whether agency is evident anywhere else in nature can only be settled empirically. Granted the reality of irreducible agency and the existence of rigorous criteria for detecting its effects, only empirical data can decide whether design is manifest in biology, cosmology, and elsewhere. Thus intelligent design is manifestly a legitimate scientific research program.

Conclusion

Agency is the Achilles' heel of scientific materialism. If materialists eliminate agency, they undermine the rationality of science. But agency also fails to reduce to materialistic categories. So, if we want to preserve the rationality of science and follow the evidence wherever it leads, we must conclude that agency is an irreducible causal category. And that is precisely the claim of intelligent design.

25

The Scientific Status of Design Inferences

Bruce L. Gordon

Scientific practice assumes that the universe, in both its origin and function, is a closed system of undirected physical processes. While many scientists reject this assumption as the ultimate truth, they still think that it is essential for *science* to function *as if* it were true. This means that they have accepted *methodological naturalism* as a necessary constraint on their practice as scientists. Methodological naturalism is the doctrine that in order to be *scientific*, an explanation must be *naturalistic*; that is, it must only appeal to entities, causes, events, and processes contained within the material universe. Even if we grant that this restriction on permissible explanations has been a fruitful strategy for science, we must still ask whether it is methodologically required by science. Arbitrarily rejecting methodological naturalism may be unwise as an explanatory strategy within science. But perhaps there is a perfectly rigorous *method* for ascertaining when such restrictions *cannot* be applied if a correct explanation for something is to be given. Would such a principled decision, subject to a strict and objective methodology, not also conform to the canons of scientific explanation?

A number of philosophers of science have attempted to give an account of what it means to offer a scientific explanation for a phenomenon. We briefly consider three such accounts: the *deductive-nomological model*, the *causal-statistical* (statistical-relevance) *model*, and the *pragmatic model*.

The *deductive-nomological* (D-N) *model* was the earliest model of scientific explanation and has been very influential. It postulates four criteria for scientific explanations:

1. The explanation must be able to be put in the form of a valid deductive argument, with the thing to be explained as its conclusion.
2. The explanation must contain at least one general law that is required for the derivation of this conclusion.
3. The explanation must have empirical content that can be tested.
4. The premises of the argument constituting the explanation must be true.

Subsequently, it became clear that the D-N model had irremediable shortcomings, falling into two categories: (1) there are arguments meeting the criteria of the D-N model that fail to be genuine scientific explanations, and (2) there are genuine scientific explanations that fail to meet the criteria of the D-N model. In short, these four criteria are neither sufficient nor necessary to guarantee that an explanation is scientific. To demonstrate this, I offer two standard counterexamples: the man and the pill, and the explanation of paresis.

That the D-N model is *insufficient* as an account of scientific explanation can be illustrated by this humorous counterexample. A man explains his failure to become pregnant over the last year, despite an amorous relationship with his wife, on the ground that he has regularly consumed her birth control pills. He appeals to the law-like generalization that every man who regularly takes oral contraceptives will not get pregnant. This example conforms to the D-N pattern of explanation. The problem is that his use of birth control is irrelevant because men do not get pregnant. So it is possible to construct valid arguments with true premises in which some fact asserted by the premises is *irrelevant* to the real explanation of the phenomenon in question.

To see that the model does *not* provide conditions that are *necessary* for a proper scientific explanation, consider the explanation for the development of paresis (a form of tertiary syphilis characterized by progressive physical paralysis and loss of mental function). In order to develop paresis, it is necessary to have untreated latent syphilis, but only about 25 percent of the people in this situation ever develop it. So we have a necessary condition for the development of the disease, but we cannot use this to derive the conclusion that paresis will develop in an individual case, or even to predict that it will. In fact, we're better off predicting that it will not develop, since it doesn't in 75 percent of the cases. Even so, the proper scientific explanation for paresis is that it results from untreated latent syphilis. This is just one example of a genuinely scientific explanation that does not conform to the D-N model.

To remedy the defects of the D-N model of scientific explanation, the *causal-statistical* or *statistical-relevance model* was proposed. Advocates of this model stress the role of *causal* components in scientific explanations and generally deny that explaining something scientifically *must* involve rigorous deductive or inductive arguments. Because they recognize that there are rational explanations for *unexpected* events (like the onset of paresis after untreated latent syphilis), they reject the idea that universal or statistical laws and empirical facts must provide conditions of adequacy for a scientific explanation of the occurrence of events.

The positive idea behind the causal-statistical model is that a scientific explanation presents two things: (1) the set of factors statistically relevant to the occurrence of that event, and (2) the causal framework or link connecting those factors with the event to be explained. *Statistical relevance* may be defined as follows: factor b is *statistically relevant* to factor a if and only if the probability of a, given that b has already occurred, is different from the probability of a occurring on its own, that is, $p(a/b) \neq p(a)$. The causal network or link connecting the factors with an event is simply an account of the underlying causal processes and interactions that bring it about. A *causal process* is a continuous spatio-temporal process; a *causal interaction* is a relatively brief event in which two or more causal processes intersect. The causal-statistical theory arose from the conviction that legitimate scientific explanations have to explain events in terms of the things that actually caused them to happen.

While the causal-statistical model seems fairly solid, it nonetheless finds a counterexample in *quantum mechanics*, the theory describing the behavior of atomic and subatomic particles. The details of why the model fails for quantum mechanics are complicated. Roughly, the causal-statistical account appeals to processes that are deterministic and continuous in space-time, while it is generally accepted that quantum mechanics is not consistent with this view of the world. Since quantum mechanics is regarded as one of the triumphs of twentieth-century science, we have a reason for thinking that this model of explanation is *too narrow*. Of course, we also have the option of saying that quantum mechanics provides us with a mathematical *description* of quantum phenomena that enables amazingly accurate predictions, but it does not *explain* these phenomena at all—a complete explanation would get to the *root cause* of experimental outcomes, not just predict them.

The shortcomings of the D-N and causal-statistical models led to a third proposal for scientific explanations, the *pragmatic model*. This approach not only denies that scientific explanations have a characteristic form (as in the D-N model), but it also denies that they supply distinctive information (as in the causal-statistical model) outside of that provided by the theories, facts, and procedures of science itself. Calling an explanation "scientific" means nothing more than saying it draws on what gets recognized as science to provide an explanation, and whether this criterion is satisfied is something determined by the community of scientists themselves. Beyond this, the pragmatic theory is highly contextual.

Bas van Fraassen, the originator of the pragmatic theory, maintains that a scientific explanation is a *telling response* to a why-question that is identifiable by its *topics of concern*, *contrast classes*, and *explanatory relevance conditions*. An explanation is a *telling response* simply if it favors the occurrence of the state of affairs to be explained. The *topic of concern* is the thing to be explained. The *contrast class* is the set of alternative possibilities, of which the topic of concern is a member, for which an explanation might be requested in a particular context. The *explanatory relevance conditions* are the respects in which an answer might be given. For example, to borrow one of van Fraassen's illustrations, our topic of concern might be why an electrical conductor is warped. In this case, the contrast class might consist of other nearby conductors that are not warped, the warping of the conductor as opposed to its retaining its original shape, and so on. The explanatory relevance conditions might be the presence of a particularly strong magnetic field, the presence of moisture on the conductor, and so on. All of these things are highly dependent on context.

The pragmatic theory is relatively simple and direct in comparison with the other two models. It also is capable of accommodating the special aspects of the other two theories of explanation, and it has a very broad range of application. Critics of the pragmatic model have questioned whether every why-question asked by a scientist requires a contrast class, whether scientific questions might sometimes involve explanations of how as well as why (for example, the question of how genes replicate), whether a telling response must always favor the topic of concern, and whether the theory is too broad and would legitimize as scientific those explanations that the community of scientists might wish to exclude (though actual acceptance by the scientific community seems to be built into the criteria of legitimacy in this case).

Notice that none of the foregoing theories of scientific explanation make mention of methodological naturalism as a constraint (though it is perhaps implicit in the definition of a causal process used by the causal-statistical approach). Some philosophers of science would say this absence points to its status as a grounding assumption for any theory of scientific explanation; others would maintain that this absence shows it is not an essential part of scientific explanation and its relevance as a condition is context-dependent. A brief consideration of the role that a rigorous theory of design inferences can play in science reveals the latter attitude to be most reasonable.

As William Dembski points out, drawing design inferences is already an essential and uncontroversial part of various scientific activities ranging from the detection of fabricated experimental data, to forensic science, cryptography, and even the Search for Extraterrestrial Intelligence (SETI). He identifies two criteria as necessary and sufficient for inferring intelligence or design: complexity and specification. *Complexity* ensures that the event in question is not so simple that it can readily be explained by chance. It is an essentially probabilistic concept. *Specification* ensures that the event in question exhibits the trademarks of intelligence. The notion of specification amounts to this: if, independently of the small probability of the event in question, we are somehow able to circumscribe and define it so as to render its reconstruction tractable, then we are justified in eliminating chance as the proper explanation for the event. Dembski calls such an event one of *specified small probability*.

If an event of small probability fails to satisfy the specification criterion, it is still attributable to chance, as is the case, for example, with any sequence of heads and tails produced by one thousand tosses of a fair coin. But if an event is genuinely one of *specified* small probability, then the proper conclusion is that the cause of that event is intelligent agency. A brief example will suffice to clarify the notion. Suppose that a bank vault lock has a quadrillion possible combinations. Each of the quadrillion possible combinations is equally improbable, yet one of them in fact opens the lock. The actual combination that opens the vault is an event of specified small probability. If a person given one chance to open the vault succeeds in doing so, then the proper conclusion is that he opened the vault by design, namely by having prior knowledge of the right combination. One of Dembski's important contributions has been to render the notion of specification mathematically rigorous in a way that places design inferences on a solid foundation.

The mathematical analysis used to determine whether an event is one of specified small probability rests on empirical observations set in the context of the theoretical models used to study the domain (quantum-theoretic, molecular biological, developmental biological, cosmological, and so on) under investigation, but the design inference itself can be formulated as a valid deductive argument. One of its premises is a mathematical result that Dembski calls *the law of small probability*. That the design inference lends itself to this precision of expression is significant because it enables us to see that a rigorous approach to design inferences conforms to even the most restrictive theory of scientific explanation, the D-N model. In fact, even though the accounts of scientific explanation we considered were inadequate as universal theories, all three of them captured important intuitions. Furthermore, it is short work to see that rigorous design inferences satisfy the conditions imposed by all of them.

Design inferences conform to the requirements of a deductive-nomological explanation because they satisfy all four criteria of this explanatory model.

1. The explanation it offers can be put in the form of a deductive argument.
2. It contains at least one general law (the law of small probability), and this law is required for the derivation of the thing to be explained (in this case the nature of the cause of the event in question).
3. It has empirical content because it depends on both the observation of the event and the empirical facts relevant to determining the objective probability of its occurrence.

4. The sentences constituting the explanation are true to the best of our knowledge because they take into account all of the relevant factors in principle available to us prior to the event we are seeking to explain.

Design inferences also satisfy the requirements of the causal-statistical model of explanation by isolating the factors statistically relevant to the explanation of the event under investigation. This is accomplished by determining that the event in question is one of small probability and by ensuring that the criterion of specifiability is satisfied, thereby eliminating natural law and chance as possible explanations. It also makes manifest the causal network undergirding this statistical regularity, since it causally connects the relevant explanatory factor (intelligent agency) to the occurrence of the event (though not necessarily by means of mechanism).

Finally, design inferences satisfy the pragmatic model of explanation because they provide telling answers to why-questions, where those questions are identifiable by their topics of concern, their contrast classes, and their explanatory relevance conditions. The topic of concern in a design inference is the observed occurrence of an improbable event that bears prima facie evidence of specification. The contrast class is constituted by the set of alternatives of which the topic of concern is a member. For example, the contrast class might include the occurrence of other, more probable events in the causal context under consideration, or equally improbable events in that context that bear no evidence of specification, and so on. The explanatory relevance conditions might be the presence of highly particular initial conditions in the physical system, indications of thermodynamic counterflow, the presence of apparently intelligent informational content, and so on. All of these things are dependent on the context, but what is sought is a correct account of the cause of the event in question. The response provided by the design inference is therefore a telling one by the standards of the pragmatic model, because when an event of demonstrably specified small probability occurs, this state of affairs is favored by design-theoretic explanations.

Since design inferences satisfy all three models of scientific explanation, there seems little reason to bar their legitimacy as a mode of scientific explanation. Indeed, when generating scientific conclusions in cryptography or forensics, the design inference is not controversial. The sticking point centers on the issue of methodological naturalism. What happens if design-theoretic analysis, when applied to certain natural phenomena, yields the conclusion that these phenomena are the result of intelligent design? And what if this state of affairs implies that there is an intelligent cause that transcends our universe? Nothing but the unacknowledged operation of a questionable double standard would bar using design-theoretic tools in this context when their employment would be uncontroversial if no such implications were in view. So *can* design inferences, when applied to nature, be a form of scientific explanation? Considered without prejudice, this question requires an affirmative answer.

26

The Vise Strategy

Squeezing the Truth Out of Darwinists

William A. Dembski

A decade ago, Phillip Johnson used to boil down his critique of evolution to analyzing three words: *science*, *evolution*, and *creation*. According to Johnson, by suitably equivocating over the meaning of these words, Darwinists were able to confuse the public and themselves into consenting to a theory that ordinary standards of evidence rendered completely absurd.

The debate has progressed considerably since the early 1990s, when Johnson mainly focused on critiquing evolution. Intelligent design (ID) now offers a positive alternative to conventional evolutionary theory. I therefore propose that we add two words to Johnson's list: *design* and *nature*.

Darwinists have a long history of evading critical scrutiny. To interrogate Darwinists with the aim of opening up discussion about evolution in the public square (e.g., discussing its strengths, weaknesses, and alternatives in the high school biology curriculum), I therefore propose subjecting them to a sustained line of questioning about what they mean by each of these five terms: *science*, *nature*, *creation*, *design*, and *evolution*.

Accordingly, the vise strategy consists in subjecting Darwinists to a sustained line of questioning about these five key terms in settings where they have no choice but to answer the questions (as in a legal deposition). Hence the "vise" metaphor. The aim of this line of questioning is to make clear to those reading or hearing the Darwinists' answers that their defense of evolution and opposition to ID are prejudicial, self-contradictory, ideologically driven, and above all unjustifiable on the basis of the underlying science. Here are the questions:

Is it fair to say that you regard intelligent design as not a part of science? Would you agree that proponents of intelligent design who characterize it as a "scientific discipline" or as a "scientific theory" are mistaken?

Would you characterize intelligent design as a "pseudoscience"?

Would it be fair to say that, in your view, what makes intelligent design a pseudoscience is that it is religion masquerading as science? If ID is something other than science, what exactly is it?

Are you a scientist?

Do you feel qualified to assess whether something is or is not properly a part of science? What are your qualifications in this regard? [*Take your time here.*]

Do you think that simply by being a scientist, you are qualified to assess whether something is or is not properly a part of science?

Have you read any books on the history and philosophy of science?

[*If yes*:] Which ones? [e.g., *Herbert Butterfield*, *Ronald Numbers*, *Thomas Kuhn*]

Would you agree that in the history of science, ideas that started out as "pseudoscientific" may eventually become properly scientific, for example, the transformation of alchemy into chemistry?

Is it possible that ID could fall in this category, as the transformation into a rigorous science of something that in the past was not regarded as properly scientific? [*If no, return to this point later.*]

Are there precise criteria that tell you what belongs to science and what doesn't?

[*If no*:] Then on what basis do you preclude ID from being science? In that case, isn't your exclusion of ID from science purely a subjective judgment? How do you rule it out as nonscience if you have no criteria for judging what's in and what's outside of science?

[*If yes*:] Please list all the criteria you can think of that demarcate science from nonscience. [*Take your time with this.*] Are you sure these are all of them? If you are not sure these are all of them, how can you be sure that your criteria are the right ones?

Do these criteria work in all cases? Do they tell you in every instance what's inside and what's outside the bounds of science? Are there no exceptions?

[*If yes*:] Tell me about the exceptions. [*After several of them*:] Are there any more exceptions? Is that everything? [*Take your time with this.*]

Let's consider one very commonly accepted criterion for what's inside and what's outside the bounds of science, namely, *testability*. Would you say that *testability* is a criterion for demarcating science? In other words, if a claim isn't testable, then it's not scientific. Would you agree with this?

Would you give as one of the reasons that ID is not science that it is untestable? [*Return to this.*]

Let's stay with testability for a bit. You've agreed that if something is not testable, then it does not properly belong to science. Is that right?

Have you heard of the term *methodological materialism* (also sometimes called *methodological naturalism*)?

Do you regard methodological materialism as a regulative principle for science? In other words, do you believe that science should be limited to offering only materialistic explanations of natural phenomena?

[*If you experience resistance to this last question because the Darwinist being questioned doesn't like the connotations associated with "materialism" try*:]

This is not a trick question. By *materialistic explanations* I simply mean explanations that appeal only to matter, energy, and their interactions as governed by the laws of physics and chemistry. Do you regard methodological materialism in this sense as a regulative principle for science? [*It's important here to get the Darwinist to admit to methodological materialism—this is usually not a problem; indeed, usually they are happy to embrace it.*]

Could you explain the scientific status of methodological materialism? For instance, you stated that testability is a criterion for true science. Is there any scientific experiment that tests methodological materialism? Can you describe such an experiment?

Are there theoretical reasons from science for accepting methodological materialism? For instance, we know on the basis of the second law of thermodynamics that the search for perpetual motion machines cannot succeed. Are there any theoretical reasons for thinking that scientific inquiries that veer outside the strictures of methodological materialism cannot succeed? Can you think of any such reasons?

A compelling reason for holding to methodological materialism would be if it could be demonstrated conclusively that all natural phenomena invariably submit to materialistic explanations. Is there any such demonstration?

[*Suppose here the success of evolutionary theory is invoked to justify methodological materialism—that is, so many natural phenomena have submitted successfully to materialistic explanation that it constitutes a good rule of thumb or working hypothesis. In that case we ask*:]

But wouldn't you agree that there are many natural phenomena for which we haven't a clue how they can be accounted for in terms of materialistic explanation? Take the origin of life. Isn't the origin of life a wide open problem for biology, one that gives no indication of submitting to materialistic explanation?

[*If they claim that it isn't an open problem, continue*:]

Are you claiming that the problem of life's origin has been given a successful materialistic explanation? If so, please state the "theory of life's origin" comparable to the neo-Darwinian theory for biological evolution. Can you sketch this widely accepted theory of life's origin? How does it account for the origin of biomacromolecules in the absence of the biosynthetic machinery that runs all contemporary living cells? Furthermore, how does such a theory provide a materialistic explanation for how these biomacromolecules came together and organized themselves into a living cell in the first place?

Would you agree, then, that methodological materialism is not scientifically testable, that there is no way to confirm it scientifically, and therefore that it is not a scientific claim? Oh, you think it can be confirmed scientifically? Please explain, exactly how is it confirmed scientifically? I'm sorry, but pointing to the success of materialistic explanations in science won't work here because the issue with materialistic explanations is not their success in certain cases but their success across the board. Is there any way to show scientifically that materialistic explanations provide a *true* account for *all* natural phenomena? Is it possible that the best materialistic explanation of a natural phenomenon is not the true explanation? If this is not possible, please explain why not. [*Keep hammering away at these questions until you get a full concession that methodological naturalism is not testable and cannot be confirmed scientifically.*]

Since methodological materialism is not a scientific claim, what is its force as a rule for science? Why should scientists adopt it? [*The usual answer here is "the success of science."*]

But if methodological materialism's authority as a rule for science derives from its success in guiding scientific inquiry, wouldn't it be safe to say that it is merely a *working hypothesis* for science? And as a *working hypothesis*, aren't scientists free to discard it when they find that it "no longer works"?

It's sometimes claimed that the majority of scientists have adopted methodological materialism as a working hypothesis. But have *all* scientists adopted it? Is science governed by majority rule?

If [*as the Darwinist will by now hopefully have admitted*] methodological materialism is not a scientific claim, how can it be unscientific for ID theorists to discard it as a working hypothesis for science? In the absence of methodological materialism as a regulative principle for science, what else is there that might prevent ID from being developed into a full-fledged science? You claimed earlier that ID is not testable. Is that the reason you think ID cannot be developed into a full-fledged science?

But how can you say that ID is not testable? Over and over again, Darwin in his *Origin of Species* compared the ability of his theory to explain biological data with the ability of a design hypothesis to explain those same data. Moreover, Darwin stressed in the *Origin* that "a fair result can be obtained only by fully stating and balancing the facts and arguments on both sides of each question." How, then, can you say that ID is not testable when Darwin clearly claimed to be simultaneously testing a design hypothesis against his own theory?

Let's talk about creation and creationism a bit. Is it fair to say that you think ID is a form of creationism? Why do you think that?

Does ID try to harmonize its scientific claims with the Bible? If so, please indicate.

Is it fair to say that ID is not in the business of matching up its scientific claims with the Genesis record of creation or any other system of religious belief? If otherwise, please indicate.

Is it fair to say that ID is not *young earth creationism*, also known as *scientific creationism* or *creation science*? [*The important thing with this line of questioning is to get the Darwinist to agree that ID is not creationism in any conventional sense.*]

Is it possible to hold to ID and not be a Christian, Jew, or Muslim? Is it possible to be a Buddhist and hold to ID? Is it possible to be a Hindu and hold to ID? [*The answer in all these cases is yes, and there are respected scientists from all these systems of religious belief who hold to ID.*]

Is it possible to hold to ID for philosophical reasons that have nothing to do with conventional belief in God? In other words, can one hold to ID and not believe in God, much less a creator God?

Would you agree that Aristotle, who held to an eternal universe and an inherent purposiveness within nature (i.e., a purposiveness not imposed on nature from the outside), did not have a conventional belief in God but would today properly be regarded as an ID advocate? Are you familiar with Antony Flew's recent embrace of intelligent design despite his rejection of conventional belief in God (for instance, he explicitly rejects personal immortality)?

Your main beef with ID therefore seems to be not that it holds to a religious doctrine of creation but rather that it takes material causation to be an incomplete category of scientific explanation. Is that true or is there any other criticism that you think is more significant? If it is true, how can you claim that ID is creationism? Creationism suggests some positive account of an intelligence creating the world, but your problem with ID seems to be its denial that a certain category of causation can account for everything in nature.

Are you merely a methodological materialist or are you also a metaphysical/philosophical materialist? In other words, do you pretend that everything happens by material causation merely for the sake of science, but then bracket that assumption in other areas of your life (say on Sundays when you go to church)? Or do you really hold that everything happens by material causation—period? If the latter, on what grounds do you hold to metaphysical materialism? Can that position be scientifically justified? How so? If you claim merely to be a methodological materialist, then whence the confidence that material causation is adequate for science? [*This cycles back to previous questions.*]

What is the nature of nature? Does nature operate purely by material causation? If not, how could we know it?

Consider the following riddle (posed by Robert Pennock): "If you call a tail a leg, how many legs does a dog have?" Wouldn't you agree that the answer is four? Calling a tail a leg doesn't make it one. Accordingly, wouldn't it be prejudicial to define nature as a closed system of material entities in which everything happens by material causation? Wouldn't you agree that nature is what nature is, and it is not the business of scientists to prescribe what nature is like in advance of actually investigating nature?

Let's return to the issue of testability in science. Do you agree that for a proposition to be scientific it must be testable? Good.

Would you agree, further, that testability is not necessarily an all-or-nothing affair? In other words, would you agree that testability is concerned with confirmation and disconfirmation, and that these come in degrees, so that it makes sense to talk about the degree to which a proposition is tested? For instance, in testing whether a coin is fair, would finding that the coin landed heads twenty times in a row more strongly disconfirm the coin's fairness than finding that it landed only ten heads in a row? [*Keep hammering on this until there's an admission that testing can come in degrees. Examples from the history of science can be introduced here as well.*]

Okay, so we're agreed that science is about testable propositions and that testability of these propositions can come in degrees. Now, let me ask you this: Is testability symmetric? In other words, if a proposition is testable, is its negation also testable? For instance, consider the proposition "it's raining outside." The negation of that proposition is the proposition "it's not the case that it's raining outside" (typically abbreviated "it's not raining outside"—logicians form the negation of a proposition by putting "it's not the case that . . ." in front of a proposition). Given that the proposition "it's raining outside" is testable, is it also the case that the negation of that proposition is testable?

As a general rule, if a proposition is testable, isn't its negation also testable? [*If you don't get a firm yes to this, continue as follows*:] Can you help me to understand how a proposition can be testable but its negation not be testable? To say that a proposition is testable is to say that it can be placed in empirical harm's way—that it might be wrong and that this wrongness may be confirmed through empirical data, wouldn't you agree? Testability means that the proposition can be put to a test, and if it fails the test, then it loses credibility, and its negation gains in credibility. Wouldn't you agree? [*Keep hammering on this until the point is conceded.*]

Doesn't it then follow that whenever a proposition is testable, so is its negation, with a test for one posing a test also for the other?

Let me therefore ask you, are the following propositions scientific and, as a consequence, testable: (1) Humans and other primates share a common ancestor. (2) All organisms on Earth share a common ancestor. (3) Life on Earth arose by material causes. Are the negations of these propositions therefore scientific and testable? If not, why not?

Let's focus on the third of these propositions, namely, that life arose by purely material causes. How is it tested? How would its negation be tested? If its negation is not testable, how can the original proposition be testable? Wouldn't it then be just like arithmetic—simply a necessary truth and not something in contact with empirical data?

Let's now turn to evolution. Back in 1989 Richard Dawkins remarked that those who don't hold to evolution are "ignorant, stupid or insane (or wicked, but I'd rather not consider that)." Is Dawkins right?

Evolutionists distinguish between common descent (also known as universal common ancestry) and the mechanisms of evolution. Common descent is a historical claim. It says that all organisms trace their lineage back to a last universal common ancestor (sometimes abbreviated LUCA). Do you hold to common descent? Why? Please be as detailed as you can in describing the scientific evidence that leads you to that belief.

No doubt you have heard of the Cambrian explosion. Isn't it the case that fossil evidence reveals most extant animal phyla first appear over a period of 5 to 10 million years in the Cambrian rocks without evident precursors?

Consider an octopus, a starfish, an insect, and a fish. To what phyla do these belong? Is there solid fossil evidence that these share a common ancestor? If so, please provide the details. [*Watch for a snow job; no compelling evidence exists.*]

Do you regard the Cambrian explosion as providing a challenge to common descent? If not, why not?

Let's turn next to the mechanisms of evolution. What are the mechanisms of evolution? [*Get as many out of the evolutionist as possible. Natural selection and random mutation will be at the top of the list, with genetic drift, lateral gene transfer, and developmental factors also receiving mention.*] Are these all of them? [*Take your time. Wait until the Darwinist admits that these are all he or she can think of.*]

So you're not sure that these are all the mechanisms that drive the process of biological evolution. Is intelligence a mechanism? If you can't be sure that you've got all the relevant mechanisms of evolution, how can you rule out intelligence as a factor in biological evolution?

Okay, you're convinced that the neo-Darwinian mechanism of natural selection and random genetic change is the most important factor in biological evolution. Why is that? What is the evidence that it deserves this place in evolutionary theorizing?

Are you familiar with the molecular machines that are in all cells and without which cellular life would be impossible (the one that has been most discussed is the bacterial flagellum, a miniature, bidirectional, motor-driven propeller that moves certain bacteria through their watery environments)?

Are you familiar with the writings of James Shapiro (who is on faculty at the University of Chicago) and Franklin Harold (who is an emeritus professor at Colorado State University)? Shapiro is a molecular biologist, Harold a cell biologist. They both claim that there are no detailed Darwinian accounts for the evolution of molecular machines like the flagellum. Do you agree with their assessment? Are there any other evolutionary mechanisms that yield a detailed, testable scenario for the origin of such molecular machines?

Theodosius Dobzhansky, one of the founders of the neo-Darwinian synthesis remarked toward the end of his life that nothing in biology makes sense except in the light of evolution. Do you accept this statement?

But isn't it the case that for systems like the bacterial flagellum, evolutionary biology has no clue how they came about? [*If the Darwinist balks, keep pressing for detailed evolutionary accounts of such complex molecular machines.*] So was Dobzhansky wrong?

Earlier you expressed reservations about ID being testable. Do you also share such reservations about the testability of evolutionary theory? No? Could you explain how evolutionary theory is testable? What sort of evidence would count against evolutionary theory?

The evolutionist J. B. S. Haldane once remarked that what would convince him that evolutionary theory was wrong was finding a rabbit fossil in

Precambrian rocks. Would such a finding convince you that evolutionary theory is wrong? And wrong in what sense? Would it show that common descent is wrong? If such a fossil were found in Precambrian rocks, why not simply explain it as an evolutionary convergence?

Suppose, for the sake of argument, we accept common descent. In that case, why should we believe that natural selection and random genetic change are the principal mechanisms driving biological evolution? Is that claim testable?

Do you accept that there are other mechanisms involved in biological evolution besides natural selection and random genetic change? If so, how do biologists know that the totality of these mechanisms account for all of biological complexity and diversity? Is the claim that these mechanisms account for all of biological complexity and diversity itself testable? Have you tested it? How so? How can it be tested? If it should be tested and disconfirmed (as can always happen to testable propositions), then what is the alternative hypothesis that correspondingly is confirmed? Wouldn't it have to be a design hypothesis? If not, why not?

Section Three

The Question of Jesus

27

Did Jesus Really Exist?

Paul L. Maier

"No, he didn't!" some skeptics claim, thinking that this is a quick, powerful lever with which to pry people away from "the fable of Christianity." But the lever crumbles at its very first use. In fact, there is more evidence that Jesus of Nazareth certainly lived than for most famous figures of the ancient past. This evidence is of two kinds: internal and external. In both cases, the total evidence is so overpowering, so absolute, that only the shallowest of intellects would dare to deny Jesus's existence. And yet this pathetic denial is still parroted by "the village atheist," bloggers on the internet, or such organizations as the Freedom from Religion Foundation.

The Internal Evidence

Aside from the many messianic predictions in the Old Testament, not one of the four Gospels or the twenty-three other documents in the New Testament would make an ounce of sense if Jesus had never lived. Did the whole cavalcade of well-known historical personalities in the first century AD who interacted with Jesus deal with a vacuum? Did Herod the Great try to terminate an infant ghost? Did the Jewish high priests Annas and Caiaphas interview a spirit? Did the Roman governor Pontius Pilate judge a phantom on Good Friday, or did Paul and so many apostles give their lives for a myth?

No one doubts that the above names are well-known from both sacred and secular sources, as well as archaeological evidence, and are therefore historical. The same is clearly true of Jesus of Nazareth. But why, then, is Jesus not permitted the luxury of actually having lived as did the rest of these? Why the double standard here?

From the internal, biblical evidence alone, therefore, Jesus's existence is simply categorical. And yet there is an *abundance* of additional extrabiblical information on this question.

External Evidence: Christian

Another long paragraph could be devoted to writings of the early church fathers, some of whom had close contact with New Testament personalities. Jesus's disciple John, for example, later became bishop of the church at Ephesus. One of his students was Polycarp, bishop of Smyrna, and a student of his, in turn, was Irenaeus of Lyons. The centerpiece in all of their writings was Jesus the Christ ("Messiah").

Apart from such living personal links to Jesus, both geographical and temporal tangencies appear in Justin Martyr. Born of pagan parents around AD 100 in Nablus (between Judea and Galilee), Justin tried and abandoned various philosophical schools until he found in Christianity the one true teaching. As a native of the Holy Land, Justin mentions sites associated with Jesus, such as the Bethlehem grotto in which he was born, and even such details as Jesus's working as an apprentice carpenter in the shop of his foster father, Joseph, where they specialized in producing such agricultural implements as yokes for oxen and plows.

External Evidence: Jewish

The Jewish rabbinical traditions not only mention Jesus, but they are also the only sources that spell his name accurately in Aramaic, his native tongue: Yeshua Hannotzri—Joshua (Jesus) of Nazareth. Some of the references to Jesus in the *Talmud* are garbled—probably due to the vagaries of oral tradition—but one is especially accurate, since it seems based on written sources and comes from the *Mishnah*—the earliest collection of writings in the *Talmud*. This is no less than the arrest notice for Jesus, which runs as follows:

> He shall be stoned because he has practiced sorcery and lured Israel to apostasy. Anyone who can say anything in his favor, let him come forward and plead on his behalf. Anyone who knows where he is, let him declare it to the Great Sanhedrin in Jerusalem.[1]

Four items in this statement strongly support its authenticity as a notice composed *before* Jesus's arrest: (1) the future tense is used, (2) stoning was the regular punishment for blasphemy among the Jews whenever the Roman government was not involved, (3) there is no reference whatever to crucifixion, and (4) that Jesus was performing "sorcery"— the extraordinary or miraculous with a negative spin—is quite remarkable. This not only invokes what historians call the "criterion of embarrassment," which proves what is conceded, but accords perfectly with how Jesus's opponents explained away his miraculous healings: performing them with the help of Beelzebul (Luke 11:18).

Moreover, the first-century Jewish historian Flavius Josephus twice mentions "Jesus who is called the Christ," in his *Jewish Antiquities*. In the second of these, he tells of the death of Jesus's half brother James the Just of Jerusalem.[2] And two books earlier, in the longest first-century nonbiblical reference to Christ, he tells of Jesus, midway through his discussion of events in Pontius Pilate's administration:

> At this time there was a wise man called Jesus, and his conduct was good, and he was known to be virtuous. Many people among the Jews and the other nations became his disciples. Pilate condemned him to be crucified and to die. But those who had become his disciples did not abandon his discipleship. They reported that he had appeared to them three days after his crucifixion and that he was alive. Accordingly, he was perhaps the Messiah, concerning whom the prophets have reported wonders. And the tribe of the Christians, so named after him, has not disappeared to this day.[3]

This is the recent, *un*interpolated text that replaces the traditional version, which, unfortunately, had suffered early interpolation.

External Evidence: Secular

Cornelius Tacitus, one of the most reliable source historians of first-century Rome, wrote in his *Annals* a year-by-year account of events in the Roman Empire under the early Caesars. Among the highlights that he reports for the year AD 64 was the great fire of Rome. People blamed the emperor Nero for this conflagration since it happened "on his watch," but in order to save himself, Nero switched the blame to "the Christians," which is the first time they appear in secular history. Careful historian that he was, Tacitus then explains who "the Christians" were: "Christus, the founder of the name, had undergone the death penalty in the reign of Tiberius, by sentence of the procurator Pontius Pilatus."[4] He then goes on to report the horrors that were inflicted on the Christians in what became their first Roman persecution.

Tacitus, it should be emphasized, was not some Christian historian who was trying to prove that Jesus Christ really lived, but a pagan who despised

Christians as a "disease," a term he uses later in the passage. Had Jesus never even existed, he would have been the first to expose that pathetic phantom on whom such cultists placed their trust. Were no other references to Jesus available, this passage alone would have been sufficient to establish his historicity. Skeptics realize this and so have tried every imaginable means to discredit this passage—but to no avail. Manuscript analysis and computer studies have never found any reason to call this sentence into question, nor its context.

Gaius Suetonius Tranquillus also recorded events of the first century in his famous *Lives of the Twelve Caesars*. He too regarded the Christians as a sect "professing a new and mischievous religious belief"[5] and doubtless cited "Christus" as well, spelling his name "Chrestus."[6] That the vowels *e* and *i* were often interchangeable is demonstrated by the French term for "Christian" to this day: *chretien*.

Pliny the Younger was the Roman governor of Bithynia—today, the northwestern corner of Turkey—and about the year 110 he wrote the emperor Trajan (AD 98–117), asking what to do about the Christians, a "wretched cult" whom he mentions eight times in his letter. Christ himself is cited three times, the most famous instance referring to Christians "who met on a fixed day to chant verses alternately among themselves in honor of Christ, as if to a god."[7] Trajan's response, interestingly enough, suggests that Christians not be hunted out.[8] But again, if Christ were only a mythical character, these hostile sources would have been the first to emblazon that fact in derision.

Other ancient secular sources, such as Theudas and Mara bar Serapion also bear witness to the historicity of Jesus. But any further evidence clearly comes under the "beating a dead horse" category so far as this article is concerned. Nothing more is necessary in view of the overpowering evidence that Jesus of Nazareth was no myth, but a totally historical figure who truly lived. Skeptics should focus instead on whether or not Jesus was *more* than a man. That, at least, could evoke a reasonable debate among reasonable inquirers rather than a pointless discussion with sensationalists who struggle to reject the obvious.

28

The Credibility of Jesus's Miracles

Craig L. Blomberg

For some people, the miracles in the Gospels form the most incredible part of the New Testament accounts. Modern science, they say, has demonstrated that the universe is a closed continuum of cause and effect. The ancients may have believed in the possibility of supernatural forces in the world, but we know better today.

In fact, this cluster of opinions proved more common a half-century ago than today. Philosophers of science have stressed that by definition all science can adjudicate is that which is repeatable under controlled conditions. If there is a God of the kind in which Jews, Christians, and Muslims have historically believed, then we would expect him occasionally to bypass the laws of nature. The real question becomes whether there is good reason to believe in God in the first place.

One of the most exciting and encouraging developments in recent years in this respect is the intelligent design movement.[1] Pointing to numerous examples of fundamental entities in the natural and biological worlds that display irreducible complexity, even some scientists who are not Christians at all have acknowledged that there must be an intelligent being behind this creation. The entire big bang theory for the beginnings of the universe leads to the question of what or who produced that bang.

For others, philosophical arguments like those of the famous seventeenth-century Scotsman David Hume turn out to be more persuasive. While not alleging that miracles are impossible, the claim now is that the probability of a natural explanation will always be greater than that of a supernatural one. Phenomena could mislead, witnesses could be mistaken, and besides, explanations of events must have analogies to what has happened in the past. But it is not at all clear that any of these arguments mean that the evidence could *never* be unambiguous and the witnesses unassailable. And if every event must have a known analogy, then people in the tropics before modern technology could never have accepted that ice exists![2]

Today perhaps the most common scholarly objection to the credibility of Jesus's miracles is that stories and myths from other religions that competed with Christianity in the first-century Roman Empire are similar enough that it makes best sense to assume that the Christian miracle stories likewise teach theological truth through fictional narrative. It is curious how often laypeople and even some scholars repeat the charge that the Gospel miracles sound just like the legends of other ancient religions without having carefully studied the competing accounts. For example, it is often alleged that there were virgin births and resurrection stories all over the ancient religious landscape. But in fact, most of the alleged parallels to special births involve ordinary human sexual relations coupled simply with the belief that one of the persons was actually a god or goddess incognito. Or, as with the conception of Alexander the Great, in one legend almost a millennium later than his lifetime, a giant python wrapped itself around Alexander's mother on her honeymoon night, keeping his father at a discrete distance and impregnating the young woman.[3]

In the case of resurrections, there are stories about gods or goddesses who die and rise annually, often corresponding to the seasons and the times of harvesting and planting respectively. Greco-Roman writers use the term metaphorically at times to talk about the restoration to health of someone who was gravely ill or about the restoration to status of someone who was disgraced or deposed for a time from some position. But there are no stories from the ancient world (or the modern world, for that matter) of people known to have been real human beings, which began to circulate during the lifetimes of their followers, in which those individuals died completely, rose bodily to life again, and were declared to have atoned for the sins of the world.[4]

In fact, the closest parallels to Jesus's miracle-working activity in the ancient Mediterranean world all come from a little after the time during which he lived. Apollonius of Tyana, who lived in the late first century, was said to have worked two or three miracles very similar to Jesus's healings and resurrections. The charismatic Jewish wonder-worker Hanina ben Dosa, whose stories appear in later rabbinic literature, likewise reportedly worked a couple of miraculous healings similar to Christ's. The second-century Gnostic myth of an ascending and descending redeemer sometimes explicitly inserted Jesus instead of (or as) Sophia, or "Wisdom," as its hero. Mithraism began to resemble Christianity only in the late second and early third centuries. But all of these developments are too late to have influenced the first Christian writers; if anything, they may have been born out of a desire to make their heroes look more like Jesus and therefore more credible in a world in which Christianity was coming to have ever greater influence.

If all the main reasons for *not* believing in the Gospel miracle stories fail to convince, what are positive reasons for *believing* in them? To begin with, they are deeply embedded in every layer, source, and finished Gospel in the early Christian tradition. Jewish sources likewise attest to Jesus's miracles. Faced with the opportunity to deny the Christian claims that Jesus performed such amazing feats, Josephus and the Talmud instead corroborate them, even though they don't believe he was heaven-sent. The rabbis often made the charge that Jesus was a sorcerer who led Israel astray, much like certain Jewish leaders in the Gospel accounts (Mark 3:20–30) accused Christ of being empowered by the devil.

In addition, the nature of Jesus's miracles contrasts markedly with most of those from his milieu. There are a fair number of exorcisms and healing accounts from Jewish, Greek, and Roman sources but none where a given wonder-worker consistently and successfully works his miracles without the use of magical formulas, paraphernalia, or proper prayer to God or the gods.[5] The more spectacular miracles over nature have fewer parallels in the Greco-Roman world; where similar accounts exist there are also often reasons for disbelieving them. For example, the fountain in the temple of Dionysus in Ephesus flowed with wine once a year rather than with water. But Lucian explained that the priests had a secret underground tunnel that enabled them to enter while the building was locked at night and replace the water supply for the fountain with one of wine. This is hardly the background for Christ's miracle of turning water into wine.

Apocryphal *Christian* miracles form part of narratives that tend to fill in the gaps of the Gospel record. What was Christ like as a boy? How did the virgin birth occur? What happened when Jesus descended to the dead? The answers at times are quite frivolous compared to those in the canonical Gospels—Jesus the child fashioning birds out of mud and water and breathing life into them so that they might fly away, or cursing a playmate who has been mocking him so that he withers up. Indeed, even within Matthew, Mark, Luke, and John, the primary purpose for Jesus's miracle-working activity is to demonstrate that the kingdom is arriving, that the messianic age has come (Matt. 12:28 and parallels). But if the kingdom is coming, then the King must be coming. If the messianic age has arrived, then the Messiah must be present. The miracles are not primarily about what God can do for *us*.

The closest parallels to the miracles of Jesus are in fact in the Old Testament. Feeding the multitudes with miraculously supplied bread, God's sovereignty over wind and waves, Elijah and Elisha raising people from the dead all appear as crucial background for understanding the New Testament texts.

If anything, such parallels should inspire confidence in the reliability of the New Testament accounts.

At the same time, nothing in Christian theology requires one to argue that only the *biblical* miracles ever occurred. Nothing in the Bible requires us to imagine that God uses only his people to work the supernatural, and both demonic inspiration and human manufacture can account for other preternatural works. Nothing requires them to be without parallel in later Christian tradition either. At the same time, historians should not and need not have a more credulous attitude toward biblical miracles than toward extrabiblical ones. When we apply the same criteria of authenticity to both, the biblical miracles simply enjoy more evidential support.

When all is said and done, one of the most meticulous historians among contemporary biblical scholars makes the following significant observation:

> Viewed globally, the tradition of Jesus' miracles is more firmly supported by the criteria of historicity than are a number of other well-known and often readily accepted traditions about his life and ministry. . . . Put dramatically but with not too much exaggeration: if the miracle tradition from Jesus' public ministry were to be rejected in toto as unhistorical, so should every other Gospel tradition about him.[6]

29

The Son of Man

Darrell Bock

This title, Jesus's favorite according to the Gospels, is one of the most discussed elements about Jesus's ministry in New Testament studies. Its use in the Old Testament is fairly limited, as the phrase simply means a "human being," with *son of man* being an expression like *son of Adam*, which simply means Adam's son. So *son of man* means *son of a human being*. It is used most often in address to Ezekiel as a human (Ezek. 2:1). This prophet uses the phrase ninety-four times. Other texts also illustrate this meaning. God is not a man (Num. 23:19) that he should lie. The suffering servant was so disfigured he did not look like a human (Isa. 52:14). Psalm 8 also uses the term this way. The most famous use, however, comes in Aramaic, not Hebrew. Here one *like* a "son of man" is a figure who comes to the Ancient of Days to receive authority (Dan. 7:13). The "son of man" figure is not a title here. The figure contrasts with the previous descriptions of various pagan nations in Daniel 7 as a variety of mixed animal forms. The representative of God and man is made in God's image and receives kingdom authority.

Now another element of background is that in Aramaic the expression is an idiom. It can mean "someone" or "some human being." It is debated whether it can be an indirect way to refer to oneself. This use is not clearly attested in the first century.

In Judaism the expression came to be used of a figure of salvation, a transcendent salvation figure as it appears frequently in 1 Enoch. However, this use cannot be dated with certainty before the time of Christ. Nonetheless, such usage shows that even some Jews pushed the figure of Daniel into a title.

The term appears eighty-two times in the New Testament. It is always spoken by Jesus in the Gospels. "One like a son of man" appears in Revelation 1:13 and 14:14. Stephen sees the Son of Man standing in Acts 7:56. All other uses are by Jesus.

Scholars have classified this expression in various ways.

One way is to discuss whether the use of the title comes with a clear use of Daniel 7, an indirect use, or no use, since this is the only Old Testament passage that is connected to the title specifically in the New Testament. Most uses of the title do not make an explicit connection to Daniel 7. In fact the explicit uses that do come appear in two places: (1) the eschatological discourse where Jesus discusses the return of the Son of Man and (2) at Jesus's examination by the Jewish leadership, where he speaks of the Son of Man seated at God's right hand coming on the clouds, a remark that combines Daniel 7 and Psalm 110:1. This means that in most uses in the Gospels Jesus used the title but did not give a reference as an explanation. Both of the explicit uses come late in Jesus's ministry.

Another way to discuss the sayings is to look at what the Son of Man is doing in the saying. This has led to a threefold classification: (1) present ministry sayings, (2) suffering Son of Man sayings, and (3) future return or apocalyptic sayings. For each Synoptic Gospel the breakdown of such use is: Matthew—30 times with 7 earthly, 10 suffering, and 13 apocalyptic sayings; Mark—14 times with 2 earthly, 9 suffering, and 3 apocalyptic sayings; Luke—25 times with 7 earthly, 8 suffering, and 10 apocalyptic sayings. The uses in John's Gospel do not break out into these categories but it uses the term 12 times. The connections to Daniel 7 appear in the apocalyptic sayings.

What does all of this mean for the use of the title? It would seem that Jesus chose a seemingly ambiguous expression, the idiom, and used it to describe his ministry as a representative human being. However, as he came to the end of his ministry, he made clear, as its earlier use had suggested, that the term referred to a specific representative who had salvation authority, as Daniel 7 suggests, that would be displayed when Jesus returned to judge.

An illustration of such a use is the story of the healing of the paralytic (Matt. 9:6; Mark 2:10; Luke 5:24). Here Jesus speaks of the authority of the Son of Man to forgive sin as he uses the healing of the paralytic to point to his personal authority, an authority that was regarded by Jews to belong to God alone. Jesus says that he heals in order that they all may know that the Son of Man has authority on earth to forgive sin. In other words, Jesus uses what one can see (a healing) to illustrate the authority God has given a specific human being concerning forgiveness of sins, something one cannot explicitly see. An interesting feature about all but one of Jesus's uses of this expression is that in Greek it is always "the" Son of Man, with explicit use of a definite article to show that a particular use is in view.

The significance of this choice is that the Son of Man is a unique combination of human and divine features in Daniel 7. The son of man–like figure in that passage points to a human, but the riding of the clouds refers to something in the Old Testament that only God or the gods are said to do (Exod. 14:20; 34:5; Num. 10:34; Ps. 104:3; Isa. 19:1). Thus the expression combines humanity and divine activity with a glimpse at the giving of authority to this figure at a moment of exaltation. The combination makes it a crucial expression for Jesus as it uniquely combines the various elements that reflect his person and ministry. Jesus's use of it in a variety of contexts that cover the scope of his ministry allows him to develop the portrait. Particularly the disciples, who would have heard him use it again and again, would have come to appreciate what it meant. It seems that they preserved his unique use of it by restricting its use to him alone.

So the Son of Man is a title Jesus used to refer to himself and his authority. He revealed its full import toward the end of his ministry. But the title referred to Jesus as the representative of humanity who also engaged in divine activity. It was a way of saying I am the One sent with divine authority who will also be the representative of humanity. In this context, all of Jesus's ministry and work, including his suffering on the cross for sin, takes place.

30

The Son of God

Ben Witherington III

One of the big mistakes in Christian apologetics is just focusing on what Jesus publicly claimed to be. The truth is that what a person is and what they claim to be can be two very different things. In the case of Jesus, public claims are but a small subset of what Jesus taught his inner circle, and that also was but a small subset of what Jesus believed about himself and revealed in various ways, including in some rare cases by public claims. We need to understand as well the nature of the culture in which Jesus lived. Jesus did not live in late Western culture, which stresses individualism or striving to be an individual. Rather, in the first century, one's identity was defined by one's key relationships. Notice that almost all of the so-called titles predicated of Jesus are actually relational terms—Jesus is Son in relationship to God, he is Son in relationship to humankind, he is God's Anointed (the meaning of Messiah/Christ), he is Lord in relationship to those he rules, he is Son in relationship to David. One of the crucial reasons that Jesus did not run around Israel making enormous direct claims for himself to total strangers is because they were bound to be badly misunderstood in a world where standing out from the crowd was seen as abnormal and undesirable. So, for example, even with his disciples Jesus asks them, "Who do people say that I am?" (Mark 8:27 NASB). Normally in Jesus's world, people were defined by others and by the tribe they were a part of.

The phrase *Son of God* often connotes divinity in modern Christian discussions, but it seldom did so in Jewish antiquity. It is true that sometimes angels were called sons of God (see Gen. 6:2), but when Jews thought about a son of God they normally thought of a king anointed by God. For example, it is perfectly clear in Psalm 2 that the discussion is about the Davidic king who has been anointed by the high priest and thereby coronated as king. "The kings of the earth take their stand / and the rulers gather together / Against the LORD / and against his Anointed One. . . . The Lord scoffs at them. . . . 'I have installed my King / on Zion, my holy hill.'" Then the king himself declares, "I will proclaim the decree of the LORD. . . . You are My Son; today I have become your Father. / Ask of me, / and I will make the nations your inheritance" (Ps. 2:2–8 NIV). These last verses should be familiar since they are quoted in part at Jesus's baptismal event (see Mark 1:11 and parallels). In Judaism it was believed that the king had a special relationship with God, and was in fact adopted by God as his own child at the point of coronation. What is especially interesting about Mark 1:11 is that the second phrase "today I have become your Father" is omitted because Mark does not want to suggest that Jesus was merely adopted as God's Son at the point of his baptism. Rather, the baptism is the juncture where the Father confirms to the Son the identity he has always had and that will now be publicly revealed.

There can be no doubt however, that Jesus did not view his relationship to God as simply identical to the relationship King David had with God. For one thing, it tells us a lot about Jesus that he prayed to God as *Abba*, which is the Aramaic term of endearment, which means dearest Father. (See Mark 14:36: *Abba* is not slang; it does not mean "Daddy.") This is frankly inexplicable if Jesus only saw himself as a king or a prophetic figure, because no Jew, not even the kings before Jesus's day, prayed to God as "my dearest Father." This would have sounded like shocking familiarity. Notice that God is very seldom called Father in the Old Testament, and never prayed to as *Abba*. This is something new, and it reveals something special about how Jesus viewed his relationship to God. He believed he had a distinctively intimate relationship with God the Father. Even more striking is the fact that he taught his own disciples to pray to God as *Abba*, suggesting he could give them an intimate relationship with God unlike any they had had before. This is why we find several places in our chronologically earliest New Testament documents, the letters of Paul, where Paul says that Christians pray to God as *Abba*, indeed the Holy Spirit prompts them to do so, for they have become sons and daughters of God like Jesus, though on a lesser scale, through their relationship with Jesus (see Gal. 4:6; Rom. 8:15). And of course the very first word of the Lord's Prayer, which Jesus taught to his disciples in Aramaic, was *Abba* (see Luke 11:2). One has to ask, What sort of person could Jesus be if he thought he could not only save people but give people alienated from God a relationship with God unlike any that human beings had had previously? This in itself implies a lot about Jesus's self-understanding.

A further insight into Jesus's view of himself as God's Son comes from a close examination of a text like Matthew 11:27 (NIV), "No one knows the Son except the Father, and no one knows the Father except the Son and those to whom the Son chooses to reveal him." The first half of this maxim is unexceptional. Anyone could say, "No one really knows me except God my maker, who knows all." But it is the second half of the saying that reflects Jesus's distinctive self-understanding. He sees himself as knowing God in a way and to a degree that others do not, and furthermore he sees himself as the conduit or unique mediator of that knowledge to other human beings. Not only so, but Jesus is said to get to choose whom he reveals this intimate knowledge to. While this does not in itself prove that Jesus thought of himself as divine, this saying puts Jesus in a unique and unprecedented position when it comes to the knowledge of God, and also in his role as the dispenser of the knowledge of God. It is not a surprise that Paul, some thirty-five or so years later, would stress, "For there is one God and one mediator between God and men, the man Christ Jesus, who gave himself as a ransom for all" (1 Tim. 2:5–6 NIV). Later Christian theology was right to draw the inference that if Jesus was indeed the mediator of the saving knowledge and power and presence of God, and it was right to see him as a mediator, then he had to be able to represent God to humankind, and humans to God. In short, he had to partake of both the nature of God and the nature of human beings.

One of the important though indirect ways that Jesus revealed his identity to his disciples and others was through various forms of wisdom, or sapiential speech, for example the telling of parables. Mark 12:1–12 immediately comes to mind. In this parable the last and climactic agent and emissary of God to his vineyard is his Son. The vineyard was of course a longtime symbol of God's Jewish people (see Isaiah 5) and the tenders of the vineyard were of course the religious leaders of Israel, whether prophets, priests, or kings. Notice how the Son is called "the one whom he loved." The Jewish phrase "beloved son" was often used as a synonym for "only begotten son" and hence especially cherished. Jesus, then, in this parable sees himself as a son of God in some way that is distinctive from other Jews such that he could be called "the beloved Son." Did he understand that he had a unique relationship to the Father because of his distinctive origins (see Matthew 1 on the virginal conception)? This seems a plausible deduction.

The title Son of God, while more frequently conveying royalty than divinity in early Judaism, nonetheless had overtones of divinity for the very good reason that in the wider culture that surrounded Israel, kings were quite readily believed to be God's son in a divine sense. Certainly, when this title was used by someone like Paul to speak of Jesus to gentiles in the Greco-Roman world, the title must have sometimes carried this sort of significance. It is important to recognize then that it was Jesus's own use of the term Son of God that set this train of thought in motion, even though it was more fully amplified, explained, and expounded on after Jesus's death by Paul and various others as the Jesus movement spread west across the empire and increasingly became a gentile phenomenon. For more on this subject one should consult my book *The Many Faces of the Christ*.[1]

31

Jesus as God

Ben Witherington III

The discussion of whether Jesus saw himself as God is often plagued by anachronism, the reading back into the discussion of later ideas. It is safe to say that no Jew before the time of Jesus viewed God as a Trinity, or three persons sharing one divine nature. The term god wherever it occurs in the Old Testament refers to Yahweh, or to some false pagan god. In the New Testament as well, the term *theos* refers almost always only to God the Father, though there are some seven places in the New Testament where this Greek term is used of Jesus (see Rom. 9:5). Two of these places are in the Gospel of John (see John 1 and John 20). John 20:28 is especially important, as it is very clear in that text that the acclamation is being applied to the human being known as Jesus, whereas this is less clear in John 1.

If we try to think as Jesus thought, in his own environment, it becomes clear why Jesus did not parade around Galilee saying, "Hi, I'm God." The reason is obvious—this would have been understood to mean, "I am Yahweh" or as Christians would put it, "I am the Heavenly Father" and would have led to his being stoned on the spot. Jesus of course never claims to be the Father, much less to be Yahweh. Even the Johannine phrase "I and the Father are one" (John 10:31 NIV) does not mean "I and the Father are identical" or "I and the Father are one person." Jesus chooses different ways, less prone to misunderstanding, to reveal his special and divine identity, ways that would work in his Jewish culture and setting.

One of these ways is clear enough in Mark 12:35–40. Jesus in this discussion suggests that Messiah will be David's Lord. He of course chooses the method of indirection, so the audience will have to tease their minds into active thought to figure out what he means, but the implication is there nevertheless. But this implication is in fact clearer by the frequent, if not constant, way Jesus uses the phrase *Son of Man*, with its allusions to Daniel 7:13–14, the discussion of a person who is to be worshiped and who will rule over all forever. Oddly enough, the title with the most divine overtones is *Son of Man* rather than *Son of God*.

But there are other indirect ways that Jesus signals who he is. For example, Jesus uniquely chooses to precede his own pronouncements with the term *amen*, a term normally used by the congregation to affirm the truthfulness of what someone else says after they say it. Not so with Jesus. He vouches for the truthfulness of his own words in advance of offering them! He does not need others to bear witness to him in order to validate the truthfulness of his words. Notice as well that Jesus never uses the prophetic formula, "thus sayeth the Lord." Why is this? It is because Jesus, when he makes dramatic pronouncements, is not merely speaking for God; he is speaking as one who has the same divine authority. This tells us a lot about Jesus's self-understanding indirectly, as does the fact that Jesus speaks on his own authority—the phrase "you have heard it said . . . but I say to you" (see Matt. 5:21–22) speaks volumes in a culture where everybody cited earlier authorities to validate their points. Then there is the further fact that Jesus feels free to

1. say that some of the Mosaic Law is obsolete (e.g., its teaching on working on the Sabbath or on clean and unclean in Mark 7:15 or on divorce in Matthew 19);
2. intensify the requirements of the Law (what it says about adultery in Matthew 5); or
3. offer up new teaching that not merely went beyond the Law but went against it and in a wholly different direction (e.g., his teaching on non-retaliation as opposed to measured or equivalent response—an eye for an eye.) One has to ask, What kind of person could approach his own words and God's Word with this sort of sovereign freedom and authority?

The modern discussion of the difference between functional and ontological terminology for God when applied to Jesus is both anachronistic and unhelpful, as it was not the way early Jews thought about such issues. If someone actually functioned as God, that person must have the character or nature to do so. As Jesus himself put it, "each tree is known by its own fruit" (Luke 6:44 HCSB). Put another way, it was believed that what one did or how one behaved revealed one's character. This being the case, if someone acted like God come to earth, he had either better be God or be gone, because otherwise it would be a clear case of dealing with a fraud or a delusional person, subject to stoning in the former case and being cast out from normal society in the latter.

Some of Jesus's parables reveal just how unique Jesus thought he was. For example, in Mark 12:1–12 he is depicted as the last emissary of God the Father to earth, his only and beloved Son. Or in Matthew 25:31–46, the Son of Man is depicted as the one who will come and judge the earth as only God can or should. One has to ask, What sort of person believes that he will return from heaven to judge the world, something also clearly suggested by Mark 14:62? Or again, What sort of person feels free to cleanse the outer precincts of the temple, or better said, perform a prophetic sign of the coming judgment on the temple, as Mark 11 says he did?

It is certainly true that the full formulation of trinitarian doctrine came after New Testament times, but it is equally clear that Jesus set in motion the christological reformulation of monotheism by predicating of himself words, deeds, and character that had previously only been predicated of Yahweh. It was not Paul who invented the idea that Jesus should be prayed to in the Aramaic phrase *marana tha*, which means "Come O Lord" (see 1 Cor. 16:22). This was already the prayer of Jesus's earliest disciples in Jerusalem, who spoke Aramaic and longed for his return. Early Jews knew better than to pray to a deceased rabbi to come or come back from beyond the grave. Only God should be prayed to. Likewise the earliest Christians sung hymns of praise to Jesus as divine as both the Logos hymn in John 1 and the christological servant hymn in Philippians 2:5–11 show. These ideas were not the invention of Paul or other early Christians. They went back to the "intimations of immortality" and the impressions of divinity Jesus left on his disciples. Most importantly, the reconfirmations of these impressions came through the personal encounters with the risen Jesus who came to be confessed (in the earliest such confession) as "the risen Lord" (see 1 Cor. 12:3) throughout the early church. This was in part because of who Jesus revealed himself to be during his ministry, and more because of who he revealed himself to be after the crucifixion.

To paraphrase Eduard Schweizer, Jesus was the man who fit no one formula, title, or pigeonhole. He chose to reveal his identity in his own way, without trying to conform to the preconceived notions of others. He revealed his divine identity in ways that suited his early Jewish context, not the much later context of the christological controversies in the fourth and fifth centuries. Our problem today is that we need to read New Testament texts through early Jewish eyes, not through the later eyes of polemical Christian discussions and formulations. When we do so, we will come to the conclusion that Jesus, unique among his contemporaries, chose to reveal his divine nature in his own way, in his own words, and in his own good time, and for good measure he came back on Easter Sunday morning to reconfirm these truths to his frightened and flawed disciples. For more on this see my book *Jesus the Seer*.[1]

32

Did Jesus Predict His Violent Death and Resurrection?

Craig A. Evans

Throughout the twentieth century, Gospel critics have frequently asserted that Jesus's predictions of death and resurrection are *vaticinium ex eventu*, formulated by the early church. Form critic Rudolf Bultmann accurately summarized scholarly opinion of his day when he said that the "predictions of the passion and resurrection . . . have long been recognized as secondary constructions of the church."[1]

The predictions to which Bultmann was referring are those found in the Synoptic Gospels (see Mark 8:31; 9:31; 10:33–34; and parallels in Matthew and Luke). It must be admitted that these predictions have been edited in the light of the events that overtook Jesus. But there are very good reasons to believe that Jesus did in fact anticipate his violent death and his vindication by means of resurrection. Let us consider the evidence for Jesus's anticipation of his violent death.

Anticipation of Violent Death

First of all, the fate of John the Baptist surely portended to Jesus his own fate. The close association of Jesus and John is highly probable, so it is reasonable to assume that in continuing John's proclamation of repentance and the appearance of the kingdom of God, Jesus surely recognized his danger. Indeed, in a saying evidently responding to threats emanating from Herod Antipas, the tyrant who executed John, Jesus retorts, "Go and tell that fox, 'Behold, I cast out demons and perform cures today and tomorrow, and the third day I reach My goal. Nevertheless I must journey on today and tomorrow and the next day; for it cannot be that a prophet would perish outside of Jerusalem'" (Luke 13:32–33 NASB). In the context of the temple precincts, where Jesus draws attention to John (see Mark 11:27–33), Jesus tells the parable of the Wicked Tenants (see Mark 12:1–12), implying that the "son" of the vineyard owner (i.e., Jesus) will be murdered.

Perhaps the most compelling evidence that Jesus anticipated his death is seen in the garden prayer, on the eve of his arrest, in which Jesus exhibits his fear in view of impending events. Falling on his face, Jesus says: "Abba! Father! All things are possible for You; remove this cup from Me; yet not what I will, but what You will" (Mark 14:36 NASB).

This short, pithy prayer is certainly authentic. It is difficult to imagine why an early Christian would invent an utterance in which Jesus appears frightened and reluctant to go to his death.[2] One only need make comparison with the serene and composed Jesus in the fourth Gospel, who with the greatest dignity reviews with his heavenly Father the glory that they have shared from all eternity (see John 17). A starker contrast with the anguished Synoptic prayer could not be imagined. Indeed, even in his death, the Johannine Jesus maintains this surreal calm and dignity, proclaiming from the cross, "It is finished!" (John 19:30 NASB). The Johannine tradition thus documents the ecclesiastical proclivity to portray Jesus in a more dignified and commanding light. The Synoptic garden prayer betrays no such tendency.

The Gospels also say that Jesus told his disciples to take up the cross and come after him (see Mark 8:34). Jesus anticipates violent death. In view of this grim fate can his disciples follow him? What is interesting here is that, in a sense, Jesus himself fails to do what he taught his disciples. When the time came to take up his cross, he could not do it; someone else carried his cross (see Mark 15:21). The tension between the saying and what later actually happens strongly argues for the authenticity of the saying, for post-Easter fiction would have Jesus say something fully consistent with the events of the passion.

There are also Jewish models of the suffering of the righteous, resulting in benefit for the people of Israel. One thinks of the mysterious priest Taxo and his seven sons, whose martyrdom precedes the appearance of the kingdom of God and the demise of Satan.[3] The deaths of the Maccabean martyrs are also remembered as clearing the way for Israel's redemption (see 2 Macc. 7:32–33).

In view of the evidence of the Gospels, which is clarified in important ways by the religious context in which Jesus lived and ministered, it is quite probable that Jesus at some point spoke of his violent death and tried to explain its significance.

Anticipation of Resurrection

Did Jesus anticipate his resurrection? It is probable that he did.[4] Once he began speaking of his death, Jesus very likely began speaking of his vindication through resurrection. Had he not anticipated it, it would have been very strange, for pious Jews very much believed in the resurrection of the dead. There are three factors that must be taken into account.

First, Jesus, like many Jews of his day, believed in the resurrection of the last days.[5] Jesus defends the resurrection in his reply to the Sadducees (see Mark 12:18–27). He tells his host at a dinner party, "When you give a reception, invite the poor, the crippled, the lame, the blind, and you will be blessed, since they do not have the means to repay you; for you will be repaid at the resurrection of the righteous" (Luke 14:13–14 NASB). Moreover, because Jesus believed the eschatological hour was at hand and that the rule of God was beginning to be felt, he probably also believed that the general resurrection itself was not far off. The same idea is attested in the Dead Sea Scrolls, where Messiah and general resurrection are linked.[6] It is in this light that we should interpret Jesus's prediction of his own vindication.

Second, Jesus's prediction of his resurrection "after three days" or "on the third day" was almost certainly based on Hosea 6:2, as reflected in the Aramaic paraphrase. This is the product of the Aramaic-speaking, Scripture-interpreting Jesus, not the Greek Scripture-reading, proof-texting Christian community after Easter. Whereas the Hebrew reads: "He will revive us after two days; on the third day he will raise us up that we may live before him" (and the Greek reads similarly), the Aramaic reads: "He will give us life in the days of consolations that will come; on the day of the resurrection of the dead he will raise us up." Jesus presupposed the interpretive orientation reflected in this later Aramaic paraphrase. He alluded to this passage in his expression of confidence that he would be raised up "after three days" (or "on the third day"), that is, "on the day of the resurrection of the dead," which given the nearness of God's kingdom, must surely be at hand. This passage from Hosea is nowhere actually quoted or paraphrased in the Gospels, which tells against seeing it as a Christian proof-text. Indeed, there is no indication that the disciples fully understood Jesus's allusion and curious exegesis or were in any way reassured by his prediction(s). Despite his assurances, his movement lost its momentum.

Third, there is a strong tradition of pious Jewish martyrs who expect vindication through resurrection after their violent and cruel deaths.[7] This is seen especially in 2 Maccabees 7, in the gruesome stories of the torture and execution of the seven brothers, who refuse to violate the Mosaic law. One of the brothers angrily replies to Antiochus, "You accursed wretch, you dismiss us from this present life, but the King of the universe will raise us up to an everlasting renewal of life, because we have died for his laws" (v. 9). Another brother warns the tyrant, “One cannot but choose to die at the hands of men and to cherish the hope that God gives of being raised again by him. But for you there will be no resurrection to life!” (v. 14). If these young men anticipated resurrection, why wouldn’t Jesus?

The evidence taken as a whole supports the conclusion that Jesus did anticipate his resurrection, perhaps as part of the general resurrection, and that this resurrection would take place soon after his death. Much to the surprise of his disciples, his resurrection indeed did take place, and “on the third day” at that.[8]

33

Can We Be Certain That Jesus Died on a Cross?

A Look at the Ancient Practice of Crucifixion

Michael R. Licona

All four New Testament Gospels report that Jesus was crucified and that he died as a result. Is the evidence sufficient to warrant the conclusion that these reports are accurate? Before investigating for an answer, I would like to note the importance of this question. The atoning death and resurrection of Jesus is the cornerstone doctrine of Christianity. If either failed to occur, the Christianity preached by the apostles was false. For if Jesus did not die on the cross, there is no sacrificial death on behalf of our sins, as the New Testament teaches. Moreover, since the term *resurrection* refers to the transformation of a corpse into an immortal body, if Jesus did not die, there was no corpse to be transformed by a resurrection.

Without a resurrection, Christianity is falsified. The apostle Paul taught: "If Christ has not been raised, your faith is worthless" (1 Cor. 15:17 HCSB). The Gospels report that Jesus likewise said that his resurrection would serve as proof that his claims about himself were true (see Matt. 12:39–40; John 2:18–22). Thus, according to Jesus and Paul, if the resurrection of Jesus did not occur, it is time to find another worldview. Accordingly, since a resurrection requires death, Jesus's death by crucifixion is a link that cannot be broken if Christianity is to be regarded as true.

In this article, I would like to provide four reasons that support the credibility of the claim that Jesus died as a result of being crucified.

First, Jesus's execution is reported in a number of ancient sources: Christian and non-Christian. In addition to the four Gospels and a number of letters contained in the New Testament, all of which were written in the first century, Jesus's execution is even reported by a number of ancient non-Christian sources. Josephus (late first century), Tacitus (early second century), Lucian (early to mid second century), and Mara bar Serapion (second to third centuries) all report the event. The fact that these non-Christians mentioned Jesus in their writings shows that Jesus's death was known outside of Christian circles and was not something the Christians invented.

Second, the probability of surviving crucifixion was very low. Crucifixion and the torture that many times preceded it may have been the worst way to die in antiquity. Many of us saw Mel Gibson's film *The Passion of the Christ* and witnessed the brutal practice of scourging. A number of ancient sources describe it, such as Josephus, a Jewish historian in the first century who tells of a man who had been whipped so severely that he was filleted to the bone.[1] Elsewhere he reports that a group was whipped until their intestines were exposed.[2] In a second century text named the *Martyrdom of Polycarp*, the Roman whip is said to expose a person's veins and arteries.[3] The victim was then taken outside the city walls where soldiers using nails would impale him to a cross or a tree.[4] Then he was left hanging in excruciating pain. In fact, the word *excruciating* comes from the Latin *excrucio*, literally, "out of the cross." In the first century, a Roman philosopher named Seneca described crucified victims as having battered and ineffective carcasses, maimed, misshapen, deformed, nailed, and "drawing the breath of life amid long-drawn-out agony."[5]

Only one account exists of a person surviving crucifixion. Josephus reported seeing three of his friends crucified.[6] He quickly appealed to his friend the Roman commander Titus who ordered that all three be removed immediately and provided the best medical care Rome had to offer. In spite of this action, two of the three still died. Thus, even if Jesus had been removed prematurely and medically assisted, his chances of survival were bleak. Even with that, no evidence exists that Jesus was removed while alive or that he was provided any medical care whatsoever, much less Rome's best.

Third, professional medical opinions are unanimous in concluding that Jesus certainly died as a result of being crucified.[7] While some debate remains regarding the actual cause of death by crucifixion, the majority opinion is that he died by asphyxiation—from a lack of oxygen. Our historical understanding of crucifixion supports that conclusion. A number of ancient sources report the practice of breaking legs in order to expedite death on the cross.[8] How would this expedite death? I have two friends, each of which is a director of the emergency room at two metropolitan hospitals.[9] I asked each of them if there were any medical reasons for why breaking the legs of a crucified victim would expedite their death. They answered that a few possibilities exist, but that these would certainly be rare. So how would breaking a crucified victim's legs expedite their death?

During the First and Second World Wars, the Germans often tortured victims by a practice called *aufbinden*, during which they would tie victims by their wrists and lift them up so that only their toes could touch the ground if they tried. When the victim tired, they would relax. As a result, they would find it difficult to breath. Since the muscles used for inhaling are stronger than the muscles used for exhaling, carbon dioxide would build up and the victim would die an uncomfortable death. Experiments on live volunteers, suspended with the inability to touch the ground, revealed that one could not remain conscious longer than twelve minutes in this position, as long as their arms were at a forty-five-degree angle or less. Breaking the legs of a crucified victim would prevent them from pushing up against the nail in their feet, an excruciating move, in order to make it easier to breath, albeit temporarily. It is the opinion of my two ER physician friends that, due to the trauma already experienced by a crucified victim, once he had died on a cross from a lack of oxygen, and had remained dead in that position for five minutes, there would be no chance of resuscitating him. In addition the Gospel of John reports that one of the guards pierced Jesus to confirm that he was already dead (see John 19:34–37), a practice likewise mentioned by Quintillian, a Roman historian in the first century.[10]

Is there reason to believe that the Romans would desire to expedite Jesus's death on the cross? Josephus mentions that prior to the destruction of Jerusalem by the Romans in AD 70, it was the custom of the Jews there to remove the crucified from their crosses and bury them prior to sunset.[11] There are reports of a crucified victim living as long as three days on his cross and of victims left on their crosses for a lengthy period of time after death to serve as food for birds, dogs, and insects. However, this was not the practice in Jerusalem prior to its destruction in AD 70. Jesus was crucified in either AD 30 or 33. Thus we have very good reason for believing that Jesus's death was ensured by the Romans prior to sunset on the day he was executed.

Fourth, even if Jesus had somehow managed to survive crucifixion, he would not have inspired his disciples to believe that he had been resurrected. Imagine Jesus, half dead in the tomb. He revives out of a coma and finds himself afraid in the dark. He places his nail-pierced hands on the very heavy stone blocking his exit and pushes it out of the way. Then he is met by the guards, who say, "Where do you think you're going, pal?" He answers, "I'm out of this hole." He then beats up the guards, after which he walks blocks if not miles on pierced and wounded feet in order to find his disciples. Finally, he comes to the house where they are staying and knocks on the door. Peter opens the door and sees Jesus hunched over in his pathetic and mutilated state and says, "Wow! I can't wait to have a resurrection body just like yours!" The historian must ask how likely it is that Jesus could have convinced his disciples in his wounded condition that he was the risen Lord of life in an immortal body. Alive? Barely. Risen? No way.

In summary, the historical evidence is very strong that Jesus died by crucifixion. It is attested to by a number of ancient sources, some of which are non-Christian and thus not biased toward a Christian interpretation of events; the chances of surviving crucifixion were very bleak; the unanimous professional medical opinion is that Jesus certainly died due to the rigors of crucifixion, and even if Jesus had somehow managed to survive crucifixion, it would not have resulted in the disciples' belief that he had been resurrected.

Even the highly skeptical cofounder of the Jesus Seminar John Dominic Crossan concludes, "That [Jesus] was crucified is as sure as anything historical can ever be."[12] Then on three occasions in the same book, Crossan affirms that this event resulted in Jesus's death. Similarly, the atheist New Testament critic Gerd Lüdemann writes, "Jesus' death as a consequence of crucifixion is indisputable."[13] Thus, given the strong evidence for Jesus's death by crucifixion, without good evidence to the contrary, the historian must conclude that Jesus was crucified and that the process killed him.

34

The Empty Tomb of Jesus

Gary R. Habermas

An intriguing development in recent theological research is that a strong majority of contemporary critical scholars seems to support, at least to some extent, the view that Jesus was buried in a tomb that was subsequently discovered to be empty. I will list several of the more than twenty arguments that have been cited in favor of the empty tomb.

Major Arguments for the Empty Tomb

First, perhaps the most powerful argument favoring the empty tomb concerns its location and the events surrounding it. The Gospel accounts are unanimous that Jesus was buried in a tomb that was located in Jerusalem. Few critics question this, holding that Jesus died and was buried in the city. Most also agree that early Christian preaching took place here, leading to the birth of the church.

But it is precisely since Jesus's grave was located nearby that we have a serious problem if it was anything but empty. Unless Jesus's tomb was unoccupied, the early Christian preaching would have been disproved on the spot. How could it be preached that Jesus had been raised from the dead if that message were starkly confronted by a rotting body? Exposing the body would kill the message and be an easy disproof of Christianity before it even gained momentum. Thus Jerusalem is the last place for the early Christian teachings to gain a foothold unless Jesus's grave was empty. A Sunday walk to the tomb could have settled the matter one way or another.

A creative response might be to assert that perhaps the body was indeed in the tomb, but that, very soon afterward, the body would have been unrecognizable, due to its decomposition. Or perhaps the tomb was still simply closed without being opened for inspection.[1] But these questions entirely miss the point of the Christian preaching that the tomb was empty. Therefore, if any body was found in Jesus's tomb, whether Jesus's or even someone else's, or if it were still closed, this would have contradicted the teaching that it was *empty*. In Jerusalem, the mistake would have been exposed in no time.

Second, the most-mentioned argument in support of the Gospel accounts is the unanimous agreement that women were the first witnesses to the empty tomb. While it is not strictly true that women were disallowed from testifying in a court of law, it was clearly the case that there was a strong prejudice against using female testimony for important matters.[2]

Notwithstanding this common stance, the Gospel accounts insist in their proclamation that the women were the star witnesses to the empty tomb. But why should these writers highlight female testimony unless the women really were the first to discover this fact? To do so would be to weaken their case considerably in the eyes of most listeners. Given this situation in first-century Palestine, we can only conclude that the Gospel authors were clearly convinced that the women had discovered the empty tomb. They were more interested in reporting the truth than they were in avoiding criticism. This argument is very widely recognized and few scholars have challenged it, which testifies to its strength.

Third, while the empty tomb accounts in the Gospels are later than Paul's writings, it is crucially important that the empty tomb accounts are witnessed by many. In other words, whichever major view of Gospel origins one takes, the empty tomb narratives arose from more than one independent source. In fact, scholars think that there could be as many as three or four independent traditions in the Gospels, which very strongly increases the likelihood that the reports are both early and historical. Along with the Jerusalem location and the testimony of the women, I think that these are the best arguments in favor of the empty tomb.

Fourth, most recent scholars seem to agree that, while Paul does not explicitly mention the empty tomb, the early tradition that this apostle reported to others in 1 Corinthians 15:3–4 implies an empty tomb. The listing of the Gospel content moves from Jesus's death, to his burial, to his resurrection from the dead, to his appearances. This sequence strongly suggests that, however it may have been transformed, Jesus's body that died and was buried is the same one that was raised afterward. Thus what was placed in the ground is precisely what emerged. In short, what went down is what came up. Such a process would have resulted in the burial tomb being emptied.

That Paul does not specifically mention the empty tomb keeps this from being as strong a point as it could have been. Still, to say so clearly that Jesus's dead body was buried, raised, and appeared would be a rather strange process unless the tomb had been vacated in the process.

Fifth, many scholars also concede that Acts 13 may very well contain another early tradition, an early sermon account that was included in a book that was written at a later date. This report, found in Acts 13:29–31, 36–37, is attributed to Paul and clearly teaches that Jesus's body was placed in a tomb. Then he was raised and appeared to his followers without undergoing any bodily decomposition. If so, here we would have an early text where Paul even more strongly acknowledged the empty tomb, because Jesus appeared and his body did not experience any decay.

Sixth, according to reports found in Matthew 28:11–15, Justin Martyr, and Tertullian, for almost two centuries or more, the Jewish leaders tried to explain that the tomb was empty because Jesus's disciples stole his body.[3] This means that the Jewish hierarchy even acknowledged the fact that Jesus's body was no longer there!

However, even skeptics freely recognize that the explanation provided by the Jewish leaders was exceptionally weak. For example, if the disciples stole Jesus's body, how can we account for their incredible transformations, such as forfeiting their family years, as well as their jobs, health, and even their peace, all for the right to be chased for decades around the Roman Empire, just so they could preach a message that they clearly knew was a false tale? Further, how do we explain their willingness to die for what they knew was a false proclamation of Jesus's resurrection? Moreover, how does this explanation allow us to account for the conversion of Jesus's brother James, who had rejected Jesus's message? And we also lack any convincing reason for Paul's conversion from Judaism. So, all for the sake of providing a clearly unconvincing alternative account, the Jewish leaders even admitted the empty tomb!

Seventh, a word should be said about the scholarly thesis of N. T. Wright and others. In the ancient world—whether pagan, Jewish, or Christian—writings up until the second century AD were in complete agreement that the very definition of resurrection was clearly a bodily notion. In fact, there are almost no exceptions to this ancient view that being raised from the dead is something that, if it ever occurred, could happen only to the body. So it had this same meaning throughout the Old Testament and Gospel accounts, as well as in Paul's writings and the rest of the New Testament teaching about Jesus. This would indicate that Jesus's resurrection was conceived in a bodily manner, necessitating that the tomb was empty.[4]

Conclusion

These are some of the reasons why a majority of contemporary scholars recognize the fact of the empty tomb. Still other arguments could be provided as well. That is why historian Michael Grant concludes that "the historian . . . cannot justifiably deny the empty tomb" because if we apply the same historical criteria that we use elsewhere, then "the evidence is firm and plausible enough to necessitate the conclusion that the tomb was indeed found empty."[5]

In light of arguments such as those we have produced here, this conclusion seems to be very difficult to avoid. The normal application of historical rules to the various data indicates that, just shortly after his death, Jesus's tomb was indeed found empty.

35

The Resurrection Appearances of Jesus

Gary R. Habermas

When the New Testament defines and identifies the Gospel data, at least three items are always mentioned: the deity, death, and resurrection of Jesus.[1] The key to Jesus's resurrection is his postdeath appearances. Critical scholars agree that the entire enterprise of the early church—worship, writings, and witness—would never have come about if Jesus's followers were not absolutely convinced that he had conquered death by appearing to them afterward.

Throughout this essay, I will not assume the inspiration or even the reliability of the New Testament writings, though I think these doctrines rest on strong grounds. I will refer almost exclusively to those data that are so well attested that they impress even the vast majority of nonevangelical scholars. Each point is confirmed by impressive data, even though I can do no more than offer an outline of these reasons.

We must be clear from the outset that not only do contemporary scholars not mind when data are taken from the New Testament writings, but they do so often. The reason is that confirmed data can be used anywhere it is found.

Using almost solely those data that are well attested and recognized, I will list ten considerations that favor Jesus's resurrection appearances. Each angle has this in common: it indicates that one or more persons were utterly convinced that they had seen Jesus again after his death. Although I cannot defend the additional thesis here, I and others have argued elsewhere in much detail that this conviction cannot be viably accounted for by any natural means. Perhaps surprisingly, comparatively few skeptical scholars even favor these alternative hypotheses.[2] Therefore, the most likely conclusion is that the disciples and others really did see the risen Jesus.

Here is the absolute crux of my case: These ten arguments point to the disciples and others having actual, visual experiences. When juxtaposed with the failure of viable natural alternatives, we have an especially powerful indication that, after his death, Jesus actually appeared to many persons. These appearances were to both individuals and groups. In other words, if multiple evidences point to visual experiences, and natural attempts fail to explain them otherwise, the most likely explanation is that Jesus rose from the dead. Briefly, *the early disciples' experiences plus the failure of naturalistic theories equals the resurrection appearances of Jesus.*

Our first four arguments are drawn from Paul's epistles. The remaining six are taken from other New Testament sources.

First, for a number of reasons, when recent scholars discuss the resurrection appearances of Jesus, they begin with the apostle Paul. He had been a powerful opponent of the early Christian message (1 Cor. 15:9; Gal. 1:13–14; Phil. 3:4–7). Paul explains that he was converted from his high rank in Judaism. Clearly, the reason for his change was his belief that he had seen the risen Jesus (1 Cor. 9:1; 15:8; Gal. 1:16). Jesus's appearance to Paul certainly qualified him, being a scholar on both Judaism and Christianity, as an exceptionally strong witness to the resurrected Jesus.

Second, beyond his scholarly and eyewitness testimony, Paul contributes far more to a case for Jesus's resurrection appearances. Few conclusions in current study are more widely held by scholars than that, in 1 Corinthians 15:3, Paul recorded a very ancient tradition that actually predates his book, probably by a couple of decades. It could very well predate even Paul's conversion to Christianity. After explaining that he received this from others, Paul succinctly reports the Gospel that was preached in early Christianity: Christ died for our sins and was buried. Afterward he was raised from the dead and appeared to many witnesses.

Paul tells his readers that he was handing down this teaching that he had received from others (see 1 Cor. 15:3). His explicit statement here is important, due to the respect that scholars have for Paul's testimony. Further, his claim has been vindicated because there are many textual indications that the words that follow were not composed by him. For example, this list of appearances exhibits a parallel structure, as if it were an ancient catechism whose purpose was to be passed on and learned. Moreover, to identify a few other characteristics, the Greek sentence structure, diction, and some of the words are not Paul's, judging from his other epistles.

Most scholars who address the subject think that Paul received this material about AD 35 just three years after his conversion, when he made his first trip to Jerusalem. Paul explains that he visited Peter and James the brother of Jesus (see Gal. 1:18–19). In the immediate context both before and after, Paul is discussing the nature of the gospel (see Gal. 1:11–2:10). Additionally, Paul's choice of words in verse 18 shows that he was interviewing or questioning the two apostles in order to gain information. Here we have an exceptionally early tradition from almost immediately after Jesus, centering on the gospel report and clearly including Jesus's resurrection appearances.

Third, Paul was so careful to assure the truth of the gospel message that he returned to Jerusalem fourteen years after this initial visit (see Gal. 2:1–10). Amazingly, his purpose was to be absolutely sure that what he preached was true (see Gal. 2:2)! For a second time, Paul conducted his research. Besides Peter and James, another major apostle, John, was also present. Could Paul possibly have consulted three Christian leaders more prominent than these? Crucially, these four witnesses were the most influential in the early church. And with a single voice, they testified at this early date to the resurrection appearances of Jesus. The bottom line was that Paul's gospel teaching, which included the resurrection (see 1 Cor. 15:1–5), was approved by the other three apostles. They added nothing to his message (see Gal. 2:6, 9). Paul's two trips to Jerusalem provided the data and the confirmation that he desired.

Fourth, in 1 Corinthians 15:11, Paul added still another layer of personal testimony. We already learned that the other major apostolic leaders had approved Paul's gospel message. Now Paul asserts that he also knew what the others were preaching. And as they had confirmed his message years before, Paul now testified that they also taught the same truth that he did regarding Jesus's resurrection appearances (1 Cor. 15:11). In fact, Paul had just recorded separate appearances to two of them: Peter (see 1 Cor. 15:5) and James (see 1 Cor. 15:7). Together with John, all the apostles preached the same truth—they were witnesses of the risen Jesus's appearances (see 1 Cor. 15:12, 15).

Scholars uniformly regard Paul as the earliest and best witness to the resurrection appearances. Considerations such as these four provide some indications of the value of Paul's testimony to Jesus's resurrection appearances. But Paul's writings are far from the only evidence. There are at least six more confirmations that work together to form an even tighter latticework.

Fifth, besides 1 Corinthians 15:3, scholars usually agree that many other New Testament books also contain early traditions that predate the texts in which they appear. Many of the best examples are found in the book of Acts, where succinct summaries of early preaching are embedded.[3] The center of these early statements is the death and resurrection of Jesus Christ.

Sixth, virtually no one, friend or foe, believer or critic, denies that it was their convictions that they had seen the resurrected Jesus that caused the disciples' radical transformations. They were willing to die *specifically for their resurrection belief*. Down through the centuries many have been willing to give their lives for political or religious causes. But the crucial difference here is that while many have died for their *convictions*, Jesus's disciples were in the right place to know the truth or falsity of the event for which they were willing to die.

Seventh, it is almost always acknowledged that during Jesus's ministry, his brother James was a skeptic (see John 7:5). He was probably one of the family members in Mark 3:21–35 who thought that Jesus was insane! But how do we account for the surprising reports that James later led the Jerusalem church (Gal. 1:18–2:10; Acts 15:13–21)? According to the creedal comment in 1 Corinthians 15:7, Jesus appeared to James, yet another pointer to a resurrection appearance.

Eighth, the tomb in which Jesus was buried was found empty shortly afterward. The early apostolic preaching of the resurrection began in Jerusalem, where a closed or occupied tomb would have been disastrous! Moreover, the unanimous agreement that women were the earliest witnesses to the empty tomb is another strong consideration, since the widespread prejudice against female testimony indicates that the reports were not invented. Although the empty tomb does not prove the resurrection appearances, it does strengthen the disciples' claim to have seen the risen Jesus.

Ninth, that Jesus's resurrection was the *very center* of early Christian faith also indicates its reality, since, for this reason, it was repeatedly affirmed by believers and challenged by unbelievers. For example, Paul visited the Jerusalem apostles at least two or three times in order to make sure that his gospel message was truthful; indeed, there was no Christianity without this event (see 1 Cor. 15:14, 17). It was the church's central proclamation (see Acts 4:33). Unbelievers attacked this centerpiece of faith but could not disprove the rock on which it was founded: Jesus's appearances.

Last, two thousand years of attempts by nonbelievers to explain what happened to Jesus in natural terms have failed. The Jewish leaders in Jerusalem had the power, motive, and location to investigate thoroughly the proclamation of the resurrection appearances. They knew of Jesus's death and his burial. Though they were ideally situated to expose the error, they did not refute the evidence. Even many of today's skeptical scholars are without an explanation of what occurred.

For reasons like these ten, the vast majority of contemporary scholars conclude that Jesus's disciples and others thought that they had seen Jesus after his crucifixion. This is what the earliest believers claimed, and this teaching is confirmed by an amazing variety of details from a number of perspectives. We might even say that the disciples were overpowered by these evidences themselves, which convinced them that they had seen the risen Jesus. Given that natural theses cannot explain these experiences, Jesus's resurrection appearances remain the best explanation of the historical facts. The early disciples' experiences plus the failure of naturalistic theories equals the resurrection appearances of Jesus.

36

Were the Resurrection Appearances of Jesus Hallucinations?

Michael R. Licona

All of us are wired differently. For me, one of the things I don't like about myself is that I'm a perpetual second-guesser. I can't even purchase a bottle of cologne without questioning whether I should have purchased a different type before I leave the store. Although raised in a strong Christian home, I began questioning the truth of Christianity in my early twenties. I realized that my choice about God could be the most important one of my life. After all, although countless exceptions exist, we largely tend to believe what we were raised to believe. I had been confident that I had a good relationship with God in which I was doing my best to please him and that he led me through life and answered most of my numerous prayers. But followers of some other religions have a similar confidence. Could it be that I had conditioned myself to believe and see things from a certain perspective? How could I *know* with reasonable certainty that Christianity is true?

This question plagued me to the point of throwing my future plans into chaos. Why devote my life to a belief system toward which I had serious doubts? A prominent Christian philosopher whose name is Gary Habermas and who had devoted his academic career to studying the resurrection of Jesus led me to that topic. And it's an important one. After all, the truth of Christianity stands or falls on whether Jesus actually rose from the dead. The apostle Paul himself, who is perhaps the earliest known Christian author, wrote, "If Christ has not been raised, your faith is worthless" (1 Cor. 15:17 NASB).

Much attention has been devoted to the subject of whether Jesus of Nazareth truly rose from the dead. Gary Habermas has compiled a bibliography of more than 3,400 academic books and journal articles written on the subject since 1975. Another specialist, Dale Allison, refers to the topic of the historicity of Jesus's resurrection as the "prize puzzle" of New Testament research.

In the previous chapter, Gary Habermas argued compellingly that the preponderance of historical evidence strongly suggests that Jesus's disciples and even a couple of skeptics had experiences that they were convinced were appearances of the risen Jesus to them. And the best historically attested experience is the appearance to the twelve disciples within a group setting. One might ask, however, whether it's more likely that these experiences were psychological in nature rather than actual appearances of the risen Jesus. After all, psychological phenomena are common occurrences, and many have been proposed to account for the appearances. But space allows us to cover only the most prominent proposed in the literature: hallucinations.

A hallucination may be defined as "a false sensory perception that has the compelling sense of reality despite the absence of an external stimulus."[1] In other words, a hallucination is the perception of something that isn't actually there. Hallucinations can occur in a number of modes. Percipients believe they see, hear, touch, smell, or taste something that is absent in reality. Sometimes hallucinations may occur in multiple modes, such as when a percipient thinks that she or he both sees and hears something. However, multiple-mode hallucinations are not as common as those occurring in a single mode.

About 15 percent of the population experience one or more hallucinations during their lifetime. Research has shown that some personality types are more prone to experiencing them. Women are more likely to experience them than men. And the older we get, the more likely we are to experience a hallucination. So it should come as no surprise to discover that senior adults who are in the midst of bereaving the loss of a loved one belong to a group that experiences one of the highest percentages of hallucinations: a whopping 50 percent![2]

With these things in mind, let's consider the possibility that Jesus's disciples, the church persecutor Paul, and Jesus's skeptical half brother James experienced hallucinations of the risen Jesus. All of the twelve disciples, Paul, and James were men, who were probably of different age groups and probably of different personalities. That the Twelve were grieving is certain. Yet proposals that the disciples were hallucinating must argue that more than 15 percent of them had the experience. In fact, more than the whopping 50 percent we find among bereaving senior adults would have experienced them. Indeed, it would have been a mind-blowing 100 percent! Moreover, it must likewise be proposed that when these hallucinations occurred, they just happened to do so simultaneously. And it just so happened that they must have experienced their hallucinations in the same mode for them to believe that they had seen the same Jesus. In other words, if a group hallucination had actually occurred, it would have been more likely that the disciples would have experienced their hallucinations in different modes and of at least slightly differing content. Perhaps one would have said, "I see Jesus over by the door," while another said, "No. I see him floating by the ceiling," while still another said, "No. I only hear him speaking to me," while still another said, "I only sense that he's in the room with us." Instead, what we have are the reports that the disciples *saw* Jesus.

But there are more problems. Paul, who had taken it upon himself to persecute Christians, was in no state of grief over Jesus's death and thus was an unlikely candidate for a hallucination.

Further problems involve the group appearances. Since a hallucination is an event that occurs in the mind of an individual and has no external reality, one person cannot participate in another's hallucination. In this sense, they are like dreams. I could not wake my wife in the middle of the night and say, "Honey, I'm having a dream that I'm in Hawaii. Go back to sleep. Come join me in my dream and let's have a free vacation!" We might go back to sleep and both dream that we are in Hawaii. But we would not be participating in the same dream, doing the same activity, in the same location, and carrying on the same discussion with precisely the same words. This is because a dream occurs in the mind of an individual and has no corresponding external reality. Hallucinations are similar in that sense as a psychological phenomenon.

Gary A. Sibcy is a licensed clinical psychologist with a PhD in clinical psychology who has an interest in the possibility of group hallucinations. He comments,

> I have surveyed the professional literature (peer-reviewed journal articles and books) written by psychologists, psychiatrists, and other relevant healthcare professionals during the past two decades and have yet to find a single documented case of a group hallucination, that is, an event for which more than one person purportedly shared in a visual or other sensory perception where there was clearly no external referent.[3]

There is at least one more difficult problem for those claiming that the appearances of Jesus were only hallucinations: Jesus's tomb was empty. If Jesus had not in fact been raised from the dead, and the appearances were hallucinations, one must still account for how Jesus's tomb had become empty. Aside from the fact that hallucinations are horribly inadequate at explaining the appearances, as we observed above, even if that were not the case they cannot account for Jesus's empty tomb.

In summary, the proposal that hallucinations can account for the post-resurrection appearances of Jesus fails on several accounts. Although at least a few if not all of Jesus's disciples may have been in an emotional state that rendered them candidates for a hallucination, the nature of some of the experiences of the risen Jesus, specifically those that occurred in group settings and to Jesus's enemy Paul, and the empty tomb strongly suggest that these experiences were not hallucinations.

37

The Trinity

Bill Gordon

The doctrine of the Trinity is one of the most important beliefs of Christianity. It is central to the Christian understanding of God and is accepted by all Christian groups.

The doctrine of the Trinity is the belief that there is only one living and true God. Yet the one God is three distinct persons: God the Father, God the Son, and God the Holy Spirit. These three have distinct personal attributes, but without division of nature, essence, or being. They enjoy eternal communion and are coeternal and coequal.

The doctrine of the Trinity denies tritheism, the belief that there are three gods. There is only one God. The doctrine of the Trinity also refutes modalism. Modalism is the belief that God is only one person who appears in different modes at different times. The three persons of the Trinity exist simultaneously. They are distinct and eternal persons in the one God.

While the word *Trinity* is not found in the Bible, its truth is expressed in many biblical passages. The Bible recognizes the Father as God, the Son as God, and the Holy Spirit as God.

The Doctrine of the Trinity in Early Church History

Many people who reject the doctrine of the Trinity argue that it developed after the time of the apostles. Most critics of the Trinity point to the Council of Nicea in 325 and the Council of Constantinople in 381 as the events that introduced the doctrine of the Trinity into the church. This claim is not supported by the historical record. This can be shown by examining the writings of Christians before the Councils of Nicea and Constantinople.

Clement of Rome wrote a letter to the church at Corinth around 96. In this letter he explains God in terms compatible with the doctrine of the Trinity. He writes, "Do we not have one God, one Christ, one Spirit of grace which was poured out on us?"[1] Clement also writes, "For as God lives, and as the Lord Jesus Christ lives and the Holy Spirit (on whom the elect believe and hope)."[2] In addition the trinitarian formula of Matthew 28:19 is quoted twice in the *Didache*, a church manual written around 90–100.

Ignatius of Antioch wrote several letters before his death in 117. He affirmed both the humanity and deity of Jesus Christ in his letter to the Ephesians. "The source of your unity and election is genuine suffering which you undergo by the will of the Father and of Jesus Christ, our God"[3] In the same letter he also writes, "There is only one physician—of flesh yet spiritual, born yet unbegotten, God incarnate, genuine life in the midst of death, sprung from Mary as well as God, first subject to suffering then beyond it—Jesus Christ our Lord."[4] In his letter to the Romans, Ignatius also refers to Jesus Christ as "our God."[5] Another early Christian named Justin wrote his *First Apology* about 155. In this writing, he declares that the Son is divine.[6]

The doctrine of the Trinity is also implied in Athenagoras's plea to Emperors Marcus Aurelius and Lucius Aurelius in 176–77, "The Son is in the Father and the Father in the Son by the unity and power of the Spirit."[7] Athenagoras repeats his trinitarian position later in his plea, "We speak of God, of the Son, his Word, and of the Holy Spirit; and we say that the Father, the Son, and the Spirit are united in power."[8]

Irenaeus of Lyons wrote his work *Against Heresies* in the late second century. He writes, "Christ Jesus our Lord and God and Savior and King, according to the pleasure of the invisible Father."[9] At about the same time, Tertullian argued that the Father, Son, and Holy Spirit are one God, in his treatise *Against Praxeas*.[10] Other early Christians also affirmed their belief in the doctrine of the Trinity, including Origen (185–254) and Novatian of Rome (mid third century).[11]

Biblical Evidence for the Doctrine of the Trinity

The Bible recognizes the Father as God. Psalm 89:26 (NIV) says, "He will call out to me, 'You are my Father, / my God, the Rock my Savior.'" Peter in his first epistle writes of those "who have been chosen according to the foreknowledge of God the Father" (1 Pet. 1:2 NIV; see also Matt. 6:9; 7:11; Rom. 8:15; 1 Pet. 1:17).

The Bible also calls Jesus (the Son) God in John 1:1 (NIV): "In the beginning was the Word, and the Word was with God, and the Word was God." The phrase "the Word was God" cannot legitimately be translated "the word was a god" as do the Jehovah's Witnesses in their New World Translation of the Holy Scriptures.[12] The lack of the definite article in the Greek text simply identifies the word *God* as the predicate of the sentence. The claim by Jehovah's Witnesses that it indicates that Jesus is an inferior deity to the Father is false. Such a claim is not only contrary to Greek grammar but would have been unthinkable to a first-century Jew. The Jehovah's Witness position actually advocates a form of polytheism that consists of a big god and a little god.

When Thomas addresses Jesus as "My Lord and my God" (John 20:28 NIV), Jesus does not correct him. Paul and Barnabas act very differently when the people of Lystra start giving them divine homage in Acts 14:8–18. They go to great lengths to convince the people they are not divine beings. According to John in the book of Revelation, the angel he starts worshiping also refuses to accept divine obeisance. The angel insists that John stop, saying, "Do not do it! I am a fellow servant with you and with your brothers who hold to the testimony of Jesus. Worship God!" (Rev. 19:10 NIV).

Titus 2:13 (NIV) declares that Jesus Christ is God: "We wait for the blessed hope—the glorious appearing of our great God and Savior, Jesus Christ." It is very difficult to understand how this passage could refer to the appearing of the Father since John 1:18 (NIV) says, "No one has ever seen God, but God the One and Only, who is at the Father's side, has made him known." Titus 2:13 indicates that Jesus Christ is both God and Savior. This same truth is also taught in 2 Peter 1:1 (NIV), where Jesus Christ is called "our God and Savior." These passages declare that Jesus Christ is truly God.

The writer of Hebrews, quoting Psalm 45:6 says, "But about the Son he says, 'Your throne, O God, will last forever and ever, / and righteousness will be the scepter of your kingdom'" (Heb. 1:8 NIV). In Hebrews 1:10, the writer quotes Psalm 102:24–25, a passage referring to God, and applies it to the Son. The inspired writer of Hebrews therefore identifies the Son as God.

The Bible also identifies the Holy Spirit as God. Peter does so in Acts 5:3–4 (NIV): "Then Peter said, 'Ananias, how is it that Satan has so filled your heart that you have lied to the Holy Spirit? . . . You have not lied to men but to God.'" The Bible describes the Holy Spirit as having attributes that only belong to God (Ps. 139:7–13; Luke 1:35; Rom. 15:19; 1 Cor. 2:10; Heb. 9:14). The Holy Spirit does the work of God (Gen. 1:26–27; Job 33:4; John 3:5–6; Acts 16:6–7, 10; Rom. 1:4; 1 Pet. 3:18; 2 Pet. 1:21). He also receives honor due only to God (Matt. 28:19; 2 Cor. 13:14).

The Bible Describes the Father, Son, and Holy Spirit as Distinct Persons

The Father and the Son are distinct persons. The Bible distinguishes Jesus from the Father (John 1:14, 18; 3:16). Since the Father sends the Son, the two are distinguished from one another (John 10:36; Gal. 4:4).

Furthermore the Father and the Son are described as persons distinct from the Holy Spirit. Jesus distinguished the Holy Spirit from himself and the Father (John 14:16–17). The Holy Spirit proceeds from the Father (John 15:26) and is sent from the Father and the Son (John 14:26; 15:26).

The Holy Spirit is a person. Although the Greek word for "spirit" is neuter, the masculine pronoun is used when referring to the Holy Spirit in John 15:26 and John 16:13–14. The work of the Holy Spirit as Comforter, Helper, and Teacher suggests that he must be a person (John 14:16, 26; 15:26). His name is mentioned with other people, which implies his own personality (Matt. 28:19; John 16:14–15; Acts 15:28; 2 Cor. 13:14; 1 Pet. 1:1–2), and the Spirit performs deeds that imply his personality (Gen. 6:3; Luke 12:12; Acts 2:4; 13:2; 16:6–7; Rom. 8:26; 1 Cor. 2:10–11). His personality is also indicated in that he is affected by the acts of others (Matt. 12:31; Acts 5:3–4, 9; 7:51; Eph. 4:30).

The three persons of the Trinity are eternal. The person of the Son existed before his incarnation (John 1:1–3; 8:58; 17:5, 24; Phil. 2:6; Col. 1:15–17; Rev. 1:4). Other biblical passages reveal the eternality of the Holy Spirit (Gen. 1:1–2; Heb. 9:14).

The doctrine of the Trinity is not a form of tritheism. Christians do not believe that the Father, Son, and Holy Spirit are three gods but that they are three persons in one God. While they are distinct persons, they are one in essence. God is not three and one, but rather three in one (John 5:17, 19; 14:9; 15:26; 17:21–23; 2 Cor. 5:19).

The three persons of the Trinity are coequal. The Father is equal to the Son, who is equal to the Spirit (Rom. 8:11–14; 2 Cor. 4:4; Gal. 3:26; 4:4–6; Heb. 1:3; 2 Pet. 1:21). Several passages speak of the Father, Son, and Holy Spirit in the same context (Matt. 28:19; 1 Cor. 12:4–6; 2 Cor. 13:14; Eph. 4:4–6; Titus 3:4–6). All three persons of the Trinity raised Jesus from the dead (John 2:19; 1 Cor. 6:14; 1 Pet. 3:18).

The Work and Teachings of Jesus Christ

The Old Testament not only predicted the birth of Jesus but also affirmed his deity. Concerning his birth, Matthew 1:23 (NIV) quotes Isaiah 7:14 and calls Jesus "'Immanuel'—which means, 'God with us.'" The virgin birth also reveals Jesus's divine and human natures. The preexistence of Jesus affirms his divinity (John 1:1; 8:58; 17:5, 24; Phil. 2:5–11).

Jesus claimed equality with God the Father. In John 5:17 (NIV) he says, "My Father is always at his work to this very day, and I, too, am working." His Jewish listeners understood this as a claim of deity and sought to kill him. When Jesus called God his Father (John 5:17–18), he was affirming his own deity. Jesus spoke of his special relationship with the Father when he referred to him as "my Father" (John 20:17 NIV).

In John 5:23 (NIV) Jesus also claimed equality with God when he said, "He who does not honor the Son does not honor the Father, who sent him." Likewise he also asserted his deity in John 10:30 (NIV) when he said, "I and the Father are one." His Jewish listeners again picked up stones to stone him to death because they believed that in claiming equality with God he had committed the sin of blasphemy. Jesus's assertion of divinity is also seen in his "I am" sayings. In John 8:58 Jesus not only claimed preexistence but equality with the God who is the "I AM WHO I AM" (Exod. 3:14 NIV).

While affirming the full equality of Jesus with the Father, the Scriptures do indicate that Jesus voluntarily submitted himself to the Father. Philippians 2:6–8 (NIV) indicates that Jesus was equal with God the Father, even though he did give up his heavenly glory when he came to earth:

> Who, being in very nature God,
> did not consider equality with God something to be grasped,
> but made himself nothing,
> taking the very nature of a servant,
> being made in human likeness.
> And being found in appearance as a man,
> he humbled himself
> and became obedient to death—
> even death on a cross!

This voluntary submission to the plan of the Father explains those occasions where Jesus revealed that the Father had sent him (John 6:38; 12:44–45; 14:24; 17:3). It also clarifies what Jesus meant when he said, "The Father is greater than I" (John 14:28 NIV).

Jesus's divinity is also evident in his actions. He did things that only God can do. He forgave sins (Matt. 9:6), which was blasphemy to the Jews because only God could forgive sins. He claimed all authority (Matt. 28:18). He claimed to be the only way of salvation (John 3:36; 14:6). He claimed authority to judge the world (John 5:22). Genesis 1:1 (NIV) indicates that "In the beginning God created the heavens and the earth." Yet the New Testament reveals that Jesus created the world (John 1:3; Col. 1:16–17).

The only conclusion is that the Christian doctrine of the Trinity accurately describes the biblical testimony about God. Finite humans cannot rationally explain the doctrine of the Trinity. This should not surprise us since there are many things the Bible teaches about God that we cannot fully understand. For example, the Bible affirms the existence of God, the creation of the universe, atonement from sin, and the resurrection of the dead, despite the fact that none of those truths can be totally understood by finite minds. As with the doctrine of the Trinity, Christians do not accept these teachings because they can rationally explain them, but because the Bible teaches them.

38

Is Jesus Superior to All Other Religious Leaders?

Tal Davis

David, a nineteen-year-old Southern Baptist, was in his first year at State University. His basic studies program required that he take several electives in humanities or religion. He had scanned the course catalog and found a class in comparative religion, a particular interest of his, taught by the school's most distinguished professor of religion.

The professor, a graduate of a famous Ivy League theological seminary, began the class with a statement that caught David by surprise: "We will be examining the history and beliefs of the major religious movements of the world; but let me say at the outset, we will begin with the presupposition that every one of them is a legitimate expression of the cultural, social, psychological, and existential experience of its adherents. Though they may differ in external and formal statements of doctrine and practice, they all express a similar essence of the awe and mystery in life and the universe. Furthermore, we will assume that each of the founders of the religions were all, in their various ways, expressing similar and universal moral and spiritual concepts. Thus, we will assume they are all equal in their authority and revelational validity."

David looked around the room. Was anyone else in the class as stunned by the teacher's pronouncement as he? Apparently not, as every other student looked straight ahead, showing no sense of surprise or concern.

Unfortunately, David's experience is a common one for college students. Often raised in Christian homes and conservative churches, they are confounded when tenets of their faith are challenged by authoritative figures such as college professors.

Thankfully, David did not take his teacher's pronouncement as an incontrovertible fact. He decided to investigate the truth claims of the various faiths and the assertion that all their leaders were the same. After several months of study, he came to the conclusion that all religions were not equal and that Jesus Christ was and is superior to the founders of the other major religions of the world. His conclusion was based on five lines of truth.

Jesus Christ Is the Only Major World Religion Founder Who Had No Beginning in Time or Space

The Bible teaches that Jesus Christ, unlike any other person who has ever lived, had no beginning in time or space. That is, Jesus eternally preexisted as God the Son in the Godhead with God the Father and God the Holy Spirit. Christians believe that, though they are separate persons, they are one God (see Matt. 28:19–20; 1 Cor. 8:6; 12:4–6; 2 Cor. 1:21–22; 13:14; 1 Pet. 1:2).

The Gospel of John states, "In the beginning was the Word, and the Word was with God, and the Word was God. He was with God in the beginning. Through him all things were made; without him nothing was made that has been made" (John 1:1–3 NIV). The apostle Paul, in Colossians 1:15–17 (NIV) states, "He is the image of the invisible God, the firstborn over all creation. For by him all things were created: things in heaven and on earth . . . all things were created by him and for him."

Jesus himself, when questioned as to his own origin, made the audacious claim, "Before Abraham was born, I am!" (John 8:58 NIV).

The Bible teaches that Jesus existed eternally and had no chronological origin. No other religious leader can make such a claim. Gautama Buddha (560–480 BC), Mohammed (AD 570–632), Confucius (551–479 BC), and all other religious founders began their life at birth. Jesus already existed, as deity in heaven, prior to his earthly birth.

Jesus Christ Is the Only Major World Religion Founder Who Came into the World as He Did

Though Jesus preexisted eternally as God, the Bible indicates that he entered this world in a unique way. He was born into the world physically as a result of a virgin birth.

According to Matthew 1:20–21 (NIV), an angel of the Lord informed Joseph not to fear taking his pregnant betrothed, Mary, as his bride "because what is conceived in her is from the Holy Spirit. She will give birth to a son, and you are to give him the name Jesus, because he will save his people from their sins."

Matthew explains (1:22–23 NIV), "All this took place to fulfill what the Lord had said through the prophet: 'The virgin will be with child and will give birth to a son, and they will call him Immanuel—which means, God with us.'"

The Gospel of Luke records that Mary herself was informed by the angel Gabriel that she would become pregnant and give birth to a son (see Luke 1:26–33). Luke says her response was incredulity, "How will this be . . . since I am a virgin?" (Luke 1:34 NIV).

The angel explained (Luke 1:35–37 NIV), "The Holy Spirit will come upon you, and the power of the Most High will overshadow you. So the holy one to be born will be called the Son of God. . . . For nothing is impossible with God."

Thus Jesus, among all the religious leaders, was conceived miraculously and born of a virgin. Even the great Hebrew prophet Moses had an earthly father.

Muhammad, founder of Islam, also was born of a man and woman and made no claims to divinity. Bahā' Allāh (1817–1892), the supreme prophet of the Baha'i faith, was conceived and born in the ordinary way.

Jesus Christ Is the Only Major World Religion Founder Who Lived a Perfect and Sinless Life

To be fair, Christians agree that many of the world's religions' founders taught high standards of morality and justice. For example, Buddha taught the Eightfold Path as a way to wisdom and morality. Bahā' Allāh taught high principles of justice, world peace, and human rights. Moses, of course, provided the Ten Commandments and the books of law.

In none of these religions, nor in any other non-Christian faith, do the followers claim their founders to be perfect or without sin. Only Christians claim, as the Bible teaches, that Jesus Christ was totally without the stain of sin. The writer of Hebrews states, "For we do not have a high priest who is unable to sympathize with our weaknesses, but we have one who has been tempted in every way, just as we are—yet was without sin" (Heb. 4:15 NIV).

Likewise, the apostle Paul in commenting about the effectiveness of Christ's atonement, states, "God made him who had no sin to be sin for us, so that in him we might become the righteousness of God" (2 Cor. 5:21 NIV). Even Pontius Pilate, the Roman governor who unjustly condemned Jesus to die, admitted, "As for me, I find no basis for a charge against him" (John 19:6 NIV).

Jesus Christ, of all the world's religious founders, was without sin and lived a perfect life. Thus he alone was qualified to do what was necessary to make salvation available to humanity.

Jesus Christ Is the Only Major World Religion Founder Who Died as a Sacrificial Atonement for the Sins of Humanity

Muhammad taught that to receive forgiveness of sins, one needs to ask for it sincerely and, if Allah wills (and you can never be sure of that), he may grant it. Buddha taught that sins cannot really be "forgiven," only that the desires of this life must be overcome by enlightenment.

The Bible, however, teaches that the only way sins may be forgiven is for an atonement to be made to cover them. The Old Testament taught that a sacrificial system using animals could temporarily atone for some sins. The New Testament, however, teaches that the ultimate sacrifice for sin was made by Jesus Christ by his death on the cross. He died as a sacrificial atonement for the sins of the world.

As John 3:16 (NIV) states, "For God so loved the world that he gave his one and only Son, that whoever believes in him shall not perish but have eternal life."

Romans 8:3 (NIV) states, "For what the law was powerless to do in that it was weakened by the sinful nature, God did by sending his own Son in the likeness of sinful man to be a sin offering."

Only Jesus was qualified to be our sacrifice, as he was without sin. Further, he gave himself willingly to rescue us from our sinful lives and from hell. Jesus said, "No one takes it from me, but I lay it down of my own accord" (John 10:18 NIV).

Jesus Christ Is the Only Major World Religion Founder Who Rose from the Dead to Demonstrate His Power and Authority

Ever wonder what would rank as the most important event in all of world history? Would it be the invention of the wheel, the rise of the Roman Empire, World War II, or the fall of Communism?

Clearly the most important event of all time, and one of the best attested historically of ancient times, was the physical resurrection of Jesus Christ from the dead. The Bible indicates that the third day after his crucifixion he rose from the dead and then, for forty days afterward, was seen alive by a number of witnesses.

The apostle Paul reported to the Corinthians after Jesus's death "that he was buried, that he was raised on the third day according to the Scriptures, and that he appeared to Peter, and then to the Twelve. After that, he appeared to more than five hundred of the brothers at the same time, most of whom are still living, though some have fallen asleep. Then he appeared to James, then to all the apostles, and last of all he appeared to me also, as to one abnormally born" (1 Cor. 15:4–8 NIV).

Paul, along with the writers of the four Gospels and the other New Testament writers, was absolutely convinced of the fact of Jesus's resurrection. Paul even states that if it were not true, then the Christian faith is false: "If Christ has not been raised, our preaching is useless and so is your faith. More than that, we are then found to be false witnesses about God, for we have testified about God that he raised Christ from the dead" (1 Cor. 15:14–15 NIV).

Indeed, Christianity stands or falls on the truth of Christ's resurrection. It is the one historical event that validates both the claims of Jesus about himself and the message that Christians proclaim. No other religious leader validated his truth claims in such an undeniable way. Moses, as great a prophet as he was, is dead. Muhammad is dead. Buddha is dead. Confucius is dead. Bahā' Allāh is dead. Any and all the founders of the world's religions are dead. Only Jesus Christ overcame death itself with this ultimate miracle, establishing once and for all the truth of his deity and lordship.

Jesus demonstrated his superiority to all others by his birth, life, death, and resurrection. Thus no other person who has ever lived can or should capture our allegiance as Jesus does. He alone offers us the way of salvation and the assurance of eternal life. As the apostle Peter boldly stated so long ago, "Salvation is found in no one else, for there is no other name under heaven given to men by which we must be saved" (Acts 4:12 NIV). Jesus himself said, "I am the way and the truth and the life. No one comes to the Father except through me" (John 14:6 NIV).

When sharing Christ with those of other faiths, those who are agnostics, or atheists, we must focus on why we believe Christianity is superior to all others—we must be cautious, however, not to belittle or demean other faiths or their leaders. That will usually only magnify the barrier that may already exist. Rather, examine common principles we share with other faiths but clearly show how Christ alone is the full expression of God's revelation in the world and the only way of salvation.

Christianity does not stand or fall on its moral principles or depth of mystical experience. If that were true, then it would be no better than any other religion in the world, and Jesus Christ would be only another great religious or moral teacher. No, Christianity stands or falls entirely on the person and work of one man: Jesus Christ. Either he was who he claimed to be, the Lord of the universe, who came to earth as man, lived a sinless life, died on the cross as an atonement for our sins, and rose again from the dead, or the entire Christian faith is a gigantic lie.

Additional Resources Concerning the Uniqueness of Christ

Colson, Chuck. *Answers to Your Kids' Questions*. Wheaton: Tyndale, 2000.

Geisler, Norman, and Ronald Brooks. *When Skeptics Ask*. Wheaton: Victor Books, 1990.

Habermas, Gary R., and Michael R. Licona. *The Case for the Resurrection of Jesus*. Grand Rapids: Kregel, 2004.

Lewis, C. S. *Mere Christianity*. New York: Macmillan, 1957.

McDowell, Josh. *More Than a Carpenter*. Wheaton: Tyndale, 1977.

———. *The New Evidence That Demands a Verdict*. Nashville: Thomas Nelson, 1999.

Strobel, Lee. *The Case for Christ*. Grand Rapids: Zondervan, 1998.

———. *The Case for Faith*. Grand Rapids: Zondervan, 2000.

39

Is Jesus the Only Way?

Michael R. Licona

Mark Twain once said, “It ain’t those parts of the Bible that I can’t understand that bother me, it is the parts that I do understand.” I must admit that of all the biblical teachings, the claim that Jesus is the only way to God is one of the most troubling for me. Is God being unfair in requiring others to believe only in Jesus in order to get into heaven? Or is it merely a matter of some Christians interpreting the Bible in this manner?

There is widespread evidence that Jesus himself claimed to be the only way to God. Not only are his claims multiply attested, his earliest followers Peter and Paul taught that he is the only way (Matt. 11:27; Luke 10:22; 12:8–9; John 3:36; Acts 4:12; Rom. 10:1–2; 2 Thess. 1:8–9; 1 Tim. 2:5; Heb. 10:26–27). In fact, there are no claims to the contrary by the earliest Christians. Consider these statements of Jesus:

> I am the way, and the truth, and the life; no one comes to the Father but through Me. (John 14:6 NASB)

> For unless you believe that I am who I say I am, you will die in your sins. (John 8:24, my translation)

These are pretty amazing claims. Imagine if Rick Warren were to appear on *Larry King Live* and utter similar statements about himself. We might still regard him as a nice guy who has given much to help the poor and destitute. But make no mistake about it. We would also think of him as being a few french fries short of a Happy Meal! Jesus's claims appear as outrageous today as they did to many of those who heard him and his disciples utter them. So what are we to do with Jesus's unrestrained claims to be the only way to God?

Since many have made similar claims to having the exclusive truth about God, we may first ask whether these claims of Jesus are true. When asked for proof that he was whom he claimed to be, Jesus replied that he would provide only one: his resurrection from the dead. This is a pretty good test and differs from those offered by other religions. The Qur'an tells us that its divine inspiration can be known when one attempts to create a sura comparable in beauty to one in it (a sura is an independent chapter, like a psalm). The Book of Mormon tells us that God will inform us of its truth if we read it and ask God with a sincere heart to show us whether it's true.

For anyone interested in taking these tests, read Qur'an 108:

> Lo! We have given thee Abundance;
> So pray unto thy Lord, and sacrifice.
> Lo! It is thy insulter (and not thou) who is without prosperity.

It is not difficult to conceive of something else having at least equal beauty and meaning. Consider Psalm 117 (NASB):

> Praise the Lord, all nations;
> Laud Him, all peoples!
> For His lovingkindness is great toward us,
> And the truth of the Lord is everlasting.
> Praise the Lord!

Or how about the following early Christian hymn preserved in 1 Timothy 3:16 (NASB)? It says that Jesus

> Was revealed in the flesh,
> Was vindicated in the Spirit,
> Seen by angels,
> Proclaimed among the nations,
> Believed on in the world,
> Taken up in glory.

A Muslim may claim that Qur'an 108 contains superior linguistic beauty when read in Arabic. But a Christian or Jew may counter that Psalm 117 is a song that contains similar linguistic beauty when read in Hebrew. The hymn in 1 Timothy 3:16 was Greek in its original form and has beauty in both its sound and grammatical structure when read in that language. So the test provided by the Qur'an boils down to a matter of personal taste. Do you prefer the beauty of Arabic, Hebrew, or Greek? This is similar to choosing between Bach, Beethoven, and Bernstein.

I have also read much of the Book of Mormon while praying sincerely that God would show me through his Spirit whether it is true. Although I read and prayed, God was silent, while a number of archaeological facts weighed against its divine inspiration. So the tests provided by the Qur'an and the *Book of Mormon* are quite subjective.

The test Jesus provided, however, is quite impressive: his resurrection from the dead. Such a test does not depend on one's personal taste or a warm feeling. He either rose from the dead, confirming his personal claims, or he didn't, revealing himself to be just another false prophet. Space does not permit me to provide a historical case for Jesus's resurrection. Gary Habermas and I have done so in *The Case for the Resurrection of Jesus*. If we may assume for the moment that Jesus was truly who he claimed to be, this goes a long way toward reconciling his claim to being the exclusive route to God with the uneasiness it brings. Notwithstanding, there are still a number of objections that I would like to address. It is my opinion that we can come to terms with most objections to Jesus's claims to being the *only way* by answering three rudimentary questions.

What Is Truth?

When Jesus was brought before the Roman governor Pilate, he said he had come into the world to proclaim the truth. Pilate asked him, "What is truth?" Many today are upset when a Christian repeats Jesus's claim to be the only true way to God and may answer, "Truth is broader than your narrow concept and differs between people." So what is truth?

A statement is true to the extent that it corresponds with reality. My wife, Debbie, and I have been married for twenty-one years. Our ideas of comfort differ. She has a lot of German blood and is comfortable in cooler temperatures, while I'm more comfortable in warmer temperatures (my dad was from Honduras). If it's seventy degrees in our house, she's turning on the fans, and I'm putting on a sweater! In this case, truth is both personal and relative: Debbie is warm, and Mike is cool. But there is a truth irrespective of our perceptions: It's seventy degrees in the room.

This applies in other areas. I've always been fascinated with space. When I was a child I wanted to be an astronaut. I was glued to the television, as were most Americans, when Neil Armstrong and Buzz Aldrin walked on the moon. When the Hale-Bopp comet neared Earth in 1997, it was visible to the naked eye. We were the first to view this comet since the Spartans in 383 BC! There was also some news at the time related to the comet: a speck appeared in the sky next to it that astronomers identified as the planet Mars. But the leader of a small cult, Marshall Applewhite, convinced thirty-eight of his followers that the speck was a spaceship trailing the comet and that it would rescue them from Earth before destroying it. Applewhite's followers trusted him so much that they followed him in committing suicide, believing that the spaceship would take their souls to another galaxy named Heaven.

Let's assess the truth claims of the Heaven's Gate cult. The earth was not destroyed, as Applewhite had predicted. And Applewhite was a shady character: he was arrested at age forty-three for stealing credit cards, and he was fired from his job as music professor because of "health problems of an emotional nature." There was a truth that is personal and relative: members of the Heaven's Gate cult obtained feelings of peace, hope, and fulfillment from following Applewhite. But there is an objective truth that holds true for everyone: Applewhite was a false prophet, and his followers were duped. Their sincere belief, to the point of taking their own lives, did not change the truth.

If we can assess the truth claims of the Heaven's Gate religion, we can assess the truth claims of other religions. Followers of other religions may find that their religious beliefs and practices bring them feelings of peace and hope and give them a purpose for living. In fact, here is a true statement: a number of valuable benefits have been realized by followers of non-Christian religions. However, if Jesus's claim to be the exclusive way to God is true, then the following statement is false: Muhammad provided an effective way to be acceptable to God. In other words, a religion can be true in a subjective sense while being false in an objective one. I am interested in following religious teachings that are true in both senses.

I realize that this can be quite offensive. But we must not be so captive to our politically correct culture that we are led astray from truth. Since the truth of a statement can be measured by how closely it corresponds with reality, if Jesus claimed to be the exclusive way to God and rose from the dead in order to confirm his claims, the following statement has a very high probability of being true: Jesus is the exclusive way to God.

What Is Ethical?

Any Western Christian who has shared his or her faith with others understands that claiming Jesus is the only way can be perceived as being intolerant of and offensive to others. A few years ago I had a public discussion with a Muslim professor on a university campus. During my speech that evening I shared that I was a Christian today because I had investigated Christianity historically and discovered that Jesus's claims to deity, his death by crucifixion, and his resurrection could all be confirmed by historical research. During the question and answer period one of the audience members asked me why the Muslim professor and I hated one another. Now we had been very collegial to each other during the evening's event. So I responded that I did not hate him and did not sense that he hated me. I added that if I were to claim that his views were equally valid or true as my own, he would not respect me, and I would not respect him if he were to say the same to me. I added that such a comment would be rather insulting, since both of us are strongly persuaded that our own religious tradition is true to the exclusion of the other. Accordingly if I were to assert that the Muslim view is as valid as the Christian view, he would understand my comment as a demotion of Islam. I ended by stating that it is certainly possible for us to disagree in the strongest sense with the other's cherished views while acknowledging and even defending their right to have them. The point I want to make is this: when someone claims that my belief that Jesus is the only way is intolerant and offensive, they ignore the fact that their pluralist approach is likewise intolerant and offensive. They are being intolerant of exclusivist views and offensive to those who hold them.

Amy-Jill Levine is a distinguished professor of New Testament Studies at Vanderbilt University and is Jewish. Professor Levine opines that the Christian claim that Jesus is the only way is *not* morally dubious. She adds, "What I would find more 'morally dubious' is my insisting to another that his or her reading or presuppositions, because they are not pluralistic, are somehow wrong. . . . The evangelical Christian should be free to try to seek to convert me to Christianity: such an attempt is biblically warranted and consistent with evangelical (exclusivist) theology. I remain free to say 'thank you, but no thanks.' I would not want someone telling me that my 'cherished confessional traditions' have only limited value. I would not presume to do the same to another.[1]

Moreover, there are times when truth should not be sacrificed for the sake of avoiding offense. While the *Titanic* was sinking, since lifeboats were available, it would have been *unethical* for the crew, in the interest of reducing panic for the moment, to have told all of the passengers to go back to their cabins and sleep through the night because everything would be fine in the morning. Truth is important. Decisions of greater importance should drive us to discover the truth rather than dilute or deny it in our efforts not to offend, which as we have seen is a no-win situation. However, when sharing our faith with others, Christians should remember to do it "with gentleness and respect" (1 Pet. 3:15 NIV). We should love others and be graceful in our efforts to share the greatest news ever told.

What Is Required?

Perhaps you have heard the following: "It doesn't matter what you believe. The way to heaven is paved with sincerity, goodness, and belief in God." This statement attempts to shed the offense of the exclusivity claims of Jesus. However, it introduces new problems. In claiming that sincerity, goodness, and belief in a generic God are the true requirements for God's acceptance, one is making a religious claim: "This is how one can appease God." When someone says that to me, I simply ask, "On what foundation is such a belief based? It's not from the Bible, the Qur'an, or any other holy book. Why should I believe it? Have you heard personally from God?"

There is another problem with this assertion: How much sincerity and goodness are required? Most people would agree that despots who were responsible for the mass murder of millions, like Hitler, Stalin, Mao, and Pol Pot, certainly don't make the cut. But the line blurs after that. What about Muslim terrorists who blow up innocent people in the process of doing what they believe is a service to God? Someone may suggest that we just need to keep the Ten Commandments; how many of them must we keep? Did you ever steal as a child, ever break a Sabbath, use God's name in a disrespectful manner, dishonor your parents, falsely accuse your sibling, or have an obsessive desire for something belonging to someone else? If you have, you've already violated six of the ten! Where should the line be drawn? If God is the one who draws it, shouldn't we seek to know where he has drawn it?

The Christian gospel lays out the requirements for acceptance by God: It's nothing any of us can do (Rom. 6:23); it's all about what God has done for us in Jesus (Eph. 2:8–9); we must entrust our eternal destiny to Jesus (John 14:6); and we must believe in Jesus's deity, atoning death, and resurrection (John 8:24; Rom. 10:9). We may also recognize that Jesus said that the road to heaven is narrow and few follow it (Matt. 7:13–14).

How can I share the gospel with others, given their aversion to the exclusive claims of Jesus? I'd like to suggest three actions. First, understand the answers to the three rudimentary questions we have discussed: What is truth? What is ethical? What is required? Second, clothe Jesus's message with love. Be winsome and humble. People don't care how much you know until they know how much you care.

Third, recognize that timing is important. Some may think you're being narrow-minded now. However, if a time comes when their life is falling apart or they have just learned that they have cancer, they may want you to give them the answer and will respect you for holding true to your faith.

40

What About Those Who Have Never Heard the Gospel?

Michael R. Licona

As I discussed in the previous chapter, the New Testament is clear that Jesus believed the only way to God is through him. However, one may ask whether this is fair to those who have never heard the gospel. Will they be condemned to be separated from God eternally when they were unable to embrace a message they never had presented to them? And what is the fate of babies and the mentally handicapped who have died without embracing the gospel of Christ? Will they be eternally separated from God for their failure to embrace a message they were unable to understand?

These are difficult questions deserving thoughtful replies. Since the Bible does not address these issues directly, we will have to engage in speculation. In the end, we can provide plausible solutions to these difficult questions by recognizing two divine principles.

We'll start by addressing the question pertaining to the fate of those who die without ever having heard the gospel. Let's suppose that a friend telephones me and tells me he has just received two free tickets to a musical and wants to know if I would like to go. Since musicals do not interest me, I decline his kind offer. Now since I did not respond to his general invitation, he is under no obligation to give me specifics pertaining to *which musical* is in town. For example, it would not have made any difference to me whether it was *Cats*, *Wicked*, or *A Chorus Line*.

Now let's suppose instead that my friend had told me he had just received two free tickets to see a baseball game and wants to know if I would like to go. Since I'm a baseball fan, I may ask him who's playing before accepting. In this case, since I responded to his general invitation, he will provide the specific details concerning the event.

According to Romans chapter one, God has made some of his invisible attributes known through the world in which we live. The stars, the sun, the moon, the ocean, and many other wonders of nature were not the work of a bull, a horse, a calf, or a man. These are the products of a cosmic designer of immense intelligence. In Romans chapter two, Paul tells us that God has instilled basic knowledge of his moral laws in our conscience, so that, instinctively, we know that actions such as rape, murder, stealing, and falsehood are immoral. We all are accountable to God for immoral actions we have committed of varying degrees. Theologians refer to this type of knowledge as *general revelation*. In other words, given our universe and our conscience, we should be aware that a God of some sort exists and that we have failed to live up to his moral law.

Unfortunately, it is the sad testimony of history that most people are indifferent when it comes to God. It's as though he has offered us a ticket to see a musical, and we have declined. Solomon is known as a man who possessed extraordinary wisdom. He estimated that less than one in a thousand people truly care about God (Eccles. 7:27–29). Whether he meant this literally or exaggerated for effect is difficult to tell. But most would agree with his general conclusion: The large majority of people don't genuinely care about God. That's not to say they are evil. It is to say they are at least indifferent toward God. And for these, God is under no moral obligation to provide them with what theologians refer to as *special revelation*, that is, specific information pertaining to God's identity. Those who are indifferent toward God in general would not respond to the specific message about his Son Jesus, even had they heard it. So they will be without an excuse when they stand before God's judgment.

This places our quagmire in a different light. It is daunting when we consider the number of people in the world who have never heard the gospel. However, when we also consider that the vast majority of them are indifferent toward God, it is difficult to regard God as being unfair for not revealing to them the specifics of who he is since he is under no moral obligation to provide details to those who are indifferent to him.

But what about those individuals who truly care about serving and pleasing God but who die without ever hearing the gospel? In Acts 17, Paul speaks before a group of philosophers in ancient Athens. He notices an altar with the inscription, "To an unknown god" and uses it as a springboard into a discussion of the gospel. The God who made the universe and everything in it determined that all should seek God, perhaps even grope around for him before finding him. Since we are God's offspring and are not made of gold or stone, God is not made of gold or stone. He has been willing to overlook human ignorance concerning himself. However, the epoch of ignorance has passed and the time to repent is now, since God has revealed himself through Jesus, has provided evidence of this fact via Jesus's resurrection from the dead, and has ordained that this specific revelation be spread throughout the entire world.

Those who have not heard of God's revelation of himself to mankind in the person of Jesus and his resurrection remain in a sort of era of ignorance. In this case, God will apparently judge them according to how they responded to the knowledge they received, the general revelation. So those who die without ever having heard the gospel, but who had responded in a positive manner to the testimony of nature and their conscience that they stand accountable to a Creator for their moral failures and sought his mercy, will be spared from God's judgment. So we have our first divine principle that provides an answer to the question pertaining to the fate of those who die without ever having heard the gospel: *God will judge us according to our response to the knowledge we received.*

Although the answer just provided is the one that I presently embrace, other reasonable answers have been proposed. Some hold that God knew before he even created the world who would respond to the gospel and caused them to be born in a location where they would one day hear it. Still others hold that God is able to communicate the gospel to those truly seeking truth by sending missionaries and by communicating the gospel through dreams and visions. In fact, there are many stories of those who came to know Christ by these means. In this view, no one who genuinely seeks to know the truth with a sincere heart will die without hearing the gospel.

This leaves us with the question pertaining to God's response to babies and the mentally handicapped, who die without having accepted the gospel. The Bible does not specifically address this question. So we will need to speculate based on how God responded to other situations in which we get a glimpse into his character. In other words, we will seek examples that identify principles that may be used to suggest that God will respond in a similar manner in other situations.

God had delivered Israel from her captivity in Egypt and had provided for her needs while in the wilderness. When she finally came to the land God had promised her, twelve spies were sent in order to report if the land was as God had promised. All twelve reported that it was. However, ten warned that its present inhabitants were much larger than the Israelites and that an attempt to take the land would be met with certain destruction. The other two spies encouraged the Israelites to proceed, reminding them that the God who had promised to give them the land would cause them to be victorious. After deliberation, the Israelites refused to take the land and, as a result, God rebuked them and commanded them to turn back into the wilderness where everyone would die except the families of the two obedient spies, and "your little ones who you said would become a prey, and your sons, who this day have no knowledge of good or evil, shall enter there, and I will give it to them and they shall possess it" (Deut. 1:39 NASB). This gives us a glimpse into the character of God and provides us with our second divine principle: *God does not hold accountable those who lack the mental capacity to choose between good and evil.*

Let's summarize. We've faced the difficult questions pertaining to the fate of those who die without ever having heard the gospel as well as that of babies and the mentally handicapped who lack the mental capacity to understand the gospel. Since the Bible does not directly address either of these questions, speculation pertaining to possible solutions is our only course of action. However, we may look at other situations in which God has acted and get a glimpse into his character. We observed two divine principles: (1) God judges us according to our response to the knowledge about him that we are given. At minimum, this knowledge consists of the fact that there is a Creator to whom we will stand accountable for our moral failures. (2) God does not hold accountable those who lack the mental capacity to choose between good and evil.

What we have observed here is that God does not act unreasonably toward those who die without receiving the specific message of the gospel of Jesus and toward those who are mentally incapable of understanding the gospel. The other side of this answer, however, is that God does hold us accountable for what we have received and understand. In most cases, this is a full knowledge of the gospel of Jesus Christ. So the remaining issue is not the other person, but you. What are you going to do about Jesus?

41

Did Paul Invent Christianity?

Ben Witherington III

The question, Did Paul invent Christianity? has frequently been asked. In fact, some have been so sure that Paul was the originator of this religion that they called him the first great corrupter of the simple religion of Jesus. We still hear today the cry "back to Jesus," which has as its flip side, "and away with Paul." You hear this for example from various members of the Jesus Seminar. Like so many caricatures, this one deserves to be put in its place.

To a large extent the answer to this question depends on what one means by *invent* and also what one means by *Christianity*. Certainly Nicene or Chalcedonian Christianity did not fully exist in the first century AD. Neither did Catholicism or Protestantism for that matter. All the earliest followers of Jesus were Jews, and all the books of the New Testament were written by Jews, with one or two possible exceptions (e.g., the author of Luke and Acts). Certainly the very earliest followers of Jesus did not see themselves as creating a new religion. They were sectarian Jewish followers of Jesus. However, through a process that involved a variety of factors (growth, evangelization, and conversion of many gentiles; christocentric rather than Torah-centric focus; expulsion from various synagogues in the empire) the Jesus movement de facto became a separate entity from early Judaism, and in fact it appears that this was already the case during the lifetime and ministry of Paul. One can say that Paul was a catalyst who helped lead the Jesus movement out of Judaism and into being its own religious group. Paul was not the inventor of Christianity, but in some sense he was its midwife, being most responsible for there being a large number of gentiles entering this sectarian group, and not on the basis of becoming Jews first (i.e., having to keep kosher or be circumcised or keep the Sabbath), which in turn shifted the balance of power in the movement everywhere in the empire except the Holy Land.

But there is more to it than that. Consider a text like 1 Corinthians 9:19–23. Here Paul says he became the Jew to the Jew and the gentile to the gentile in order that by all means he might win some to Christ. Now this is a very odd way for a Jew, indeed a former Pharisee, to talk if he thinks he is still a part of Judaism. Or notice already in his earliest letter, Galatians, written about 49 AD, Paul says, "You have heard of my previous way of life in Judaism. . . . I was advancing in Judaism beyond many Jews" (Gal. 1:13–14 NIV). Judaism is apparently a thing of the past for Paul, something he is no longer "in" or "advancing in." It appears that Paul believes he is in something else—namely he is "in Christ," or put more broadly, "in the body of Christ," seen as a separate entity from Judaism.

In any religious movement that endures for any length of time there are always pioneers or trailblazers who see the way forward more clearly than others, and certainly Paul was one of these. It is clear enough that his insistence that salvation or the new birth must be by grace through faith in Jesus had implications that only a few had fully worked out in Paul's day. For one thing, in Paul's mind this meant that even Jewish Christians were no longer obligated to keep the Mosaic covenant and its law. They could do so as a blessed option, or as a missionary tactic (as Paul did), but it was not required even of Jewish Christians, much less of gentiles. The answer to the question, Must one become a Jew to be a follower of Jesus? was answered in the negative by Paul. Now in theory others such as Peter and James agreed about the basis of salvation, but when they asked the question, How then shall Christians live? there was disagreement, especially when the subject became How then shall Jewish Christians live? James and other members of the Jerusalem community believed that Jewish Christians should indeed be obligated to keep the law, if for no other reason than to be a good witness to their fellow Jews, and thereby win some of them to Christ.

Paul, however, understood the radical implications of salvation by grace through faith in Jesus. He understood that this meant that if you required circumcision and law observance of the Jewish Christians, but not the gentile ones, you were in effect creating two different Christian groups, two different ways of following Jesus. The Judaizers who dogged Paul's steps in Galatia understood this problem, which is why they more consistently argued that everyone, including gentiles, must keep the Mosaic law.

At the end of the day, Paul's view of the Mosaic law and whether it should be imposed on Christians most clearly reveals that Paul understood that being in Christ meant something more and something different from being "in Judaism." This is why in an elaborate argument in Galatians Paul compares the

Mosaic law to a nanny, who was meant to oversee the people of God until they came of age, but now that Jesus has come they are not under that supervisor any more (see Galatians 4). Paul even goes so far as to say that one of the main reasons Jesus came born under the law was to redeem those under the law, getting them out from under its sway (see Gal. 4:4-5). Those under the law are seen as being in bondage to it until Christ comes and redeems them. Now this clearly enough is sectarian language, the language of a split-off group from Judaism. Paul insists in Galatians 2:21 that if a person could be set right, or kept right, with God by the observance of the Mosaic law then "Christ died for nothing!" He even urges his converts, "I declare to every man who lets himself be circumcised that he is obligated to obey the whole law" (Gal. 5:3 NIV). This is also why, in a salvation-historical argument in 2 Corinthians 3:7–18 he speaks of the Mosaic law, and even the Ten Commandments, as a glorious anachronism, something that was glorious in its day but which is rapidly becoming obsolete.

It is this radical message, not merely about salvation through the crucified Christ but religious living without the necessity of keeping the Mosaic law, that got Paul whipped, stoned, and in general run out of one synagogue after another. Second Corinthians 11:25–27 probably also indicates that there was a contract out on Paul set up by some of his fellow Jews. The reason for this is clear. As Alan Segal, a Jewish New Testament scholar, has rightly seen, Paul was viewed as an apostate Jew, and the Jesus movement was seen as beyond the boundaries of true Judaism.[1] The upshot of all this is rather clear. There was already a parting of the ways between Judaism and Christianity, at least outside the Holy Land, by the time Paul wrote his letter to the Corinthians. In Galatians we can still see the transition period, just barely. So it is indeed right to see Paul as the midwife who helped give birth to a new form of religion centered on the worship of Jesus Christ.

This does not mean that Paul invented the idea that Jesus was divine, or the idea of the Trinity, or the idea of the atoning death of Jesus, and certainly he could not be accused of inventing the idea of the virginal conception since he never mentions it in any of his letters. Paul shared in common with all other true Christians the belief that Jesus was the risen Lord, and that he was the Son of God come in the flesh. His Christology he shared with his fellow followers of Jesus, though doubtless he explained and explored and applied these truths in fresh ways in his churches. Where Paul takes a different tack than James, for example, is in how he thinks Jewish Christians can and should live in manifesting their discipleship to Jesus. He is more consistent on insisting on salvation and Christian living by grace through faith than others were. He is also more consistent in affirming that the guide for Christian living is the "law of Christ," which is not just Christ's interpretation of the Mosaic law. It is rather Jesus's unique teachings, plus those portions of the Old Testament that Jesus affirmed and reappropriated (e.g., part of the Ten Commandments), plus the moral example of Christ, plus also some early Christian teachings that originated after Jesus's time.[2]

In the end, one can say that Paul was a shepherd leading God's people in new directions and through uncharted waters to a new promised land where Jew and gentile would be united in Christ on the very same basis and with the very same discipleship requirements. Though Paul did not call this end result Christianity, he more than any other of the original apostles was responsible for the birthing of the form of community that was to become the early church. And though he did not invent its doctrines or even its ethics, he most consistently applied its truths until a community that comported with these truths emerged.[3]

Section Four

The Question of the Bible

42

Is the Bible Today What Was Originally Written?

Andreas J. Köstenberger

The Bible was originally written in Hebrew, Aramaic (the Old Testament), and Greek (the New Testament). The Bibles we use today are translations from the original languages into English (or other languages). Jesus most likely taught in Aramaic (though he probably also knew Hebrew and Greek), so that the Greek New Testament itself represents a translation of Jesus's teaching from the Aramaic into Greek.

The question, Is the Bible today what was originally written? involves two important questions: (1) Are the available manuscripts (MSS) of the Bible accurate representations of the original MSS of the respective books of the Bible (the autographs of Scripture)? This is an issue of textual *transmission*. (2) Are the available translations faithful renderings of the Bible in the original languages? This is an issue of *translation*.

With regard to the first question, no original autographs exist of any biblical text; only copies are available. The word *manuscript* is used to denote anything written by hand rather than copies produced from the printing press. Textual evidence constitutes anything written on clay tablets, stone, bone, wood, various metals, potsherds (ostraca), but most notably papyrus and parchment (vellum).

Most ancient books were compiled and then rolled into a scroll. Since a papyrus roll rarely exceeded thirty-five feet in length, ancient authors divided a long literary work into several "books" (e.g., the Gospel of Luke and the Acts of the Apostles consisted of a two-volume set composed by Luke).

Later, sometime during the first or second century AD, the codex came into use. The codex consisted of bound sheets of papyrus and constitutes the prototype for the modern book format. Thus early Christians began to collect and collate individual books into what is now the canonical New Testament. The term Bible derives from the Greek word *biblion* (book); the earliest use of *ta biblia* (the books) in the sense of "Bible" is found in 2 Clement 2:14 (circa 150).

Even though the original autographs are lost, the extant manuscript evidence allows a high degree of confidence in the text of the Bible. Both the Old and New Testaments are attested by a large number of MSS in a variety of forms spanning many centuries.

The primary witnesses to the Old Testament come from the Masoretic texts (the Masoretes were Jewish scribes) including the Cairo Geniza (895), the Leningrad Codex (916), the Codex Babylonicus Petropalitanus (1008), the Aleppo Codex (circa 900), the British Museum Codex (950), and the Reuchlin Codex (1105). The Leningrad Codex remains the oldest complete manuscript and serves as the main source for the Hebrew text. However, since the earliest of these MSS date from the ninth century AD, they are removed from the original autographs by a considerable period of time.

Other witnesses include the Talmud (Aramaic translations and commentaries), the Septuagint (LXX, the Greek translation of the Old Testament), the Samaritan Pentateuch, and the Dead Sea Scrolls (DSS). The latter, discovered during the 1940s and '50s, provide scholars with witnesses to the Old Testament text that can be dated between 250–100 BC. Cave four (4Q), for example, has yielded about 40,000 fragments of 400 different MSS, 100 of which are biblical, representing every Old Testament book except Esther. Remarkably, a comparison of the DSS and the Masoretic text reveals a fairly small number of discrepancies.

Thus the manuscript evidence for the Old Testament firmly demonstrates that the original Old Testament texts were carefully preserved and are accurately represented in our modern Bibles.

The New Testament text remains the best attested document in the ancient world. The witnesses to the New Testament fall into three broad categories: the Greek MSS, ancient translations (versions) into other languages, and quotations from the New Testament found in early ecclesiastical writers (the church fathers). The Greek MSS, over six thousand in number, include papyrus fragments, uncials (written in all capitals without spaces or punctuation), and minuscules (small cursive-like script).

The papyri form the most significant group due to the fact that their early date implies that they are chronologically the closest to the original autographs. For example, both $\mathfrak{P}^{52}$ (containing a few verses of John 18) and $\mathfrak{P}^{46}$ (containing all of Paul's epistles except the Pastorals) are most likely dated within thirty years of the original writings.

The uncials follow the papyri in chronological importance. Codex Sinaiticus, an uncial written about 350, is the earliest extant copy of the entire New Testament. Other uncials, such as the Codex Vaticanus, Alexandrinus, Ephraemi, and Bezae, constitute significant witnesses as well.

The minuscules compose the largest group of Greek MSS, but they are dated considerably later.

Finally, the early versions and church fathers provide helpful early attestation that can aid scholars in reconstructing the most plausible original readings. The total tally of more than 6,000 Greek MSS, more than 10,000 Latin Vulgate MSS, and more than 9,300 early versions results in over 25,000 witnesses to the text of the New Testament.

This sheer multiplicity of MSS does not, however, result in absolute uniformity of the texts. Thousands of variant readings (most of them minor) exist between the MSS. While scribes exhibited great care in their effort to reproduce exact copies, they were not immune from human error. Scribal errors can take on the form of unintentional and intentional errors. Unintentional errors are the cause of the majority of textual variants. These typically include errors of the eyes (e.g., skipping words or losing one's place), hands (slips of the pen or written notes in the margins), and ears (confusing similar sounding words or misunderstanding a word). Intentional errors resulted when scribes attempted to correct a perceived error in the text or altered the text in the interest of doctrine and harmonization. These errors often became standardized through subsequent copies made from the defective copy.

All Greek MSS exhibit traits that enable scholars to classify them into text families (Alexandrian, Western, Byzantine) based on geographic origin, Greek style, and date. Through comparative analysis performed by the practitioners of a science called "textual criticism," scholars sift through all the MSS in order to reproduce the most plausible reading of the original autographs in each individual case.

Textual critics adjudicate between readings through exacting criteria such as dating, text type, attested readings (i.e., how many MSS have a certain reading), and possible reasons for variants (e.g., smoothing out a theologically difficult reading). In addition to examining the Greek MSS, textual critics also consider all other relevant witnesses (i.e., versions and the church fathers).

Although textual criticism is a very complex and at times controversial science, it has provided us with at least two assured results. First, none of the variant readings (including omissions) affect the central message or theological content of the Scriptures. Second, it can confidently be asserted that the text of the Bible today is an accurate and faithful representation of the original autographs.

The second issue, namely that of *translation*, follows as a natural corollary once the question of the textual *transmission* is settled. To assess the fidelity and accuracy of the Bible today compared to the original texts, one must investigate the issues of translation theory and the history of the English Bible. The task of translating the Bible from its source languages (Hebrew, Aramaic, and Greek) into a receptor language (English, for example) involves a plethora of issues related to the nature of language and communication. Is word meaning found in some fixed form of inherent meaning, or is meaning determined by contextual usage? Is meaning located in the formal features of the original grammar, or in the function of words within the grammar? These are just a few of the questions pertaining to translation theory.

Some translators maintain that accurate translation requires a word-for-word approach of formal equivalence (King James Version, New King James Version, New American Standard Bible, English Standard Version). Others contend that construing a straightforward one-to-one correlation between two languages actually distorts meaning. These translators employ a phrase-for-phrase approach of dynamic or functional equivalence (New Revised Standard Version, New International Version, Contemporary English Version, New Living Translation, Today's New International Version). In light of linguistic, exegetical, and stylistic considerations, translations produced in accord with dynamic or functional equivalency tend to reflect the original meaning more closely. The goal of all translators, no matter what translation theory they employ, is the production of an English version that is an accurate rendering of the text written in such a way that the Bible retains its literary beauty, theological grandeur, and, most importantly, its message.

The history of the English Bible satisfactorily demonstrates that the Bible of today does indeed faithfully represent the Scriptures in their original languages. For centuries the only Bible available to Western people was the Latin Vulgate, prepared by Jerome, who was commissioned by Pope Damasus toward the end of the fourth century AD. The Vulgate served as the official version of the Bible throughout Medieval Europe and was restricted to the clergy, monastic orders, and scholars.

A British priest and Oxford scholar, John Wycliffe (1330–1384), was the first to make the entire Bible accessible to the common English-speaking people. His translation, however, was based on the Vulgate and not on the Hebrew and Greek. William Tyndale published the first English New Testament based on the Greek text in 1526. Two close associates of Tyndale, Miles Coverdale and John Rogers, finished his work by publishing their own respective translations of the entire Bible: the Coverdale Bible (1535) and Matthew's Bible (1537). The Geneva Bible of 1560 provided a translation of the Bible entirely from the original languages. This paved the way for King James I to issue a translation that would correct the partisan nature of the Geneva Bible. Thus in 1611, the much-celebrated Authorized Version (AV or King James Version), largely based on Tyndale's work, became the unrivaled English translation for 270 years.

The twentieth century has given rise to a number of new translations. The updating and production of new translations were necessitated by new manuscript discoveries, changes in the English language, and the advancement of linguistics. Today when someone opens any English Bible (New King James Version, New American Standard Bible, New International Version, English Standard Version, Today's New International Version, Holman Christian Standard Bible), he or she may know that generations of faithful scholarship have managed to preserve and protect that Bible as it was originally given.

43

Inerrancy and the Text of the New Testament

Assessing the Logic of the Agnostic View

Daniel B. Wallace

Synopsis

This chapter addresses a popular argument that is used against those who hold to an inerrant Bible. Essentially, the argument is posed as a question: How can you claim to have an inerrant original text when we don't even have the original text? On its face, this argument has seemed so compelling that some people never get beyond it. This chapter will show the underlying assumptions behind this question and why they are fallacious.

The Problem

The fundamental doctrinal commitment of the Evangelical Theological Society—the doctrine on which this society was founded in 1949—is as follows: "The Bible alone, and the Bible in its entirety, is the Word of God written and is therefore inerrant in the autographs."[1]

This is a good representation of the modern doctrine of inerrancy. The question we are wrestling with in this section involves the last word of the statement—*autographs*. The modern definition of inerrancy usually qualifies the doctrine as relating only to the *original manuscripts*, or autographs. Copies are not inerrant, nor are translations. But the original is claimed to be. This articulation found its greatest impetus in Benjamin B. Warfield, the prolific Princeton theologian a couple generations ago (1887–1921), notably in his book *The Inspiration and Authority of the Bible*.[2]

But with this view of things there is a nagging question: How can anyone believe that the Scriptures are inerrant in the original when we do not even possess the original documents? This question is raised so often from those who do not embrace the doctrine of inerrancy that it has almost become a rhetorical question. The answer seems obvious: no thinking individual can hold to this doctrine because the originals are lost and therefore the doctrine cannot be verified. One must be agnostic *at best* about such a doctrine. Consider the following statements to this effect:

> First, the original manuscripts are not accessible today. If the scriptures derive their authority from their inspiration and inerrancy, then only the original manuscripts carry any authority, for the copies we have now are neither inspired nor inerrant. This forces the conclusion that every Bible believing Christian places his faith in an authority that doesn't exist.[3]

> It has been frequently pointed out that if God thought errorless Scripture important enough to inspire its composition, he would surely also have further inspired its copying, so that it might remain error free. Surely a God who can inspire error-free composition could also inspire error-free copying. Since he did not, it would appear he did not think our possession of error-free Scripture very important. But if it is not important for us, why was it important originally?[4]

> Presumably if we could ever recover the original manuscript of a NT book it would be very close to what its author intended. Even here, however, the text might not be completely correct. If the author wrote it himself, he could have made mistakes; if he dictated it to a scribe, the latter could have made mistakes.[5]

These are representative quotations regarding skepticism about such a doctrine. And, as mentioned above, such questions are almost framed as though rhetorical—that is, no answer is truly expected since the person asking the question assumes that no answer can possibly be given. This one question is the thinking man's trump card to inerrancy, and it is viewed as both decisive and irrefutable. But has it truly been thought through?

An important procedural point here: Regardless of whether one embraces inerrancy or not, this essay is simply addressing the argument from agnosticism, namely, that since the autographa don't exist one really can't claim the inerrancy of the originals. My fundamental point is that that argument really is not valid, as the following will make clear. I am not here attempting to defend, define, or attack inerrancy; rather, I am simply trying to focus on the first (and sometimes only!) objection to it by skeptics, to set the record straight about whether this line of reasoning is sound.

The Response

In response to this question, we will note three things. The argument here is not to be found in any one of these, as though each were a self-contained unit. Rather, the argument is inductive, and the points are linked.

We begin with the data available to us today, the extant manuscripts.

The Quantity and Age of Witnesses

The data are growing; every decade, and virtually every year, new manuscripts (MSS) are discovered. Currently, the number of Greek New Testament MSS is close to 5,700—far more than any other ancient literary text. The average classical author's writings, in fact, are typically found in less than twenty extant MSS. The New Testament—in the Greek MSS *alone*—beats this by almost 300 times! Besides the Greek MSS, there are Latin, Coptic, Syriac, Armenian, Georgian, Arabic, and many other versions of the New Testament. The Latin MSS alone number almost 10,000. All told, the New Testament is represented by approximately 1,000 times as many MSS as the average classical author's writings. And even the extraordinary authors—such as Homer or Herodotus—simply can't compare to the quantity of copies that the New Testament enjoys. Homer in fact is a distant second in terms of copies, yet there are fewer than 2,300 copies of Homer extant today.

But there's more: besides the Greek and versional witnesses, the New Testament is also reproduced in patristic commentaries and quotations. Hundreds of thousands of quotations. Indeed, if all the Greek MSS and versions were destroyed, scholars could reproduce all but about half a dozen verses of the New Testament from the patristic quotations alone.

The fundamental problem of New Testament textual criticism is not lack of data, but an embarrassment of riches.

What about the dates of these MSS? Although the vast majority of New Testament MSS are over a millennium removed from the autographs, there are significant numbers of documents in the first millennium. Naturally, the closer we get in time to the originals, the fewer the MSS. But the numbers are nevertheless impressive—especially when compared with other ancient literature.

The average ancient Greek author's writings have no copies until at least five hundred years later. In many cases, if not most, it is closer to 1,000 years. Not so with the New Testament. The earliest fragments come from the second century—within 100 years of the originals. In the 1930s, there was but one fragment of the New Testament in the early second century, $\mathfrak{P}^{52}$, a fragment of John 18 that has been dated between AD 100 and AD 150.[6] Today there are as many as a dozen or so Greek New Testament MSS from the second century. And once we approach the third century, we begin to have some of the most important MSS ever discovered for establishing the text of the New Testament. $\mathfrak{P}^{66}$, $\mathfrak{P}^{75}$, $\mathfrak{P}^{45}$, $\mathfrak{P}^{46}$ are but a few of these significant papyri, and all come from no later than the early third century. Between them, ten of Paul's letters, all four Gospels, and Acts are represented. Once we get into the fourth century—within 250 years of the completion of the New Testament—we have the great uncials: Aleph and B. Aleph (or Codex Sinaiticus), when it was discovered in 1859, was found to contain the entire New Testament. Today it is still the oldest complete New Testament by over 500 years. But even if this precious manuscript had never come to light, there are plenty of other early MSS to fill in the gaps. We are not dependent on one manuscript to determine the wording of the New Testament.

The point in all this is that we have sufficient data in the extant witnesses to construct the original New Testament in virtually every place. Most scholars, in fact, would argue that there is no place for conjectural emendation[7] in New Testament textual criticism because of the great wealth, diversity, and age of the materials that we have to work with. Whether this is entirely true, the fact remains that the New Testament is the best preserved religio-literary document of the ancient world, and if conjectural emendation is necessary, it is only necessary on extremely rare occasions.

Thus the argument against inerrancy because of the nonexistent autographs depends for its force on an unstated supposition, that is, that the original cannot be recovered from the existing materials. But that supposition is, in the opinion of most scholars, hardly the case.

The Quality of Variants

Let us play devil's advocate for a moment, taking the most extreme position. Let's assume that conjectural emendation is necessary in a few places (surely no more than a dozen) in the New Testament. If so, would that nullify evangelicals' claims that the autographs are inerrant? That depends on the quality of the variants. Regarding such, most New Testament scholars are of the opinion that no doctrine is jeopardized by textual variants. The view goes back to J. A. Bengel (1687–1752), the Swabian pietist who did much for biblical criticism. Since his day, many others have argued the same thing: no doctrine is jeopardized by textual variants.[8]

My view is not quite as optimistic, but the relevant point for our purposes in this essay is untouched. I would argue that *no cardinal doctrine is jeopardized by any viable variant*. The adjectives *cardinal* and *viable* are important here. By *cardinal* I mean any doctrine essential for salvation; by *viable* I mean any variant that has a legitimate chance of representing the wording of the autographs. Now I will be quick to add that I do not regard inerrancy as a cardinal doctrine. At the same time, I would include it in the principle that this statement espouses. Perhaps we could modify the statement as follows: No cardinal doctrine nor many other doctrines are jeopardized by any viable variant. Of course stating it this way is rather vague. The "many other doctrines" could be a number of things! Nevertheless, the point for our purposes is that even inerrancy does not seem to be jeopardized by viable textual variants.

You may recall that I began this paper by noting that I am neither defending nor attacking the doctrine of inerrancy but rather am addressing an argument against it that, to me, lacks logical force. The preceding paragraph may seem to be a denial of this neutral stance. But it is not, as you will see in the final section.

The remarkable thing to note about the minimal impact of textual variants on doctrine is that there are so many variants—hundreds of thousands of them! The best estimates today are that there are between 300,000 and 400,000 textual variants among the New Testament witnesses. For a book that has less than 140,000 words (in Greek), that is quite significant. Yet the vast majority of these variants are mere spelling differences that affect nothing of substance. Then there are synonyms and minor additions—such as replacing a pronoun with a name or adding "Christ" to the title "the Lord Jesus." These too do not materially affect the meaning of the text. To be sure, there are several hundred textual variants that affect exegesis, or the meaning of a given passage. But no viable variant affects any cardinal doctrine, and even the nonviable variants have a minimal impact on the teachings of the New Testament.

A few examples would be suitable here. One of the most notorious textual problems is the ἔχομεν/ἔχωμεν problem of Romans 5:1. Does Paul say, "We have peace" (ἔχομεν) or "Let us have peace" (ἔχωμεν)? The difference between the indicative and subjunctive is a single letter. The omicron and omega were most likely pronounced alike in Hellenistic Greek (as they are in later Greek), leaving the decision even more difficult. Indeed, scholars are split on this textual problem. But the point here is this: Is either variant a contradiction of the teaching of Scripture? Hardly. If Paul is saying that Christians have peace, he is speaking about our positional status with God the Father. If Paul is urging Christians to have peace with God, he is urging them to grab hold of the "indicatives of the faith," the foundational truths on which the Christian life is based. We have plenty of examples in the New Testament of both kinds of utterances, even within the *corpus Paulinum*: the apostles both declare our reconciled standing with God, and also urge Christians to be reconciled to God. Both utterances are true, but on different levels. The real question in Romans 5:1 is not whether either variant is true, but what Paul is talking about. The problem ultimately is one that affects exegesis, but not theology.

Or consider Matthew 18:15: Ἐὰν δὲ ἁμαρτήσῃ [εἰς σὲ] ὁ ἀδελφός σου . . . ("If your brother sins *against you* . . .") Here the εἰς σὲ ("against you") is in doubt.

Now what is at stake is a matter of orthopraxy (i.e., how church discipline is to be conducted), but not orthodoxy. That is, does Christian A have the right and responsibility to address the sin of Christian B *only* if that sin is directed against Christian A? Or does he have the right and responsibility to address the sin of Christian B if he or she was not the victim of the sin? The textual problem is difficult to solve, but it does not affect any cardinal doctrine.

The same can be said for 1 Corinthians 14:34–35, a passage that some scholars believe should be excised from the text. Gordon Fee and Philip Payne have written most cogently in this regard. But whether the passage is part of the autograph of 1 Corinthians or not, no cardinal doctrine is affected. True, the text is addressing the role of women in the church—and thus is a very important passage for them! But the doctrine of salvation does not hang in the balance.

Another illustration is the Western text of Acts 1:11, where εἰς τὸν οὐρανόν ("into heaven") is lacking in this clause: οὗτος ὁ Ἰησοῦς ὁ ἀναλημφθεις ἀφ' ὑμῶν εἰς τὸν οὐρανόν ("this Jesus who was taken up from you into heaven . . ."). There are some who claim that the Western text undercuts the doctrine of the ascension of Christ because of this verse. However, to maintain that view the Western text must lack *all* references to the ascension. Yet the first and third εἰς τόν οὐρανόν in this verse are untouched. And most other ascension texts are untouched as well.[9] It may be that the Western scribes were trying to trim words and phrases for stylistic reasons, but it is doubtful in the extreme that they were attempting to eradicate any reference to the ascension of Christ. If so, they were singularly incompetent in their attempt. Still more, it is completely unreasonable to think that the New Testament originally did not speak of the ascension of Christ and that this teaching was only added later.

Among the textual problems that are usually cited as causing the most trouble for inerrantists are the following:[10]

Matthew 1:7–8	Ἀσάφ vs. Ἀσά ("Asaph" vs. "Asa")
Matthew 1:10	Ἀμώς vs. Ἀμών ("Amos" vs. "Amon")
Mark 1:2	ἐν τῷ Ἠσαΐᾳ τῷ προφήτῃ vs. ἐν τοῖς προφήταις ("in Isaiah the prophet" vs. "in the prophets")
Mark 2:26	ἐπὶ Ἀβιαθὰρ ἀρχιερέως vs. *omit* ("when Abiathar was high priest" vs. omission of this line)[11]
Mark 5:1	Γερασηνῶν vs. Γαδαρηνῶν ("Gerasenes" vs. "Gadarenes")
Luke 23:45	τοῦ ἡλίου ἐκλιπόντος vs. καὶ ἐσκοτίσθη ὁ ἥλιος ("the sun was eclipsed" vs. "the sun was darkened")
John 7:8	οὐκ vs. οὔπω ("not" vs. "not yet")
Acts 12:25	εἰς Ἰερουσαλήμ vs. ἐξ Ἰερουσαλήμ vs. ἀπὸ Ἰερουσαλήμ ("into Jerusalem" vs. "out of Jerusalem" vs. "from Jerusalem")
Acts 16:12	conjecture vs. various readings[12]

Acts 20:4	Δερβαῖος vs. Δουβέριος ("Derbe" vs. "Doberius")
2 Peter 3:10	εὑρεθήσεται ("will be found") vs. various readings[13]

These are among the more interesting and significant textual problems in the New Testament with reference to theological formulation. But standard commentaries on the New Testament will show that the problems they raise are more apparent than real. Suffice it to underscore our previous point: no cardinal doctrine is jeopardized by any viable variant.[14]

One hundred and twenty-five years ago, F. J. A. Hort was bold enough to think that less than 1/1000th of the text was in doubt. That would mean that only about 140 or so words could not be positively confirmed. I suspect the number is significantly higher than that, but nevertheless lower than what many skeptics are willing to believe. At the upper limit, we are dealing with about 1 percent of the text of the New Testament in doubt—less than 1,400 words. And yet, in all these places, the true text can be found in *some* MSS. Further, as I have argued already, no cardinal doctrine is at stake in any of them. To put this pragmatically, when one looks at the Nestle-Aland *Novum Testamentum Graece*, he or she is looking at the original text—either in the text or in the apparatus. The argument, then, that inerrancy is an unsupportable doctrine because the autographs are gone is moot: we *have* the original somewhere on the page of the Greek New Testament.

Evangelicals and Text-Critical Theories

Finally, we come to the diversity of opinions among evangelicals concerning the text of the New Testament. By *evangelical* I mean those Christians who, inter alia, embrace the doctrine of inerrancy. To be sure, not all evangelicals hold to inerrancy, but those that are in view here do. Perhaps a better title, however, would be "Inerrantists and Text-Critical Theories," but inerrantists include many who are not evangelicals (such as members of heterodox Christian groups and many fundamentalists who don't care for the title *evangelical*). So *evangelicals* will have to do.

Within the field of New Testament textual criticism, there are several schools of thought. On the far right are those who would embrace the majority text, or the MSS that are typically Byzantine in flavor and usually comprise a majority, even a large majority. (The Byzantine/majority text generally stands behind the King James Version.) The text that such scholars construct has not been of a sort to cause them *Angst* over inerrancy. That is, *if* the majority text is the true text, then evangelicals do not all of a sudden have to abandon inerrancy.

On the other side are those who give priority to internal evidence (known as rigorous or thoroughgoing eclectics). To be sure, there are not too many evangelicals in this camp (perhaps because there are not too many textual critics in this camp!). And the text that they believe is the original has not caused them to abandon inerrancy either. Two points are important here, however. First, although this approach to textual criticism is more prone to adopting conjectural emendation than any other school, rigorous eclectics are generally quite opposed to adopting a reading that does not have at least some manuscript support.[15] Second, evangelicals are generally the least likely group of New Testament scholars to adopt conjecture. They tend to have such a high regard for the MS evidence that such an approach is unthinkable. But precisely because of this, the text that they claim to be inerrant is one that is found in the MSS, not one that is made up *ex nihilo* to safeguard inerrancy. And it should be underscored that conjecture is almost always suggested in a passage because of the discrepancies the wording seems to create. Thus, evangelicals *should* be the most prone to come up with conjectural emendation, if those discrepancies truly produced errors in the text that they couldn't live with.

In the middle are those who are best styled as reasoned eclectics. This group comprises the majority of textual critics today, whether they be evangelicals or otherwise. This approach to textual criticism stands behind most of the modern translations of the Bible. There are many permutations within this broad camp, but even accounting for them all, evangelicals are found at every point. The text that they construct as the original has not caused them to abandon inerrancy.[16]

These various schools of thought all construct a different original New Testament, yet inerrantist evangelicals are found in each school. *There is no text-critical school that, by its very nature, excludes inerrantists from membership.* In other words, evangelicals in various schools view as inerrant whatever New Testament text they adopt. And, as we mentioned earlier, evangelicals are not prone to employ conjecture to solve textual difficulties. Thus the argument that since the autographs have disappeared means that there is no way we can know if the text was inerrant becomes—*especially* for evangelicals—a faulty assumption. This line of argument could only be true (1) if conjectural emendation were a necessity in given places, (2) if in such places only the conjecture resolved a discrepancy in the text of such a nature that the doctrine of inerrancy were in jeopardy otherwise, *and* (3) if only evangelicals adopted the conjecture (for then they could be charged with special pleading). But these conditions are manifestly not met. Consequently the agnostic argument is vacuous.[17]

Conclusion

Regardless of what one thinks about the doctrine of inerrancy, at least the argument against it on the basis of the unknown autographs is logically fallacious. We have the text of the New Testament somewhere in the MSS. And the text we have in any viable variants is no more a problem for inerrancy than other problems where the text is secure. Now, to be sure, there are definitely challenges to inerrancy in the textual variants. This is not denied. But they are minor challenges compared to the bigger challenges that inerrancy faces.

Yet, evangelicals are not prone to alter the text where the big problems are. Which evangelical would not like a clean harmony between the two records of Judas's demise, uniform parallel accounts of Peter's threefold denial of Jesus, or an outright excision of the census by Quirinius? And who would not prefer that in Mark 2:26 Jesus did not speak of David's violation of the temple as occurring during the days of "Abiathar the high priest"? These are significantly larger problems for inerrancy than the few, isolated textual problems—and they are not in passages that are capable of facile text-critical solutions.[18] The argument thus is from the greater to the lesser: if these major challenges to inerrancy are not resolved via conjectural emendation by evangelicals, then the minor challenges that involve textual variants are certainly not sufficient to cause evangelicals to abandon this doctrine.

This in no way is meant to suggest that the major problems are incapable of a solution. Rather, my argument here is simply that there are bigger fish to fry for inerrantists than a few minor textual problems.

Simply put, the doctrine of inerrancy is embraced by evangelicals even in the face of a less-than-certain text of the New Testament. And that's because even though there is not 100 percent certainty over the wording of the New Testament, the words of the original text are evident—in either the text or the variants of, say, the Nestle-Aland^{27} text. Conjectural emendation is virtually unnecessary. And no viable variant in that apparatus has been persuasive enough to evangelicals as a whole to dislodge their belief in this doctrine.

As a matter of intellectual integrity, I would urge those who use the agnostic argument to retire it. As good as it sounds on the surface, once it is probed just a bit, it crumbles. Or, in the immortal words of former Texas governor Anne Richards, "That dawg won't hunt."

In sum, there is an assumption made by non-evangelicals when they pose the question of inerrancy and the autographs. It is that the wording of the autographs is, in places, completely unrecoverable—that is, unknown and unknowable. But this assumption implies that the wording of the original in some places cannot be found in the manuscripts. That is manifestly not true. Pragmatically the wording of the original is to be found either in the text *or the apparatus* of the Nestle-Aland Greek New Testament. We have the original in front of us; we're just not sure at all times whether it is above the line or below it.

We could add the second point: evangelicals belong to all major camps of textual criticism. Thus, regardless of what is considered a viable variant (i.e., one that has a genuine possibility of reflecting the wording of the autographs), evangelicals have not been shaken in their belief in inerrancy. To be sure, there are challenges to inerrancy in relation to textual criticism. But overall, these are *minor* (and it is beyond the scope of this paper to address them). They simply do not show up as the major problems for this doctrine.

44

Why All the Translations?

Denny Burk

When one wanders into the Christian bookstore to buy a Bible, the sheer number of versions available can be quite overwhelming, and yet many Christians have no criteria by which to evaluate which translation is the best. This essay proposes to set forth some of the historical reasons for new translations and to explain some of the different translation philosophies that drive the production of so many different versions in our own day. Thus we must address the question posed in the title of this article from both a historical and a philosophical perspective. Historically speaking we are compelled to consider why there has been such a proliferation of English translations of the Scripture. The question emerges why each generation undertakes the task of translation. Also we need to have an idea about the different philosophies of translation. We need to understand what it is that causes the various English versions to differ from one another in significant ways (especially the modern ones).

Historical Reasons for New Translations

As each generation of Christians has the responsibility to preach the gospel, they also have the responsibility to make the written word of God available to all. This is the task of Bible translation. Every generation witnesses changes in the textual basis for translation, in the translation language, and in other areas that require either revisions of old translations or the production of new ones. The one thing that has remained constant over the years is that the exigencies of history require new translations into English.

John Wycliffe, a powerful preacher and lecturer at Oxford University, sought to reform what he saw as the corrupt Roman papacy and church hierarchy in his day. Part of his protest movement consisted in providing a translation of the Bible for English Christians into their own language. He wanted the average layman to have access to the word of God. Up until that time, no one had ever produced an English translation of the entire Bible. Wycliffe wanted to see a revival take place in England and is reported to have said that "it helpeth Christian men to study the Gospel in that tongue in which they know best Christ's sentence."[1] So in 1382, Wycliffe completed the first edition of his handwritten English translation of the whole Bible.

While John Wycliffe's English translation of the Scripture was an important and momentous achievement in his generation, it was not the best translation that was possible. Wycliffe's translation was based not on Greek and Hebrew manuscripts (the original languages of the Bible), but on Jerome's Latin translation (the Vulgate, circa 403).[2] Later translations would correct this shortcoming. Moreover, Wycliffe's translation was in Middle English, a form of English that would be too archaic for subsequent readers.

William Tyndale, lecturer at Cambridge University, undertook his translation of the New Testament and based his work on a Greek text of the New Testament. Tyndale's was the first printed translation of the New Testament in English (1526). Tyndale completed translating portions of the Old Testament from the Hebrew text also, but he died before finishing it. Tyndale's move back to the original languages of the New and Old Testaments was a needed improvement over the work of Wycliffe. Another improvement consists in the fact that the English of Tyndale's translation belongs to the Modern English period.[3] It would not be until the work of Miles Coverdale that a complete Bible, Old and New Testaments, would emerge (1535).

There were many other translations of the Bible into English after Coverdale, but the watershed English translation is without a doubt the King James Version (1611). Whereas many of the English translations from Wycliffe forward were produced by translators working alone, the King James Version is the result of the work of about fifty translators working in committees. Translating from the original languages, some of the best and brightest biblical scholars of that day contributed to the work. King James I (1566–1625) of England commissioned these men in an effort to provide a translation that would be acceptable to both Anglicans and those following the Puritan or Reformed traditions.[4] The result of their efforts produced one of the greatest religious and literary masterpieces of the English language. Until the Revised Standard Version and the proliferation of other versions in the second half of the twentieth century, the King James Bible was without rival among English readers.

A growing understanding of the languages and cultures of the Bible, as well as a discovery of thousands of ancient Greek and Hebrew manuscripts, constitute at least part of the reason that new English versions have appeared over the centuries. Also, changes in the English language require updates of older versions that use more archaic forms of English.

Philosophical Reasons for New Translations

One of the reasons that we find so many translations being produced today is because of a variety of philosophies that govern translation. Translation involves much more than a mere substitution of words from one language to another. Any translation is at bottom an interpretation of the Bible's meaning into another language, and translators have differed with one another on the best way to render the ancient texts into English. There are basically three translation philosophies current today: the formal equivalence approach, the dynamic equivalence approach, and the paraphrase.

The formal equivalence approach is the most literal method of translation. Translations that utilize formal equivalence are essentially word-for-word translations. They attempt to reproduce the various forms of the original language with the appropriate English forms. For instance, if there is a participle in a given Greek text, a formal equivalence translation will often try to translate the participle with an English participle. The King James Version (1611), the New American Standard Bible (1971; update 1995), the Revised Standard Version (1952), and the English Standard Version (2001) all reflect this approach to translation.

The dynamic equivalence approach does not attempt a word-for-word rendering of the original but rather a thought-for-thought rendering. For example, if a translator comes across a participle in a given Greek text, he will not necessarily attempt to render it with a corresponding English participle. Often an English form is chosen that may not include a participle at all, as long as it faithfully captures the thought of the original. Translators who utilize this approach recognize that a word-for-word translation does not always adequately capture the meaning of the original text, and a dynamic equivalent rendering is necessary. Two popular translations that fall into this category are the New International Version (1978) and the New Revised Standard Version (1990).

A paraphrased version is not technically a translation because it does not seek to translate from the ancient texts. A paraphrase is a "free rendering or amplification of a passage, expression of its sense in other words."[5] Versions in this category include the Kenneth Taylor's *Living Bible* (1971) and Eugene Peterson's *The Message* (NT 1993; Old Testament Wisdom Books 1997; Old Testament Prophets 2000).

These different translation philosophies account for no small part of the various translations that have appeared over the last century. The NIV Bible, for example, is the direct result of a translation philosophy that gained popularity in the 1970s—dynamic equivalence. But a debate still rages among scholars of the Bible as to which approach is the best. Eugene Nida has been very influential in promoting a dynamic equivalence approach, while Leland Ryken and others have advocated for an essentially literal approach.[6]

45

Archaeology and the Bible

How Archaeological Findings Have Enhanced the Credibility of the Bible

John McRay

The Bible is a collection of many kinds of documents written over a period of about fifteen hundred years. Beginning with the composition of the first five books (the Pentateuch), the sixty-six total documents were completed by the end of the first century AD. They were composed in the Hebrew, Aramaic, and Greek languages in various geographical settings and different historical periods. Archaeological discoveries relating to these settings and periods have enlightened the cultural context in which many of the recorded events occurred and have enhanced the credibility of the biblical record of both the Old and New Testament periods. For example, many events recorded in the last one hundred years of this period of biblical history, during which the New Testament documents were written, have been illuminated through significant archaeological discoveries. Following are some of these impressive finds. Space limitations will not allow discussion of the fourteen hundred years of Old Testament sites.

Pool of Siloam

Hezekiah, a king of Judah in the eighth century BC, built a tunnel through Mount Ophel in Jerusalem southward from the underground Gihon Spring through almost 1,750 feet of rock to channel water to the Pool of Siloam inside the city walls. It was to this pool that Jesus sent a blind man to have him wash his eyes in its water and receive his sight, according to John 9:7.

Until recently, only a small portion of the pool has been accessible. After the site was excavated in the late nineteenth century, the people of the village of Silwan (modern spelling of Siloam) built on the northwest corner of the little pool a mosque with a minaret, which still stands above it. However, excavations at the site in the first six months of 2005 uncovered the eastern portion of a large pool, fifty meters in length (its width as yet unknown), which lies only about ten meters south of the little pool. These two are undoubtedly part of one larger complex that was called the Siloam Pool (like the Pool of Bethesda, which had two sections). It has a series of stone steps for entering the pool, which, being fed by fresh running water from the Gihon Spring through a small channel discovered on the north side of the pool, was probably a major facility for ritual purification before entering the temple. This may be the reason Jesus chose this pool for the miracle. A stone pavement has also recently been discovered, leading from the pool up Mount Ophel to the Temple Mount.

Rolling Stones at Tombs

In Matthew 28:2 it is stated that an angel descended from heaven to the tomb of Jesus, "rolled back the stone and sat upon it." Many tombs from the time of Christ have been discovered in Jerusalem, and some of them still have these rolling stones by their entrances. A tomb from the time of Jesus was built for the burial of Queen Helena of Adiabene, north of the Damascus Gate, and has the stone still in place. Another, better-preserved rolling stone still stands beside the entrance to the tomb of the family of Herod the Great, south of the King David Hotel. More than sixty rolling stone tombs have been found and studied in Israel and Jordan in recent years.

Tomb of Caiaphas

In November 1990, a tomb was discovered in Jerusalem that contains an ossuary with the name of Caiaphas carved into it. The burial cave is located in the Peace Forest, south of the Gehenna Valley, near the Government House, where the United Nations was located. The high priest before whom Jesus appeared just before his death was named Caiaphas (see Matt. 26:3, 57; Luke 3:2; John 11:49; 18:13, 14, 24, 28). Later both Simon Peter and John appeared before him in Jerusalem (Acts 4:6). Archaeologists have identified the site as the burial cave of the family of Caiaphas.

Capernaum Synagogue

When Jesus began his public ministry in Nazareth of Galilee at about thirty years of age and was rejected in the synagogue there (see Luke 3:23; 4:16–30), he went to Capernaum, a small village on the north shore of the Sea of Galilee, where he apparently lived in the home of Simon Peter, one of his disciples (see Matt. 8:14; Mark 2:1), and taught in the synagogue (see Mark 1:21; 3:1; John 6:59). Archaeological excavations conducted in Capernaum have discovered the synagogue under the fourth–fifth century limestone structure still standing there. Portions of the floor and walls of the first-century synagogue were found beneath the floor of this later building.

Acts 17:6 and Politarchs in Thessalonica

The credibility of the Bible has been challenged for many years by critics who have insisted that Luke, the author of the Acts of the Apostles, erroneously used the Greek term *politarchēs* in referring to the officials before whom Christians associated with the apostle Paul were taken in the city of Thessalonica (see Acts 17:6). It has been adamantly asserted that no such office existed at that time. However, an inscription containing this term has been found in that city and is now displayed in the British Museum. The inscription, which was attached to a first-century arch on Egnatia Street, begins "In the time of the Politarchs . . ." Thirty-five inscriptions have now been discovered that contain this term; nineteen of them come from Thessalonica, and at least three date to the first century AD. These inscriptions prove that the office of politarchs existed in Thessalonica in the time of the New Testament and that the Bible is accurate in its use of the term.

Erastus in Corinth

Before AD 50, a sixty-two-foot square area was paved with stone at the northeast corner of the theater in Corinth, Greece. Excavations there revealed part of a Latin inscription carved into the pavement, which reads: "Erastus in return for his aedileship laid [the pavement] at his own expense."

The Erastus of this inscription is identified in the excavation publication as the Erastus mentioned by Paul in Romans 16:23, a letter written from Corinth, in which Erastus is referred to as "the city treasurer." Three main points favoring the identification are set forth by the editor of the inscriptions: (1) the pavement was laid around AD 50, the time when Erastus would likely have been converted; (2) the name Erastus, an uncommon cognomen, is not found in Corinth other than in this inscription; and (3) the particular Greek word Paul uses in this passage for "treasurer" (*oikonomos*) is an appropriate term to describe the work of a Corinthian aedile.

Romans 13:3 Inscription in Caesarea Maritima

While I was excavating at Caesarea on the coast of Israel in 1972, we uncovered a large mosaic inscription of the Greek text of Romans 13:3. A shorter one had been found in 1960 by an Israeli archaeologist, Abraham Negev. The two texts, dating to at least the fifth century, are part of a mosaic floor of a large public building (perhaps a praetorium or archives building) and are identical to that passage in the Greek New Testament. These are as old as some of our oldest manuscripts of the New Testament.

Paul before Gallio at the Tribunal in Corinth

One of the most important discoveries relating to the New Testament is the tribunal (Greek *bēma*), or speaker's platform, from which official proclamations were read, and where citizens appeared before appropriate officials. It still stands in the heart of the forum in Corinth, Greece. The large stone platform was identified by portions of an inscription found nearby and dated to the period between AD 25 and 50, just prior to Paul's arrival in the city.

Paul spent eighteen months in Corinth on his second missionary journey. At the end of that time, the Jews took advantage of the inauguration of Gallio as proconsul of Achaia in May or June of AD 51 (see Acts 18:12) to bring Paul before him on the charge of violating their law. Gallio found no violation of Roman law by Paul, no "wrongdoing or vicious crime" (see Acts 18:14), and refusing to be a judge of Jewish law, drove Paul's accusers from this "tribunal" (see Acts 18:16–17), where he was seated. Gallio was the brother of Seneca, a Greek stoic philosopher who later became an adviser to the emperor Nero. Seneca perhaps informed the emperor of the fact that Paul had already been acquitted before Gallio in Corinth and thus influenced the favorable outcome of Paul's first arrest in Rome as implied in the last verses of Acts. Luke's accuracy in referring to this tribunal once again enhances the accuracy of the Bible.

Gallio was visiting Corinth from his official residence in Delphi across the Corinthian Gulf. Four fragments of an inscription carved in stone, which had been mounted on the wall of a public building in Delphi, have been excavated, which contain information about the accession of Gallio and help to determine the date of his tenure in office.

The fragments are from a copy of a letter sent from Claudius to the city of Delphi, either to the people of Delphi or to the successor of Gallio, who had the letter carved into stone and attached to the wall of the building. It contains the name of "Gallio Proconsul of Asia," in addition to that of the Roman emperor Claudius, with dates for his reign.

The letter is dated to AD 52. Since proconsuls normally held office for one year, and these provincial governors were required to leave Rome for their posts no later than the middle of April, Gallio probably began his term of office in May of AD 51. And since Paul had arrived in Corinth eighteen months earlier than his appearance before Gallio (see Acts 18:11–12), he would have entered Corinth in the winter of 49–50—perhaps in January of AD 50.

This would coincide well with Luke's statement in Acts 18:2, that when Paul arrived in Corinth on his second journey, he found Aquila and Priscilla, Jews who had "recently" come from Rome, "because Claudius had commanded all the Jews to leave Rome." This expulsion is also referred to in other ancient sources and can be dated to AD 49. Suetonius, chief secretary to the emperor Hadrian (AD 117–38), wrote a biographical account of the Roman emperors titled *The Twelve Caesars*, in which he says, "Because the Jews at Rome caused continuous disturbances at the instigation of Christ, he expelled them from the City."[1] Thus the accuracy of Luke's account in Acts is confirmed and illustrated.

46

The Historical Reliability of the Gospels

Craig L. Blomberg

Can the major contours of the portraits of Jesus in the New Testament Gospels be trusted? Many critics would argue not. The Jesus Seminar became the best-known collection of such critics during the 1990s, as they alleged that only 18 percent of the sayings ascribed to Jesus and 16 percent of his deeds as found in the four canonical Gospels of Matthew, Mark, Luke and John, plus the apocryphal *Gospel of Thomas*, bore any close relationship to what he actually said and did. At the same time, a much more representative cross-section of scholars from about 1980 to the present has inaugurated what has come to be called the Third Quest of the Historical Jesus, in which a greater optimism is emerging about how much we can know from the Gospels, read in light of other historical cultural developments of the day. This article briefly surveys the lines of evidence that, cumulatively, support the historical reliability of the Gospels, particularly the Synoptics (Matthew, Mark, and Luke). None of these arguments presupposes Christian faith; all proceed following standard historical approaches of evaluating the credibility of a wide variety of ancient documents.

More so than with any other literary work of antiquity, we can have enormous confidence in reconstructing what the original texts of the Gospels most likely said. While none of the autographs remain, the sheer volume of manuscripts (from tiny fragments to complete New Testaments)—five thousand in ancient Greek alone—far outstrips what we have for any other Jewish, Greek, or Roman literature, where historians often consider themselves fortunate to have manuscripts numbering in double figures! The art and science of textual criticism enables scholars to date, classify, compare, and contrast these documents where they differ and determine, with 97 to 99 percent accuracy, what the originals most probably contained. With the oldest known fragment of any of the Gospels, a few verses from John 18 dating to around AD 125, we are within one generation of that document's original composition. For most other ancient works, at least several centuries elapse between the originals and the oldest existing copies. None of this makes anything in the Gospels true, but it does mean we know what their writers claimed, something that we are often not at all sure of about other ancient writers.

The authors were in a position to write accurate history if they so chose. Traditional Christian claims affirm that the Gospels were written by two of Jesus's twelve closest followers (Matthew and John); a third man (Mark), who closely followed the memoirs of Peter, the leader of the Twelve; and a fourth (Luke), who carefully interviewed eyewitnesses of Jesus's life as well as consulting previously written sources (Luke 1:1–4). More skeptical scholars have often suggested that we should think of anonymous first-century Christians instead, perhaps disciples of the four men mentioned here. But either way, we are at most two removes away from eyewitness information.

Conservative scholars typically date Matthew, Mark, and Luke to the 60s and John to the 90s; liberal scholars tend to favor a date for Mark in the 70s, Matthew and Luke in the 80s, and John in the 90s. But either way, we are still talking about first-century testimony. Again, compare these last two points with the typical situation for other ancient histories and biographies. The detailed life of Alexander the Great, however, which most historians believe can be reconstructed with a fair amount of accuracy, depends on Arrian and Plutarch's late first- and early second-century biographies of a man who died in 323 BC.

But were the first two generations of Christians (circa AD 30–100) even interested in preserving historical information? This has often been doubted, primarily for two reasons. First, some argue that the perception of the possibility of Jesus's quick return to Earth to bring an end to this age as we know it would have precluded any interest in functioning as historians. Who bothers to record history, even of that believed to be sacred, if they think the world might end at any time? Well, Jews, for one, at least since the eighth century BC! Their prophets had been promising that the "Day of the Lord" was at hand for centuries, and yet God's people also recognized that a day with the Lord was as a thousand years (Ps. 90:4), so the ordinary course of human events continued. Second, some allege that the ideological (i.e., theological) bias of the Gospels' writers would have necessarily distorted the historical facts. There is no doubt that a passionate commitment to a certain ideology can lead some writers to play fast and loose with history, but certain kinds of ideologies actually require greater loyalty to the facts. Jews after World War II, for example, for precisely the reason that they were passionately committed to preventing a Holocaust such as they had experienced under the Nazis from ever happening again, objectively chronicled in detail the atrocities they had suffered. It was less committed people who produced the appalling revisionism that substantially minimized the extent of the Holocaust or even denied it altogether. Because Christian faith depended on Jesus having lived, died, and been resurrected according to the biblical claims (1 Corinthians 15), the Gospels' authors would have good reason to tell the story straight.

But could they pull it off? Even just thirty years after historical events, memories can grow dim and distorted. But first-century Judaism was an oral culture, steeped in the educational practice of memorization. Some rabbis had the entire Hebrew Scriptures (the Christian Old Testament) committed to memory. Memorizing and preserving intact the amount of information contained in one Gospel would not have been hard for someone raised in this kind of culture, which valued the memories of Jesus's life and teaching as sacred.

Why then are the Gospels not word-for-word alike? Why was more than one needed in the first place? Moreover, the verbatim similarities among the Synoptics are usually taken as a sign of literary dependence of one Gospel on another or two together on a common source. There is a whole host of reasons for these differences. Many have to do with what each author selected to include or leave out from a much larger body of information of which he was aware (John 21:25). Distinctive theological emphases, unique geographical outlines, and larger questions of literary subgenre account for many of these selections and omissions. But even where the Gospels include versions of the same event, verbatim parallelism usually remains interspersed with considerable freedom to paraphrase, abridge, expand, explain, and stylize other portions of the accounts. All this was considered perfectly acceptable by the historiographical standards of the day and would not have been viewed in any as errant. But recent scholarship also points out how the flexibility and patterns in oral storytelling would have accounted for many of the more incidental differences as Christian tradition initially passed these stories on by word of mouth.

Can we even assume, then, that the Gospel writers were trying to write something akin to an ancient history or biography rather than, say, a novel or a tragedy in drama form? Yes, for the closest parallels to Luke's prologue come in the comparatively accurate writers of history such as Josephus in the Jewish world and Herodotus and Thucydides in the Greek world.

Another pair of arguments pushes the case even further. The so-called hard sayings of Jesus suggest that the Gospel writers felt considerable constraint on what they could or could not include. Even though Luke's version of Jesus's command to hate father and mother (Luke 14:26) can be explained by its parallel in Matthew (Matt. 10:37), it would have been far easier for Luke simply to omit it altogether and avoid the apparent contradiction with the Mosaic command to honor one's parents had he felt free to do so. The same thing can be said of Jesus's claim not to know the day or hour of his return (Mark 13:32). Numerous embarrassments in the Gospels could have been avoided if their writers had anywhere close to the freedom to tamper with the tradition in the ways that the Jesus Seminar and like-minded writers have alleged they had.

Conversely the topics that Jesus never addresses in the canonical Gospels further support their accuracy. The debate over whether gentile adult males in a world without anesthesia had to be circumcised as a sign that they were keeping the whole Jewish Law en route to becoming Christians threatened to tear the first generation of Christianity wide apart (Gal. 2:1–10; Acts 15). The easiest thing in the world for one of the Gospel writers to have done would have been to quote—or invent—Jesus's teaching on the topic had they felt free to do so. But no verse anywhere in the canonical Gospels expresses Jesus's opinion on the role of circumcision among his followers. The same can be said of speaking in tongues, an issue that threatened to blow the Corinthian church sky-high (see 1 Corinthians 12–14) twenty-five years after Jesus's death.

A dozen or so non-Christian writers or texts confirm a remarkable number of details in the Gospels about Jesus's life—that he was a Jew living in the first third of the first century, born out of wedlock, a self-styled teacher who became very popular, selected certain men as his inner core of disciples, disregarded Jewish dietary laws and ate with the despised, enraged certain Jewish leaders even though believed to be the Messiah by others, was crucified by Pontius Pilate but believed by some of his followers to have been raised from the dead, and began a fledgling religion that never died out. Some might argue that this does not seem like a lot of detail, but in a world in which almost all historical and biographical writing focused on kings, emperors, military generals, people in institutional positions of religious power, famous philosophers whose "schools" had long outlived them, and more generally, the well-to-do and influential, it is remarkable that Jesus gets mentioned at all by first-through-third–century non-Christian writers. Before the legalization of Christianity in the fourth century, who would have expected this obscure, crucified rabbi to produce a following that would one day become the religion adopted by the greatest percentage of people on earth?

Archaeology confirms a whole raft of details susceptible to artifactual or epigraphic corroboration—the existence of the pools of Siloam and Bethesda in Jerusalem, the latter with five porticoes, just as John 5:2 describes; Pontius Pilate as prefect of Judea; Roman crucifixion by driving nails through the ankle bones; fishing boats large enough to hold thirteen people (like Jesus and his twelve disciples); the tomb of Caiaphas; the probable ossuary (bone box) of

James, brother of Jesus; and so on. And all of these details in the Gospels were once doubted before their archaeological confirmation came forth.

Finally, other Christian testimony confirms a whole host of details in the Gospels. Second-century Christian writers refer back to and even quote a considerable portion of the Gospel accounts with approval. More significantly, the letters of James, Peter, and Paul, all concurrent with but primarily prior to the written form of the Gospels, contain numerous allusions to and occasional quotations of Jesus's sayings, which show that they must have been circulating by word of mouth in carefully preserved form. Perhaps most telling of all, testimony to Christ's bodily resurrection was phrased in catechetical language as that which would have been received and passed on by oral tradition and thus probably formed part of what Paul was taught at his conversion, a scant two years after the death of Jesus (1 Cor. 15:1–3). These are no late Hellenistic legends that evolved long after the life of Jesus, the simple Jewish rabbi. These were the revolutionary claims being made by his followers from the very beginning!

47

The New Testament Canon

Craig L. Blomberg

Orthodox Jews often reject the New Testament because the Hebrew Scriptures repeatedly declared themselves to be eternal, suggesting that nothing more could be added to them. Liberal scholars often reject *limiting* the New Testament to its twenty-seven books, because they believe there was other inspirational Christian literature from the early years of Christianity equally worthy of inclusion. Just what factors *were* involved in the formation of the New Testament canon and how legitimate were they?

It is true that God's law and God's word last forever. But the Old Testament prophets also recognize incompleteness in his revelation. Jeremiah 31:31–34 is the clearest and most extensive text to predict a coming *new covenant*, but many texts look forward to a new, messianic age. Since the Mosaic covenant led to the writing of one "testament" (a word that in the Greek—*diathēkē*—could also mean "covenant"), it was logical to expect a written "testament" to accompany the new covenant. At least that is how Tertullian argued near the end of the second century.

But what was the process that led to this New Testament? Already in 2 Peter 3:16 we read of Paul's "letters," perhaps implying that they had begun to be collected together in the first century. By the second century, the four Gospels were circulating together at times. (By about 180, a harmony of the four Gospels had appeared.) The oldest nearly complete New Testament manuscripts still in existence date from the fourth century, but their predecessors probably emerged already in the third. Initially, there was not full agreement on the order of the books. It was natural to group the Gospels together and the letters of Paul together. Revelation naturally came at the end of the collection because it was the last one written, and it also discussed the last things of human history. Acts, Hebrews, and the General Epistles "floated" around in several places before they finally settled into where we find them today.[1]

The rationale for the existing order would appear to have been as follows. The Gospels came first because they are biographies of the life of Jesus, the founder of the Christian religion, who is the reason there is any New Testament in the first place. The order of Matthew, Mark, Luke, and John probably corresponds to the order in which several church fathers believed they were written, though Matthew was regularly credited with having written something in a Hebrew dialect, probably less than a full-fledged Gospel. Even if Mark was written first, as most modern scholars have good reason to believe, Matthew could easily have been put first because it is the most Jewish of the four Gospels and has the greatest number of links with the Old Testament.

Acts comes next because it treats the generation of Jesus's followers immediately after his death and resurrection. Then come all the epistles, grouped together, beginning with the letters of Paul, the most influential of all the first-generation Christians. Except when two epistles are adjacent because they have the same addressees, the letters of Paul are arranged in descending order of length. (Galatians also disrupts the pattern, being just slightly shorter than Ephesians.) First came letters to churches and then letters to individuals, each arranged according to this pattern. The authorship of Hebrews has been uncertain from its initial publication. Because some thought it Pauline, while many did not, it was placed immediately next to the Pauline epistles but not inserted where it would have gone, according to its length, *within* that collection. The so-called General Epistles were apparently arranged in the order of the importance or prominence of their authors in the first decades of the Jesus movement. Although Peter, as the first bishop of Rome in the 60s, would eventually eclipse James the half brother of Jesus in the eyes of later Christians, James was the lead elder of the mother church in Jerusalem in its early days. Peter follows as a close second; then John (Peter's "sidekick" in several contexts in Acts), and finally Jude, the least prominent of the four.[2]

The exact twenty-seven books were not finally agreed on until Athanasius's Easter-time bishop's encyclical letter in AD 367, and this canon was formally ratified only in 393 at the Council of Hippo and in 397 by the Council of Carthage. Although much evidence from antiquity is simply lost forever, the process leading up to the finalization of the canon may be discerned at least in part. Mid-second-century heretical offshoots of Christianity, most notably Gnosticism and Marcionism (a view that pitted the evil God of the Old Testament against the loving Jesus of the Christians), provoked the more faithful heirs of the apostolic tradition to begin itemizing the documents they believed were uniquely inspired and authoritative. Growing Roman persecution, particularly by the third century, at times meant that Christians had to decide, quite literally, which books they were willing to die for.

No debate seems ever to have surrounded the acceptance of the four Gospels, the Acts, the thirteen letters with Paul's name in their opening lines, 1 Peter, or 1 John. The other seven books that eventually "made it" into the New Testament had various questions swirl around them. Did Paul write Hebrews, or was it someone else? Does James contradict Paul on the role of faith and works? Was 2 Peter genuinely Petrine, given its dramatically different style and contents from 1 Peter? Were 2 and 3 John and Jude long enough and significant enough to merit inclusion? And just how was Revelation to be interpreted anyway?

Despite these questions, each of these seven books was eventually accepted. The late second-century Muratorian canon lists twenty-one books; early in the third century, Tertullian noted twenty-two. About the same time, Origen mentions all twenty-seven, but observes that six are disputed. Eusebius, in the early fourth century, also lists all twenty-seven and quotes Origen's references to doubts over certain ones.

At the same time, a handful of additional documents were occasionally proposed for acceptance as on a par with the other twenty-seven. The generally orthodox *Shepherd of Hermas* and *Epistle of Barnabas* were the two most frequently suggested, though not nearly as often as even the disputed books of the twenty-seven. The church eventually rejected the *Epistle of Barnabas*, in part because of its anti-Semitic content. Both letters, moreover, reflected second-century writings from the collection of works known as the Apostolic Fathers that elsewhere seemed to be conscious of originating from a later date and with lesser authority than the first-century documents that now constitute our New Testament.

Indeed, three criteria prevailed for sifting the canonical from the noncanonical. First and foremost was *apostolicity*—authorship by an apostle or a close associate of an apostle—which thus, for all practical purposes, limited the works to the first hundred years or so of Christian history. Second was *orthodoxy* or noncontradiction with previously revealed Scripture, beginning with the Hebrew Scriptures that Christians came to call the Old Testament. Finally, the early church used the criterion of *catholicity*—universal (or at least extremely widespread) usage and relevance throughout the church. This excluded, for example, the Gnostic writings, which were accepted only in the sects from which they emanated.[3]

Modern historical revisionists often use language like that of "suppression" or "censorship" to speak of the emerging Eastern Orthodox and Roman Catholic approach to extracanonical documents, as if there once was a time when some group of so-called Christians somewhere had agreed on a larger canon only to have the majority of believers whittle their canon down. Nothing could be further from the truth. The canon gradually grew up from smaller collections. It is possible that some Gnostic sect somewhere put forward some of their unique documents as on a par with Scripture, but if so, that evidence has been lost. What remains suggests that although they played a special role in the communities of those who created them, the Gnostic literature was never put forward for formal inclusion in a finalized canon of the New Testament.[4]

While Catholics and Protestants to this day disagree on the canon of the Old Testament, both branches of Christianity, along with Eastern Orthodoxy, agree on the contents of the New. For sixteen centuries there has been no significant controversy within Christianity regarding the extent of the New Testament canon. Christians are on solid ground in affirming that these twenty-seven books belong in the New Testament and that other ancient writings were excluded for good reason.

48

What Should We Think About the Coptic *Gospel of Thomas*?

Craig L. Blomberg

In the 1990s, the well-known Jesus Seminar voted on the authenticity of all of the sayings and deeds ascribed to Jesus in the *five* Gospels—Matthew, Mark, Luke, John *and Thomas*. In the church known as the Unity School of Christianity, Sunday morning Gospel lessons are sometimes taken from the *Gospel of Thomas*. And in her best seller *Beyond Belief*, Elaine Pagels rejects orthodox Christianity in favor of the more attractive religion she thinks she finds in this noncanonical Gospel.[1] Just what is the *Gospel of Thomas*, and why is it so heralded in certain circles these days?

To begin with, we must distinguish the Coptic *Gospel of Thomas*, which features in our three introductory examples, from a third-century apocryphal work often called the *Infancy Gospel of Thomas*, which contains fanciful miracles attributed to Jesus, the "boy wonder." The Coptic *Thomas* forms part of the Nag Hammadi library, a collection of scrolls found at a site by that name near Chenoboskion, Egypt, just after World War II. This "library" contains primarily, though not exclusively, Gnostic works written in Coptic, the language of ancient Egypt and parts of Ethiopia.

Gnosticism is a hybrid religion or philosophy that began with Plato's radical dualism, sharply differentiating between the material and immaterial worlds and finding only the latter redeemable. It mixed in a few Jewish concepts, quite a few Christian ones, and a pinch of additional Greek philosophy. The result was a worldview, represented by a variety of sects with varying beliefs, centered on the conviction that the creation of this universe was an act of rebellion by a lesser "god" (more technically, an "emanation" from the original Godhead). Redemption involves recognizing the spark of divinity that lies (or may lie) within one and fanning it into flame through secret "knowledge" (Greek, *gnōsis*). Because matter was inherently evil, most Gnostics became ascetics, but a few opted for hedonism. Almost all readily accepted the deity of Jesus (though they understood his deity in terms of their Greek philosophy) but balked at the notion of his humanity. They could not see how God could become truly human since they believed this would make him evil. Jesus redeemed people, therefore, not by dying a substitutionary death as a fully human being but by appearing to be human and revealing the truth about the nature of humanity and the universe that enables the elite who accept the truth to transcend this evil world.

Most of the Nag Hammadi texts that are called Gospels are little more than extensive dialogues supposedly between Jesus and various followers, primarily in secret settings after the resurrection, with language and concepts that bear little resemblance to the New Testament. Most of these documents do not predate the third century AD. But *Thomas* is different. It is made up of 114 consecutive sayings of Jesus, more than half of them introduced with nothing more than, "Jesus said . . ." Although the rest of the sayings come with brief indications of a setting, topic, or dialogue partner, only periodically do even two or three consecutive passages clearly belong together. Most of the document resembles what one finds, in part, in other Jewish or Greco-Roman sources—epitomes of the "best" of the teachings of a famous rabbi or philosopher as recalled by one or more of his followers.

The existing Coptic *Thomas* is fourth or fifth century in origin, but fragments of a Greek document discovered in the late 1800s at another Egyptian location called Oxyrhynchus and dating to the second century have turned out to represent portions of an older edition of *Thomas*. *Thomas* is therefore the oldest known noncanonical "Gospel" that has survived in any ancient language except perhaps for a few tiny fragments of one or two other documents.

Thomas differs from the other noncanonical Gospels also in that almost half of his sayings find at least a partial parallel somewhere in Matthew, Mark, Luke, or John. *Thomas* 34, for example, declares, "Jesus said, 'If a blind man leads a blind man, they will both fall into a pit'" (cf. Matt. 15:14).[2] Saying 44 reads, "Whoever blasphemes against the Father will be forgiven, and whoever blasphemes against the Son will be forgiven, but whoever blasphemes against the Holy Spirit will not be forgiven either on earth or in heaven" (cf. Mark 3:28–29). And *Thomas* 48 announces, "If you make peace with each other in this one house, they will say to the mountain, 'Move away,' and it will move away" (cf. Mark 11:23).

Almost a third of *Thomas*'s sayings are fairly clearly Gnostic in origin. Thus saying 3b states, "The Kingdom is inside of you, and it is outside of you. When you come to know yourselves, then you will become known, and you will realize that it is you who are the sons of the living Father. But if you will not know yourselves, you dwell in poverty and it is you who are that poverty." Again, *Thomas* 29 proclaims, "If the flesh came into being because of spirit, it is a wonder. But if spirit came into being because of the body, it is a wonder of wonders. Indeed, I am amazed at how this great wealth has made its home in this poverty." In other words, it is amazing that the corruptible could come from the incorruptible, but it would be even more amazing if it were the other way around.

The rest of *Thomas*'s teachings are neither demonstrably orthodox nor necessarily Gnostic. Most are ambiguous enough that they could be taken in a variety of ways. Take, for example, the shortest of the sayings in this document (saying 42): "Become passers-by." Does this mean that one should treat this fallen world as if one were just a visitor passing by it? The Jesus of the New Testament *could* have taught that. Or does it deal with the material universe as something from which people should long to *free* themselves? Now the saying becomes Gnostic. Or consider saying 56: "Whoever has come to understand the world has found (only) a corpse, and whoever has found a corpse is superior to the world." Does this mean that if people worship the fallen world system they will die, while those who recognize that they will die (and avoid serving mammon) will escape from sin? Jesus could have taught that. Or, contrary to Christian thought, does it mean that whoever clings to the material *body* holds on only to that which will die but that at least this is better than trying to hold on to the whole material *world*? Or does it mean something different altogether?

This third category of sayings has particularly intrigued scholars. Might some of the more orthodox-sounding teachings reflect genuine sayings of Jesus not preserved elsewhere? Some of *Thomas*'s sayings that have the ring of the historical Jesus include saying 98—a parable: "The Kingdom of the Father is like a certain man who wanted to kill a powerful man. In his own house he drew his sword and stuck it into the wall in order to find out whether his hand could carry through. Then he slew the powerful man." One thinks especially of the parables of the tower builder and king going to war in Luke 14:28–32. Or consider saying 82: "He who is near Me is near the fire, and he who is far from Me is far from the Kingdom." Even the Jesus Seminar, though, did not place much stock in *Thomas*'s unparalleled sayings.

The only ones they were particularly impressed with were paralleled texts, particularly parables, which appear shorter and less allegorical in *Thomas*. If length and detail are signs of developing tradition, then the Synoptic accounts must come later than *Thomas*, which may thus be dated to the mid-*first* century. But in fact the continuing oral tradition of Jesus's teachings abbreviated and eliminated allegorical elements more often than it added them, so at best these criteria prove inconclusive. Nicholas Perrin, moreover, has made a compelling case for the view that *Thomas* originated in Syriac, in dependence on the earliest known harmonization of the four canonical Gospels, Tatian's *Diatessaron* (circa 180). By translating the existing Coptic into Syriac, Perrin is able to demonstrate that the reason for *Thomas*'s seemingly random sequence of sayings is that each is linked to the next often only by one or more "catchwords"—a pattern that is observable only about half of the time in the Coptic and Greek versions of this Gospel.[3]

Thomas, or Gnosticism more generally, can at first glance appear more "enlightened" from a modern (or postmodern) perspective than parts of the New Testament. But if one is going to accept a Gnostic worldview, one has to take all of it. And the final saying of this enigmatic Gospel has Peter telling Jesus and the other disciples, "Let Mary leave us, for women are not worthy of life." Jesus replies, "I myself shall lead her in order to make her male, so that she too may become a living spirit resembling you males. For every woman who will make herself male will enter the Kingdom of Heaven." Modern appropriations of *Thomas* seldom incorporate this perspective! Indeed, *Thomas* can appear superior to the canonical Gospels only by highly selective usage of its teachings. Despite what some may claim, it does not open any significant window into first-century Christian history and origins, only into its later corruption.[4]

49

What Should We Think About the *Gospel of Peter*?

Charles L. Quarles

Skeptics frequently allege that the true story of the real Jesus appears not in the four New Testament Gospels but in other "lost Gospels," which were suppressed by the early church. One of these allegedly superior sources is the *Gospel of Peter*. This article will summarize the contents of the *Gospel of Peter*, discuss the implications of affirming the reliability of the document, and present compelling evidence that the *Gospel of Peter* is later and less reliable than the four New Testament Gospels.

The so-called *Gospel of Peter* is discussed by Eusebius of Caesarea in his *Ecclesiastical History* 3.3.1–4 (early fourth century). Eusebius indicates that the document had been a topic of debate in the church at Rhossus.[1] Although the bishop of Antioch, Serapion, had initially approved the document for reading in the church of Rhossus, upon more careful examination of its contents he rejected the work. In a letter to the church, Serapion noted that while the document was generally in accord with the New Testament Gospels, the Docetists had added some elements in support of their false teaching. Serapion wrote about the *Gospel of Peter* in approximately AD 200, and his discussion, which is preserved by Eusebius, constitutes the earliest extant reference to the work.

Until the late 1800s, nothing was known of this mysterious gospel apart from the brief mentions by Serapion and Eusebius, and one by Origen (early third century).[2] However, in excavations at Akhmim, Egypt, in 1886–87, archaeologists discovered a fragment of a Gospel in the coffin of a Christian monk. The Greek fragment consisted of some sixty verses and dated to the eighth or ninth century. Because the final verse of the fragment identifies Simon Peter as the author, most scholars have concluded that this fragment is a portion of the long lost *Gospel of Peter*.

Scholars are not sure of the length of the original document. The fragment begins with an allusion to Pilate's handwashing at the end of Jesus's trial and breaks off at the beginning of a description of an appearance of the resurrected Jesus to his disciples. This portion of the document was apparently all that was available to the scribe responsible for copying it since ornaments at the beginning and end of his manuscript indicate that the manuscript is complete. This ancient scribe copied all of the gospel that was available to him. On the other hand, Origen claimed that the tradition that Mary's husband Joseph had children by a previous marriage was preserved either in the *Gospel of Peter* or the book of James. This may imply that the *Gospel of Peter* was much more extensive and included a narrative of Jesus's birth. However, Origen's statement may not be helpful in determining the original extent of the document since he seems uncertain about the contents of the *Gospel of Peter* and since the reference appeared in the alternative source mentioned by Origen, the protevangelium of James. At the very least, the original Gospel would have contained an account of Jesus's trial, crucifixion, resurrection, and at least two postresurrection appearances to his disciples.

In its present form, the so-called *Gospel of Peter* begins as the trial of Jesus ends. After Pilate washes his hands in display of his innocence in Jesus's unjust trial, Joseph of Arimathea asks permission to bury Jesus's body. In this gospel, the Jews fill the role assigned to the Roman soldiers in the New Testament Gospels by mocking, spitting on, striking, and scourging Jesus. The author of the gospel also claims that the Jews were directly responsible for nailing Jesus to the cross, inscribing the *titulus* that adorned the cross and dividing Jesus's garments. The Jews refuse to break Jesus's legs and hasten his death in hopes of prolonging his agony and intensifying his tortures. The account emphasizes the guilt of the Jews by saying, "They fulfilled all things and completed the measure of their sins on their head" (17), and, "Then the Jews and the elders and the priests recognized what great evil they had done to themselves and began to grieve and to say 'Woe on our sins, the judgment and end of Jerusalem is near'" (25).

Several miracles occur around the time of Jesus's death and these drive many of the Jews to repent of their role in Jesus's crucifixion. At the moment of Jesus's death, the veil in the temple is torn in two. Later, when Jesus's corpse is removed from the cross and touches the ground, an earthquake occurs. Repentant Jews frighten the scribes, Pharisees, and elders by declaring that Jesus was innocent. The Jewish leaders ask Pilate to authorize a Roman guard to ensure that Jesus's disciples do not steal the body and stage Jesus's resurrection. Pilate sends a Roman *custodia* to guard the tomb. The guard is accompanied by scribes and elders. The group rolls a stone over the tomb, seals it with seven seals, sets up camp at the tomb entrance, and begins to keep watch. Early in the morning on the Lord's Day, the heavens open and two men surrounded by a bright light descend to the tomb. The stone sealing the entrance rolls aside all by itself. The men step in to escort Jesus out of the tomb. When they exit the tomb, the men from heaven are so tall that their heads bump the sky, but the resurrected Jesus is so tall that his head reaches the heavens. A cross floats out of the tomb behind them. A voice from heaven asks, "Did you preach to those who sleep?" The cross replies, "Yes."

The soldiers report the events to Pilate, but at the request of the Jewish leaders, he commands the soldiers to say nothing about the events to anyone. Early in the morning Mary Magdalene goes to the tomb and sees a young man in a shining robe sitting in the tomb, who announces that Jesus has risen. In the next pericope Peter, Andrew, and Levi leave the other grieving members of the Twelve to go to the sea and fish. Unfortunately, the text breaks off no sooner than the story is introduced.

John Dominic Crossan, cofounder of the Jesus Seminar, which is an organization residing on the theological left, has claimed that the *Gospel of Peter* was the product of a complex evolution. The earliest layer of the gospel was a hypothetical source called the "Cross Gospel." Crossan argues that this early layer served as the only written source for the narrative of Jesus's death and resurrection in Matthew, Mark, Luke, and John. After the production of the New Testament Gospels, a later editor inserted material from the four Gospels into the Cross Gospel. An even later editor noticed tensions between the original and newer material in this patchwork gospel and polished up the document.

Although Crossan's theory has convinced few in the scholarly community, one scholar recently claimed, "One can expect that all future research on Gos. Pet. will need to begin with a serious consideration of Crossan's work."[3] If true, Crossan's theory would have a devastating effect on confidence in the historical reliability of the accounts of Jesus's death and resurrection in the four Gospels. According to Crossan's theory, the sole source for the accounts of Jesus's death, burial, and resurrection in the four Gospels was a document that was already so laced with legend as to be wholly unreliable even before it reached the hands of Matthew, Mark, Luke, and John. The four Gospels would be unreliable adaptations of an unreliable tradition replete with a talking floating cross and a super-sized Jesus whose head bumps the heavens when he walks out of the tomb!

Despite Crossan's daring claim, the evidence for his theory is very slim. An impressive number of clues suggest that this gospel postdates even the latest New Testament book and belongs to the mid-second century. First, a close analysis of verbal parallels shared by the *Gospel of Peter* and the Gospel of Matthew suggests that the *Gospel of Peter* postdates Matthew and utilized that Gospel as a source. An example of these parallels is the account of the guard assigned to Jesus's tomb. Of the four canonical Gospels, only Matthew shares with the *Gospel of Peter* an account of this event. Both the account in Matthew and the *Gospel of Peter* refer to the Pharisees' gathering before Pilate to express concern about a staged resurrection on the third day. Both accounts refer to the guarding and sealing of the tomb. Both describe the Jews as "the people." One sustained verbal parallel clearly indicates a definite literary dependence of one document on the other. Both Matthew 27:64 and *Gospel of Peter* 8:30 contain the precise words "lest his disciples come and steal him." Crossan argues that the parallel demonstrates Matthew's dependence on an early form of the *Gospel of Peter* (the Cross Gospel). However, an examination of the vocabulary, grammar, and style of the two documents strongly favors the dependence of the *Gospel of Peter* on Matthew. Robert Gundry, one of the most respected experts on issues related to Matthew's style, calls the phrase a "series of Mattheanisms."[4] Similarly, John Meier notes, "When it comes to who is dependent on whom, all the signs point to Matthew's priority. . . . The clause is a tissue of Matthean vocabulary and style, a vocabulary and style almost totally absent from the rest of the *Gospel of Peter*."[5] This is consistent with a number of other Matthean features that appear in the *Gospel of Peter*, which all point to the dependence of the *Gospel of Peter* on Matthew.

Second, other features of the *Gospel of Peter* suggest that the gospel not only postdates Matthew but even postdates the latest book of the New Testament canon, the book of Revelation. For example, although Matthew indicates that the Roman guard seals the tomb of Jesus, *Gospel of Peter* 8:33 adds that it is sealed with seven seals. The reference to the seven seals conflicts with the immediate context. *Gospel of Peter* 8:32–33 states that all the witnesses present seal the tomb. However, a minimum of nine witnesses are present, leading readers to expect at least nine seals. The best explanation for the awkward reference to the seven seals is that the detail was drawn from Revelation 5:1. This allusion to Revelation fits well with the *Gospel of Peter* 9:35 and 12:50 reference to the day of Jesus's resurrection as the "Lord's Day" since this terminology only appears in Revelation in the New Testament, and first in Revelation out of all ancient Christian literature. The reference to the "Lord's Day" in the *Gospel of Peter* is a shortened form that appears to be a later development from the original form appearing in Revelation.

Still other features of the *Gospel of Peter* fit best with the historical data if the *Gospel of Peter* was produced in the mid-second century. The *Gospel of Peter* assumes the doctrine of Jesus's descent into Hades to preach to the dead. However, this doctrine first appears in the words of Justin Martyr around AD 150. The talking cross is a feature of other second-century literature. The *Epistula Apostolorum* 16 states that during the second coming Jesus will be carried on the wings of the clouds with his cross going on before him. Similarly, the Ethiopic *Apocalypse of Peter* 1 describes the returning Christ as coming in a glory seven times as bright as the sun and with his cross going before his face. In a similar fashion, beginning in the late first century, Christian texts describe Christ as possessing gigantic stature. In an allegorical depiction of Jesus's supremacy and authority over the church, the *Shepherd of Hermas* 83.1 described Christ as of such lofty stature that he stands taller than a tower. 4 Ezra 2:43, dating to the middle or late third century, refers to the unusual height of the Son of God. These shared compositional strategies and features make the most sense if these documents and the *Gospel of Peter* were composed in the same milieu.

This evidence confirms the traditional Christian claim that the four New Testament Gospels are the most reliable accounts of Jesus's trial, death, burial, and resurrection. The accounts of crucifixion and resurrection in the four Gospels are based on eyewitness testimony rather than naive dependence on an unreliable source like the alleged Cross Gospel. The *Gospel of Peter* (and the so-called Cross Gospel) is clearly later than the New Testament Gospels and is sprinkled throughout with imaginative elements and traces of legend. Although the *Gospel of Peter* is helpful for understanding the thought of some sectors of the church in the mid-second century, it is of little value for understanding the details of Jesus's final days on earth.[6]

50

What Should We Think About the *Gospel of Judas*?

Craig A. Evans

On Thursday, April 6, 2006, the National Geographic Society held a press conference at its Washington, DC, headquarters and announced to some 120 news media the recovery, restoration, and translation of the *Gospel of Judas*. The story appeared as headline news in dozens of major newspapers around the world and was the topic of discussion in a variety of news programs on television that evening and subsequent evenings. A two-hour documentary aired on the National Geographic Channel Sunday evening, April 9, and has aired several times since.

What is the *Gospel of Judas*? Why all the fuss, and what should Christians and others think about it?

The Discovery of the *Gospel of Judas*

As best as investigators can determine, a leather-bound codex (or ancient book), whose pages consist of papyrus, was discovered in the late 1970s, perhaps in 1978, in Egypt, perhaps in a cave. For the next five years the codex, written in the Coptic language,[1] was passed around the Egyptian antiquities market. In 1983 Stephen Emmel, a Coptic scholar, acting on behalf of James Robinson, formerly of Claremont Graduate University and well known for his work on the similar Nag Hammadi codices, examined the recently discovered codex in Geneva. Emmel was able to identify four tractates, including one that frequently mentioned Judas in conversation with Jesus. He concluded that the codex was genuine (i.e., not a forgery) and that it probably dated to the fourth century. Subsequent scientific tests confirmed Emmel's educated guess.

The seller was unable to obtain his asking price. After that the codex journeyed to the United States, where it ended up in a safe-deposit box in Long Island, New York, and suffered serious deterioration. Another dealer placed it in a deep freezer, mistakenly thinking that the extreme cold would protect the codex from damaging humidity. Unfortunately, the codex suffered badly, with the papyrus turning dark brown and becoming brittle.

Happily, the codex was eventually acquired by the Maecenas Foundation in Switzerland and, with the assistance of the National Geographic Society, was recovered and partially restored. I say "partially restored" because an unknown number of pages are missing (perhaps more than forty) and only about 85 percent of the much-talked-about *Gospel of Judas* has been reconstructed.

The National Geographic Society wisely commissioned a series of tests to be undertaken, including carbon 14, analysis of the ink, and various forms of imaging, to ascertain the age and authenticity of the codex. Carbon 14 dates the codex to AD 220–340. At the present time most of the members of the team incline to a date between 300 and 320 (but Emmel thinks a bit later).

In 2005, the Society assembled a team of biblical scholars to assist with the interpretation of the *Gospel of Judas*. Most of them were present at the aforementioned press conference and made statements.[2]

The Publication of the *Gospel of Judas*

An English translation of the *Gospel of Judas* has been published by the National Geographic Society in an attractive volume edited by Rodolphe Kasser, Marvin Meyer, and Gregor Wurst.[3] This volume includes very helpful introductory essays by the editors and translators, explaining the condition of the codex and the relationship of the *Gospel of Judas* to early Christian literature, including other Gnostic texts.

The *Gospel of Judas* is found on pages 33–58 of Codex Tchacos, but there are three other tractates (or writings): Pages 1–9 preserve a version of the *Letter of Peter to Philip*, which is approximately the same text as the second tractate of Nag Hammadi's codex 8. Pages 10–32 preserve a book of *James*, which approximates the third tractate of Nag Hammadi's codex 5, which there is entitled the *First Apocalypse of James*. Pages 59–66 preserve an untitled work, in which the figure Allogenes ("Stranger") appears. This tractate, which is quite fragmentary, does not appear to be related to the third tractate of Nag Hammadi's codex 11, which is titled *Allogenes*. And finally, a fragment not related to these four tractates has surfaced very recently, on which may appear the page number "108." If so, then we may infer that at least 42 pages of Codex Tchacos are missing.

The *Gospel of Judas* and Judas as "Hero"

The *Gospel of Judas* begins with these words: "The secret account of the revelation that Jesus spoke in conversation with Judas Iscariot" (page 33, lines 1–3). The tractate concludes with the words: "The Gospel of Judas" (page 58, lines 28–29). These lines are stunning enough, but what happens in between is what has given rise to most of the controversy—the idea that Judas is a hero of sorts. In what follows I will summarize the message of the *Gospel of Judas*, as understood in the first edition published by National Geographic.

Judas Iscariot is singled out as Jesus's greatest disciple. He alone is able to receive Jesus's most profound teaching and revelation. Jesus laughs at the other disciples' prayers and sacrifices. They do not fully grasp who Jesus really is and from whom and from where he has come. But Judas is able to stand before Jesus (page 35, lines 8–9). "I know who you are and from where you have come. You are from the immortal realm of Barbelo. And I am not worthy to utter the name of the one who has sent you" (page 35, lines 15–21). After this confession Jesus teaches Judas in private.

At the conclusion of this private teaching, in which Judas is invited to enter the cloud (and be transformed?), Jesus utters his most startling instruction: "You will exceed them all. For you will sacrifice the man who clothes me" (page 56, lines 18–20). That is, while the other disciples are wasting time in inferior worship and activity (sacrificing animals in the Jewish fashion, presumably), Judas will carry out the sacrifice that truly counts, the sacrifice that will result in salvation: he will sacrifice the physical body of Jesus, thus allowing Jesus to complete his mission. In this way, Judas does indeed become the greatest of the disciples.

Accordingly, the narrative concludes with the handing over of Jesus to the ruling priests: "The ruling priests murmured because he [Jesus] had gone into the guest room to pray. But some scribes were there watching carefully, in order to arrest him during the prayer, for they were afraid of the people, for Jesus was regarded by all as a prophet. They approached Judas and said to him, 'What are you doing here? You are the disciple of Jesus.' Judas answered them as they wished; and Judas received some money and handed him [Jesus] over to them" (page 58, lines 9–26).[4] There is no mention of a trial, execution, or resurrection. The *Gospel of Judas* seems to teach that Judas has assisted Jesus in fulfilling his salvific mission.

Is this what the *Gospel of Judas* really teaches? We will turn to this question later.

The Real Meaning of the *Gospel of Judas*

Writing in AD 180 Irenaeus inveighs against a group he and others call the Cainites, evidently because this group makes heroes out of biblical villains, from Cain, who murdered his brother Abel, to Judas, who handed Jesus to his enemies. Irenaeus has this to say:

> Others again declare that Cain derived his being from the Power above, and acknowledge that Esau, Korah, the Sodomites, and all such persons, are related to themselves. On this account, they add, they have been assailed by the Creator, yet no one of them has suffered injury. For Sophia was in the habit of carrying off that which belonged to her from them to herself. They declare that Judas the traitor was thoroughly acquainted with these things, and that he alone, knowing the truth as no others did, accomplished the mystery of the betrayal; by him all things, both earthly and heavenly, were thus thrown into confusion. They produce a fictitious history of this kind, which they style the *Gospel of Judas*.[5]

In other words, the so-called Cainites identify with the villains of the Old Testament. They do this because they believe that the god of this world, in stark contrast to the God of Light above, is evil. Accordingly anyone that the god of this world hates and tries to destroy—such as Cain, Esau, or the people of Sodom—must be good people, people on the side of the God of Light. The *Gospel of Judas* evidently shares this perspective.

The *Gospel of Judas* seems to be a very early exemplar of Sethian Gnosticism, a form of Gnosticism that may have roots in Jewish pessimism that emerged in the aftermath of the disastrous wars in AD 66–70 and 115–117.[6]

Media hype notwithstanding, it is highly unlikely that the *Gospel of Judas* preserves for us authentic, independent material, material that supplements our knowledge of Judas and his relationship to Jesus. No doubt some popular writers will produce some fanciful stories about the "true story," but that is all that they will produce—fanciful stories. Father Donald Senior, a Roman Catholic New Testament scholar, stated at the press conference that in his opinion the *Gospel of Judas* will have no impact on Christian theology or on Christian understanding of the Gospel story. Other scholars have expressed similar opinions.[7]

Months after the publication of the *Gospel of Judas* a number of scholars began to express serious reservations about the reconstruction, translation, and interpretation offered by Kasser, Meyer, and Wurst. The scholars raising these concerns were not clergy and laity, but scholars with expertise in Coptic Gnostic texts. These scholars include, among others, April DeConick, Louis Painchaud, Birger Pearson, and John Turner, all of whom observed doubtful reconstructions, inaccurate translations, and highly questionable interpretations.[8] DeConick was the first to publish a full-length treatment, in which these errors are clearly and systematically identified.[9]

The most significant errors include these: (1) They translate the word *daimon* as "spirit," instead of "demon," as it is normally understood in Jewish and Christian texts. In the translation by Meyer and colleagues, Jesus calls Judas the "thirteenth spirit," implying something positive. But Jesus really calls Judas the "thirteenth demon," something that is not positive. (2) Meyer and colleagues translate the text to say that Judas has been "set apart for" the holy generation, something for which all true spiritual people aspire. However, the text should be translated "separated from," that is, Judas will not gain access to the holy generation. (3) Meyer and colleagues translate the text to say that Judas will ascend to the holy generation, but the text in fact says that Judas will not ascend. (4) Meyer and colleagues translate the text to say that Judas will exceed the other disciples in sacrificing the human being whose body Jesus inhabits. The implication is that Judas's action is positive. However, the text really means that Judas is worse than the other disciples. Whereas they sacrifice animals in the Jewish fashion, Judas will sacrifice a human being, thus exceeding them in folly.

These errors, as well as a few others, distort the true meaning of the *Gospel of Judas*. A new edition and retranslation has been undertaken.

Conclusion

When the *Gospel of Judas* is properly translated and interpreted we do not find in Judas Iscariot a hero, the wisest of the disciples, who assists Jesus and then enters glory. On the contrary, Judas is a tragic figure in a dramatic retelling and reinterpretation of the Passion of Jesus, a retelling that is marked by anti-Semitism and a mockery of the apostolic Church. The disciples have failed to understand who Jesus really is. Even the one who came closest to this truth—Judas Iscariot—in the end was the worst of a bad lot, sacrificing a human being to the rulers of this fallen earth. He, like the other disciples, will not escape the corrupt world of darkness that will eventually be destroyed.

However the *Gospel of Judas* is interpreted, all scholars agree that this second-century writing provides us with no genuine information about the historical Jesus and his tragic disciple who for whatever reasons decided to betray him. The *Gospel of Judas* is second-century fiction, not first-century history.

Notes

Introduction

1. Gary A. Tobin and Aryeh K. Weinberg, "Religious Beliefs and Behavior of College Faculty," in *Profiles of the American University* (Roseville, CA: Institute for Jewish and Community Research, 2007), 73, 76–77.

2. Ibid., 86.

Chapter 1 The Cosmological Argument

1. Thomas Aquinas *Summa contra gentiles* 15.124.

Chapter 2 The Moral Argument for God's Existence

1. John Rist, *Real Ethics* (Cambridge: Cambridge University Press, 2003), 1.

2. See Paul Copan, "Is Michael Martin a Moral Realist? *Sic et Non*," *Philosophia Christi* 1, no. 2 (1999): 45–72; idem, "Atheistic Goodness Revisited: A Personal Reply to Michael Martin," *Philosophia Christi* 2, no. 1 (2000): 91–104; "The Moral Argument," in *The Rationality of Theism*, ed. Paul Copan and Paul K. Moser (London: Routledge, 2003), 149–74; "A Moral Argument," in *To Everyone an Answer: A Case for the Christian Worldview: Essays in Honor of Norman L. Geisler*, ed. Francis Beckwith, William Lane Craig, and J. P. Moreland (Downers Grove, IL: InterVarsity, 2004), 108–23; "Morality and Meaning Without God: Another Failed Attempt," *Philosophia Christi* 6, no. 1 (2004): 295–304; "God, Hume, and Objective Morality," in *In Defense of Natural Theology: A Collection of New Essays in the Philosophy of Religion*, ed. Douglas R. Groothuis and James R. Sennett (Downers Grove, IL: InterVarsity, 2005), 200–225.

3. C. S. Lewis, *The Abolition of Man* (1944; repr., San Francisco: HarperSanFrancisco, 2001).

4. Kai Nielsen, *Ethics Without God* (Amherst, NY: Prometheus Books, 1990), 10–11.

5. Michael Ruse, *The Darwinian Paradigm* (London: Routledge, 1989), 262.

6. Charles Darwin, "Letter to Wm. G. Down (3 July 1881)," in *The Life and Letters of Charles Darwin*, ed. Francis Darwin (London: John Murray, 1887), 1:315–16.

7. "Jeffrey Dahmer: The Monster Within," *Biography*, A&E, 1996.

8. J. L. Mackie, *The Miracle of Theism* (Oxford: Clarendon, 1982), 115–16.

9. In Greg Ganssle, "Necessary Moral Truths," *Philosophia Christi* 2, no. 1 (2000): 111.

Chapter 3 Near Death Experiences

1. These details and quotations are taken from two volumes by Melvin Morse (with Paul Perry), *Closer to the Light: Learning from the Near-Death Experiences of Children* (New York: Random House, 1990), 3–14; *Transformed by the Light: The Powerful Effect of Near-Death Experiences on People's Lives* (New York: Random House, 1992), 22–23.

2. For an excellent response here, see Michael Sabom, *Light and Death: One Doctor's Fascinating Account of Near-Death Experiences* (Grand Rapids: Zondervan, 1998), 213–14; cf. 104–41.

3. One fascinating example is Howard Storm, *My Descent into Death: A Second Chance at Life* (New York: Doubleday, 2005), esp. 14–23. Storm even recounts his conversion

from atheism to Christianity as a result of his near death experience (chapter 4).

4. Gary R. Habermas and J. P. Moreland, *Beyond Death: Exploring the Evidence for Immortality* (Wheaton: Crossway, 1998; repr., Eugene, OR: Wipf and Stock, 2003), chaps. 7–9.

Chapter 7 God, Suffering, and Santa Claus

1. Paul Davies, *God and the New Physics* (New York: Simon & Schuster, 1983), 189.

2. Karl Popper and John Eccles, *The Self and Its Brain* (New York: Springer-Verlag, 1977), 559–60.

3. G. K. Chesterton, *Orthodoxy* (1908; repr., New York: Doubleday, 1959), 52.

4. I should point out that, if the proponent of the argument from evil happens to be, say, a deist or an agnostic, my response would have to be modified. A deist does have an explanation for certain facts about the world (e.g., its existence and fine-tuning). A comparison of the explanatory power of deism and theism would therefore require a somewhat different analysis (and I suspect that it would come down to the evidence for miraculous events). An agnostic, by contrast, would say that he or she is free to reject theism without offering an alternative explanation, since he or she doesn't claim to know what caused the universe. However, while an agnostic is certainly free to reject theism, the purpose of the argument from evil is to show that theism is a poor explanation of things. Thus I think the same response would apply: if theists are to take the argument from evil seriously, the proponent of the argument needs to offer an alternative hypothesis that accounts for the facts about our world as well as theism does.

Chapter 9 The Pale Blue Dot Revisited

1. Carl Sagan, *Pale Blue Dot: A Vision of the Human Future in Space* (New York: Random House, 1994), 7.

2. Aristotle *De caelo* 2.14; Ptolemy *Almagest* 1.5.

3. Nicholas Copernicus *De revolutionibus* 1.6.

4. Galileo Galilei *Sidereus nuncius*, quoted in Dennis Danielson, ed., *The Book of the Cosmos: Imagining the Universe from Heraclitus to Hawking* (New York: Basic Books, 2000), 150.

5. Dennis Danielson, "The Great Copernican Cliché," *American Journal of Physics* 69 (October 2001): 1029–35.

6. Ibid., 1029.

Chapter 11 The Origin of Life

1. Antony Flew, interview, *ABC News*, ABC, December 9, 2004.

2. Nicholas Wade, "Life's Origins Get Murkier and Messier: Genetic Analysis Yields Intimations of a Primordial Commune," *New York Times*, June 13, 2000.

3. See Lila L. Gatlin, *Information Theory and the Living System* (New York: Columbia University Press, 1972).

Chapter 12 What Every High School Student Should Know about Science

1. See Stephen C. Meyer, "The Methodological Equivalence of Design and Descent: Can There Be a Scientific 'Theory of Creation'?" in *The Creation Hypothesis: Scientific Evidence for an Intelligent Designer*, ed. J. P. Moreland (Downers Grove, IL: InterVarsity, 1994), 67–112.

2. Jonathan Wells, "Definitions of Science in State Standards," Discovery Institute, November 10, 2005, http://www.discovery.org/a/2573.

3. Henry H. Bauer, *Scientific Literacy and the Myth of the Scientific Method* (Champaign, IL: University of Illinois Press, 1992).

4. Noel Swerdlow, *The Babylonian Theory of the Planets* (Princeton: Princeton University Press, 1998).

5. National Research Council, *National Science Education Standards: Observe, Interact, Change, Learn* (Washington, DC: National Academies Press, 1996), 201; emphasis added. Also available at http://www.nap.edu/readingroom/books/nses/6e.html.

6. Charles Darwin, *On the Origin of Species* (1859; Cambridge, MA: Harvard University Press, 1964), 2.

7. Stephen Meyer and Michael Keas, "The Meanings of Evolution," in *Darwinism, Design, and Public Education*, ed. John Angus Campbell and Stephen C. Meyer (East Lansing, MI: Michigan State University Press, 2003), 135–52.

8. National Research Council, *National Science Education Standards*, 2.

9. Ibid., 200.

Chapter 13 Darwin's Battleship

1. Phillip E. Johnson, *Darwin on Trial*, 2nd ed. (Downers Grove, IL: InterVarsity, 1993), 169.

Chapter 14 Debunking the Scopes "Monkey Trial" Stereotype

1. http://www.law.umkc.edu/faculty/projects/ftrials/scopes/statcase.htm.

2. Fred Hoyle, *The Mathematics of Evolution* (Memphis: Acorn Enterprises, 1999), 106.

3. George William Hunter, *A Civic Biology* (New York: American Book Company, 1914), 261–64.

4. Ibid.

5. Ibid.

6. Ibid.

Chapter 15 How Darwinism Dumbs Us Down

1. John Dewey, *The Influence of Darwin on Philosophy: And Other Essays in Contemporary Thought* (New York: Henry Holt, 1910), 9.

2. Edward Craig, *The Mind of God and the Works of Man* (Oxford: Clarendon, 1987).

3. William James, "What Pragmatism Means," in *Pragmatism: A New Name for Some Old Ways of Thinking* (1907; Amherst, NY: Prometheus, 1991), 36.

4. John Warwick Montgomery, "How Muslims Do Apologetics: The Apologetic Approach of Muhammad Ali and Its Implications for Christian Apologetics," in *Faith Founded on Fact: Essays in Evidential Apologetics* (Nashville: Thomas Nelson, 1978), available online at http://www.mtio.com/articles/bissar59.htm.

5. Ernst von Glasersfeld, *Radical Constructivism: A Way of Knowing and Learning* (New York: Routledge, 1996), 51.

6. Ibid.

7. Richard Rorty, *Truth and Progress* (Cambridge: Cambridge University Press, 1998), 48.

8. Michael Ruse, address given at the symposium "The New Antievolutionism" (Annual Meeting of the American Association for the Advancement of Science, Boston, February 13, 1993), http://www.arn.org/docs/orpages/or151/mr93tran.htm.

9. Arthur M. Shapiro, "Did Michael Ruse Give Away the Store?" *NCSE Reports* 3 (1993): 20–21.

Chapter 16 Limits to Evolvability

1. See Jonathan Wells, *Icons of Evolution: Science or Myth? Why Much of What We Teach about Evolution Is Wrong* (Washington, DC: Regnery), 137–57.

2. See Lane P. Lester and Raymond G. Bohlin, *The Natural Limits to Biological Change* (Grand Rapids: Zondervan, 1984), 103, 170.

3. Pierre-Paul Grassé, *Evolution of Living Organisms* (New York: Academic Press, 1977), 87.

4. Wallace Arthur, *The Origin of Animal Body Plans: A Study in Evolutionary Developmental Biology* (Cambridge: Cambridge University Press, 2000), 14.

5. Charles Darwin, *On the Origin of Species*, 471.

6. Susumo Ohno, "The Notion of the Cambrian Pananimalia Genome," *PNAS* 93 (1996): 8475–78.

7. Stephen Jay Gould, *Ever Since Darwin: Reflections in Natural History* (New York: W. W. Norton, 1977), 104.

Chapter 17 Evolutionary Computation

1. W. Ross Ashby, "Can a Mechanical Chess Player Outplay Its Designer?" *British Journal for the Philosophy of Science* 3.9 (1952): 44–57.

2. Nils Aall Barricelli, "Numerical Testing of Evolution Theories, Part I: Theoretical Introduction and Basic Tests," *Acta Biotheoretica* 16.1–2 (1962): 69–98. Reprinted in David B. Fogel, ed., *Evolutionary Computation: The Fossil Record* (Piscataway, NJ: IEEE Press, 1998), 166.

3. J. L. Crosby, "Computers In the Study Of Evolution," *Scientific Progress* 55 (1967): 279.

4. Randall Jean, personal communication, 2005.

5. Yu-Chi Ho, Q. C. Zhao, and D. Pepyne, "The No Free Lunch Theorem: Complexity and Computer Security," *IEEE Transactions on Automatic Control* 48.5 (May 2003): 783–93.

6. David H. Wolpert and William G. Macready, "No Free Lunch Theorems for Optimization," *IEEE Transactions on Evolutionary Computation* 1.1 (1997): 67–82.

7. Ho, Zhao, and Pepyne, "The No Free Lunch Theorem," 783–93.

8. Wolpert and Macready, "No Free Lunch Theorems."

Chapter 20 Intelligent Design

1. See my book *No Free Lunch: Why Specified Complexity Cannot Be Purchased without Intelligence* (Lanham, MD: Rowman & Littlefield, 2002).

Chapter 21 Intelligent, Optimal, and Divine Design

1. Francis Collins, interview by Brent Waters and Ron-Cole Turner, "Reading the Book of Life: Francis Collins and the Human Genome Project," *Science and Spirit*, January/February 2000, 14.

2. This short essay is an expanded and more carefully crafted version of a comment that I made to Dr. Mark Ptashne at the end of his lecture "On the Evolvability of Gene (and Other) Regulatory Systems" at the Nature of Nature Conference at the Michael Polanyi Center, Baylor University, April 12–15, 2000. I was prompted to make my remarks because I heard him, and others, consistently speak of intelligent design as though it were synonymous with optimal design, where *optimal* is defined in the sense of being the most efficient or elegant solution for the specific task at hand. Dr. Mark Ptashne is a researcher at the Memorial Sloan-Kettering Cancer Center.

Chapter 22 Molecular Biology's New Paradigm

1. "A Gene Map of the Human Genome," National Center for Biotechnology Information, http://www.ncbi.nlm.nih.gov/SCIENCE96.

2. Andy Coghlan, "Recount Slashes Number of Human Genes," *New Scientist*, October 20, 2004, http://www.newscientist.com/article.ns?id=dn6561.

3. Jonathan Hodgkin, "What Does a Worm Want with 20,000 Genes?" *Genome Biology* 2, no. 11, http://genomebiology.com/2001/2/11/comment/2008.

Chapter 23 Panning God

1. Quoted in Paul Nussbaum, "Evangelicals Divided Over Evolution," *Philadelphia Inquirer*, May 30, 2005.

2. Richard Dawkins, *The Blind Watchmaker: Why the Evidence of Evolution Reveals a Universe without Design* (New York: W. W. Norton, 1996), 93.

3. Lewis Theobald, *Shakespeare Restored* (London, 1726), 87.

4. Charles Giddon, quoted in Herbert Spencer Robinson, *English Shakespearian Criticism in the Eighteenth Century* (New York: H. W. Wilson, 1932), 26–27.

5. William Richardson and Edward Taylor, *Cursory Remarks on Tragedy, on Shakespeare, and on Certain French and Italian Poets* (London, 1774), 50, 42.

6. Robinson, *English Shakespearian Criticism*, xii.

Chapter 24 The Role of Agency in Science

1. Angus Menuge, "Dennet Denied: A Critique of Dennet's Evolutionary Account of Intentionality," *Progress in Complexity, Information, and Design* 2, no. 3 (October 2003), http://www.iscid.org/papers/Menuge_DennettDenied_103103.pdf.

Chapter 27 Did Jesus Really Exist?

1. *b. Sanh.* 43a.
2. Josephus *Jewish Antiquities* 20.200.
3. Josephus *Jewish Antiquities* 18.63.
4. Tacitus *Annals* 15.44.
5. Suetonius *Nero* 16.
6. Suetonius *Claudius* 25.
7. Pliny the Younger *Letter* 96.
8. Pliny the Younger *Letter* 97.

Chapter 28 The Credibility of Jesus's Miracles

1. See esp. Michael J. Behe, *Darwin's Black Box: The Biochemical Challenge to Evolution*, rev. ed. (New York: Free Press, 2006).

2. See Joseph Houston, *Reported Miracles: A Critique of Hume* (Cambridge: Cambridge University Press, 1994).

3. See especially J. Gresham Machen, *The Virgin Birth of Christ* (New York: Harper & Row, 1930; repr., London: James Clarke, 2000).

4. For full details, see Ronald H. Nash, *The Gospel and the Greeks: Did the New Testament Borrow from Pagan Thought?* rev. ed. (Phillipsburg, NJ: P&R, 2003).

5. See especially Graham H. Twelftree, *Jesus the Exorcist* (Peabody, MA: Hendrickson, 1991); *Jesus the Miracle Worker* (Downers Grove, IL: InterVarsity, 1999).

6. John P. Meier, *Mentor, Message, and Miracles*, vol. 2 of *A Marginal Jew: Rethinking the Historical Jesus* (New York: Doubleday, 1994), 630.

Chapter 30 The Son of God

1. Ben Witherington III, *The Many Faces of the Christ* (New York: Continuum, 2005).

Chapter 31 Jesus as God

1. Ben Witherington III, *Jesus the Seer* (Peabody, MA: Hendrickson, 2000).

Chapter 32 Did Jesus Predict His Violent Death and Resurrection?

1. Rudolf Bultmann, *The History of the Synoptic Tradition* (1921; repr., Oxford: Basil Blackwell, 1972), 152.

2. I invoke here the "criterion of embarrassment," whereby it is understood that it is improbable that the early church would have invented material that would become the source of its own embarrassment.

3. See *Testament of Moses* 9–10.

4. See my study "Did Jesus Predict His Death and Resurrection?" in Stanley E. Porter, Michael A. Hayes, and David Tombs, eds., *Resurrection*, JSNTSupp 186 (Sheffield: Sheffield Academic Press, 1999), 82–97; see also N. T. Wright, *The Resurrection of the Son of God* (Minneapolis: Fortress, 2003), 409–11.

5. See Dan. 12:1–3; 1 Enoch 22–27; 92–105; Jubilees 23:11–31; 4 Macc. 7:3; 4 Ezra 7:26–42; 2 Bar. 21:23; 30:2–5; Josephus *Jewish War* 2.8.11 §154; 2.8.14 §165–166; *Jewish Antiquities* 18.1.3–5 §14, §16, §18.

6. See 4Q521.

7. See J. W. van Henten, *The Maccabean Martyrs as Saviours of the Jewish People: A Study of 2 and 4 Maccabees*, JSJSupp 57 (Leiden: Brill, 1997). See also J. W. van Henten and F. Avemarie, *Martyrdom and Noble Death: Selected Texts from Graeco-Roman, Jewish and Christian Antiquity* (New York: Routledge, 2002).

8. James D. G. Dunn, *Jesus Remembered*, vol. 1 of *Christianity in the Making* (Grand Rapids: Eerdmans, 2003), 818–24.

Chapter 33 Can We Be Certain That Jesus Died on a Cross?

1. Josephus *Jewish War* 6.304. See also 2.612 and *Jewish Antiquities* 12.256.

2. Josephus *Jewish War* 2.612.

3. *Martyrdom of Polycarp* 2.2.

4. An overwhelming majority of ancient sources mention the use of nails in impaling the punished to a cross or tree. Since John's Gospel mentions the use of nails in Jesus's crucifixion (20:25, 27) and Luke implies it (24:39), no good reasons exist for thinking that Jesus was not nailed to his cross.

5. Seneca *Epistles* 101.

6. Josephus *The Life* 420–21.

7. A number of these are mentioned in Raymond Brown, *The Death of the Messiah* (New York: Doubleday, 1994), 2:1088.

8. Cicero *Orations* 12.12.27; *Gospel of Peter* 4:14. In the *Gospel of Peter*, breaking the legs is forbidden so that the crucified victim would suffer longer.

9. Dr. Jim Ritchie and Dr. Jack Mason.

10. Quintillian *Declamationes maiores* 11.9: "As for those who die on the cross, the executioner does not forbid the burying of those who have been pierced."

11. Josephus *Jewish War* 4.317.

12. John Dominic Crossan, *Jesus: A Revolutionary Biography* (San Francisco: HarperCollins, 1991), 145.

13. Gerd Lüdemann, *The Resurrection of Christ* (Amherst, NY: Prometheus Books, 2004), 50.

Chapter 34 The Empty Tomb of Jesus

1. Regarding the suggestion that Jesus was never buried in a tomb, see the nine criticisms listed in Gary R. Habermas, *The Historical Jesus: Ancient Evidence for the Life of Christ* (Joplin, MO: College Press, 1996), 127–29.

2. An excellent discussion of these issues is provided in Carolyn Osiek, "The Women at the Tomb: What Are They Doing There?" *Ex Auditu* 9 (1993): 97–107.

3. Justin Martyr *Dialogue with Trypho* 108; Tertullian *On Spectacles* 30.

4. Wright, *The Resurrection of the Son of God*, xix, 31, 71, 82–83, 201–6, 273, 314, 710.

5. Michael Grant, *Jesus: An Historian's Review of the Gospels* (New York: Macmillan, 1992), 176.

Chapter 35 The Resurrection Appearances of Jesus

1. For examples, see Acts 2:22–36; 3:12–23; Romans 1:3–4; 10:9.

2. See Gary R. Habermas and Michael R. Licona, *The Case for the Resurrection of Jesus* (Grand Rapids: Kregel, 2004), esp. 79–150; Gary R. Habermas, *The Risen Jesus and Future Hope* (Lanham, MD: Rowman & Littlefield, 2003), esp. chap. 1.

3. Commonly cited examples include Acts 1:21–22; 2:22–36; 3:13–16; 4:8–10; 5:29–32; 10:39–43; 13:28–31; 17:1–3, 30–31.

Chapter 36 Were the Resurrection Appearances of Jesus Hallucinations?

1. Gary R. Vandenbos, ed., *APA Dictionary of Psychology* (Washington, DC: American Psychological Association, 2007), 427.

2. See André Aleman and Frank Larøi, *Hallucinations: The Science of Idiosyncratic Perception* (Washington, DC: American Psychological Association, 2008).

3. Personal correspondence with the author, March 10, 2009.

Chapter 37 The Trinity

1. Cyril Richardson, ed., *Early Christian Fathers* (New York: Macmillan, 1970), 65.

2. Ibid., 70.

3. Ibid., 87–88.

4. Ibid., 90.

5. Ibid., 103.

6. Ibid., 285.

7. Ibid., 309.

8. Ibid., 326.

9. Ibid., 360.

10. Justo L. González, *A History of Christian Thought* (Nashville: Abingdon, 1970), 1:182–83.

11. Ibid., 226, 242.

12. *New World Translation of the Holy Scriptures* (New York: Watchtower Bible and Tract Society, 1984).

Chapter 39 Is Jesus the Only Way?

1. A. J. Levine, "Homeless in the Global Village," in *Moving beyond New Testament Theology? Essays in Conversation with Heikki Räisänen*, ed. T. C. Penner and C. V. Stichele (Helsinki: Finnish Exegetical Society/University of Helsinki, 2005), 195–96.

Chapter 41 Did Paul Invent Christianity?

1. See Alan Segal, *Paul the Convert* (New Haven: Yale University Press, 1992).

2. On all this see Ben Witherington III, *Grace in Galatia: A Commentary on Paul's Letter to the Galatians* (Grand Rapids: Eerdmans, 1995); and Ben Witherington III and Darlene Hyatt, *Paul's Letter to the Romans: A Socio-Rhetorical Commentary* (Grand Rapids: Eerdmans, 2004).

3. For a more detailed treatment, see Ben Witherington III, *The Paul Quest: The Renewed Quest for the Jew of Tarsus* (Downers Grove, IL: InterVarsity Press, 1998).

Chapter 43 Inerrancy and the Text of the New Testament

1. In recent years, the Evangelical Theological Society added a second doctrine that all members must also subscribe to: "God is a Trinity, Father, Son, and Holy Spirit, each an uncreated person, one in essence, equal in power and glory."

2. See B. B. Warfield, *The Inspiration and Authority of the Bible* (1948; repr., Philadelphia: P&R, 1970), 46: "Christians need not be worried about the fact that the autographa are lost." The reasons for this are given in n. 22 on the same page.

3. Darin M. Weil, "Inerrancy and Its Implications for Authority: Textual Critical Considerations in Formulating an Evangelical Doctrine of Scripture," *Quodlibet Journal* 4, no. 4 (November 2002): 1, also available at http://www.quodlibet.net/articles/weil-inerrancy.shtml.

Mr. Weil is an inerrantist and spends the rest of his essay addressing this and similar issues.

4. Paul J. Achtemeier, *The Inspiration of Scripture: Problems and Proposals* (Philadelphia: Westminster John Knox, 1998), 71–72.

5. Jack Finegan, *Encountering New Testament Manuscripts: A Working Introduction to Textual Criticism* (Grand Rapids: Eerdmans, 1974), 54.

6. This date and the relevance of this papyrus for dating John's Gospel have been recently disputed. See Brent Nongbri, "The Use and Abuse of 𝔓^{52}: Papyrological Pitfalls in the Dating of the Fourth Gospel," *Harvard Theological Review* 98, no. 1 (January 2005): 23–48. Nongbri concludes his article as follows(he brings in A. Schmidt's arguments for a later date. He also conducts a fairly detailed comparison between 𝔓^{52} and various other manuscripts):

> What emerges from this survey is nothing surprising to papyrologists: paleography is not the most effective method for dating texts, particularly those written in a literary hand. Roberts himself noted this point in his edition of 𝔓^{52}. The real problem is the way scholars of the New Testament have used and abused papyrological evidence. I have not radically revised Roberts's work. I have not provided any third-century documentary papyri that are absolute "dead ringers" for the handwriting of 𝔓^{52}, and even had I done so, that would not force us to date 𝔓^{52} at some exact point in the third century. Paleographic evidence does not work that way. What I have done is to show that any serious consideration of the window of possible dates for 𝔓^{52} must include dates in the later second and early third centuries. Thus, *𝔓^{52} cannot be used as evidence to silence other debates about the existence (or non-existence) of the Gospel of John in the first half of the second century*. Only a papyrus containing an explicit date or one found in a clear archaeological stratigraphic context could do the work scholars want 𝔓^{52} to do. As it stands now, the papyrological evidence should take a second place to other forms of evidence in addressing debates about the dating of the Fourth Gospel.

The thesis of the article is that the standard dating of 𝔓^{52} to AD 100–150 is disputable and thus the date of John's Gospel is again open to question. (To be sure, some scholars date it later than that, but they are in a distinct minority. C. H. Roberts, who discovered the fragment and who dated it c. 100–150, received confirmation of this date from Wilhelm Schubart and H. I. Bell [C. H. Roberts, ed., *An Unpublished Fragment of the Fourth Gospel in the John Rylands Library* (Manchester, UK: University of Manchester Press, 1935), 16; Ulrich Wilcken, "Die Bremer Papyrus Sammlung," *Forschungen und Fortschritte* 12 (1936): 90; and W. H. P. Hatch, *The Principal Uncial Manuscripts of the New Testament* (Chicago: University of Chicago Press, 1939), plate I]. Another scholar, Frederick Kenyon, thought its closest parallel was from a manuscript dated 153. Kurt Aland agreed with Roberts ["Zur Liste der neutestamentlichen Handschriften VI," *Zeitschrift für die neutestamentliche Wissenschaft* 48 (1957): 149; *Repertorium der griechischen christlichen Papyri I: Biblische Papyri: Altes Testament, Neues Testament, Varia, Apokryphen*, Patristische Texte und Studien 18 (Berlin: Walter de Gruyter, 1976)]. A. Deissmann thought it could be dated as early as the late first century ["Ein Evangelienblatt aus den Tagen Hadrians," *Deutsche allgemeine Zeitung* 564 (1935); see also the *Catalogue of Greek and Latin Papyri in the John Rylands Library 3* (Manchester: University of Manchester Press, 1938), 1–3, for citations of various scholars on the date of the fragment].) But that the long-held date of 𝔓^{52} can be so cavalierly put aside (by simply arguing for what is possible rather than by noting what is probable) seems to be a desperate measure, born out of a postmodern agenda: skepticism must reign over all matters related to the Scriptures. The prerequisites for a *certain* date that Nongbri suggests (explicit date on the manuscript or *in situ* discovery that places the fragment among other artifacts that can be dated) are of course well known. But short of certainty are many shades of probability. The author's statement that "paleography is not the most effective method for dating texts" seems to imply that a better method is available to us for this fragment. That is not the case, as Nongbri admits; indeed, he uses paleography to attempt to discredit the standard dating of this fragment! But he does not seem willing to grant the likelihood that 𝔓[52] brings a lot to the table concerning the date of John. His conclusion that the papyrus "*cannot be used as evidence*" for the date of John is certainly overdone. That the vast majority of New Testament manuscripts are dated strictly on paleographical bases, and that there are several other papyri of John from as early as the second century, suggests that Nongbri's skepticism is unwarranted.

7. That is, reconstructing the wording of the text without any manuscript support, a practice that is required for almost all other ancient literature. Kurt and Barbara Aland go so far as to say, "The principle that the original reading may be found in any single manuscript or version when it stands alone or nearly alone is only a theoretical possibility" (*The Text of the New Testament*, 2nd ed. [Grand Rapids: Eerdmans, 1989], 281), and "Textual difficulties should not be solved by conjecture, or by positing glosses or interpolations, etc., where the textual tradition itself shows no break; such attempts amount to capitulation before the difficulties and are themselves violations of the text" (ibid., 280). See also G. D. Kilpatrick, "Conjectural Emendation in the New Testament," *New Testament Textual Criticism*, ed. Eldon J. Epp and Gordon D. Fee (Oxford: Clarendon, 1981), 349–60. For a specific treatment on conjecture, in which the author rejects it outright, see David Allan Black, "Conjectural Emendations in the Gospel of Matthew," *Novum Testamentum* 31 (1989): 1–15. On the other hand, on rare occasions a New Testament scholar will put forth a conjecture. But such are not only few and far between; they are also a self-consciously uphill battle. See J. Strugnell, "A Plea for Conjectural Emendation in the New Testament," *Catholic Biblical Quarterly* 36 (1974): 543–58.

8. See D. A. Carson, *The King James Version Debate: A Plea for Realism* (Grand Rapids: Baker, 1979), 56, 65.

To be sure, not all New Testament scholars are of the same opinion. See especially Bart Ehrman, *The Orthodox Corruption of Scripture* (Oxford: Oxford University Press, 1996), as well as articles by K. W. Clark (e.g., "Textual Criticism and Doctrine," in *Studia Paulina: In Honorem Johannis de Zwaan* [Haarlem: De Erven F. Bohn, 1953], 52–65). In Ehrman's recent popular book *Misquoting Jesus: The Story behind Who Changed the Bible and Why* (San Francisco: HarperSanFrancisco, 2005), he seems to suggest that even the deity of Christ is in jeopardy by textual variants (114). In his conclusion, he argues that viable textual variants become the key factors in determining whether Jesus was angry (textual variant in Mark 1:41) or whether he was ignorant about the end of the world (textual variant in Matt. 24:36) (208). What Ehrman fails to do in the book, however, is to note that while these issues are a matter of emphasis, their reality is not questioned precisely because there are indisputable passages in which Jesus is said to be angry (e.g., Mark 3:5) or claims not to know when the end will come (Mark 13:32).

9. Some scholars (such as K. W. Clark; see previous note) attempt to show that a doctrine is suppressed in various texts, but this again does not demonstrate that a doctrine is eradicated, jeopardized, or affected. There are several textually debatable passages regarding the deity of Christ, for example, but the doctrine is not in jeopardy in the slightest because of them. This method is also what King James Version–only folks use to denounce modern translations: a manuscript here or there that does not mention the blood of Christ, that God is *our* Father, or the deity of Christ is often viewed as produced by heretics who conspired against the Word of God. The most notable text used by King James Version–only folks is the *Comma Johanneum*, 1 John 5:7–8, where the Trinity seems to be in view in the third edition of the *Textus Receptus*. The textual basis for the words here is as poor as it gets, and virtually all New Testament scholars recognize this. Further, no more than 1 percent of the members of the Evangelical Theological Society (the estimate is generous) embrace the *Comma Johanneum* as authentic. Yet *all* members of the ETS must annually sign their confession of the Trinity. If the removal of the *Comma Johanneum* is destructive of the Trinity, then how could all these members of ETS sign the confessional statement?

10. In each instance, the reading of the NA[27] text is listed first.

11. In this case, the Western text omits the phrase in order to eliminate the historical discrepancy. But few textual critics today, if any, would accept the Western reading as authentic.

12. See discussion in Bruce M. Metzger, *A Textual Commentary on the Greek New Testament*, 2nd rev. ed. (New York: United Bible Societies, 2005), 393–95.

13. See discussion in ibid., 636–37.

14. In *Misquoting Jesus* Bart Ehrman thinks he has produced other textual variants that are more significant, those that directly affect cardinal doctrines. For the most part, the passages he brings up were already mentioned in his 1993 scholarly volume, *The Orthodox Corruption of Scripture*. Yet several scholars criticized Ehrman in that tome for either being wrong in his textual choices or wrong in his interpretations.

15. So G. D. Kilpatrick, "Conjectural Emendation in the New Testament," in *New Testament Textual Criticism*, 349–60. More recently, J. K. Elliott, Kilpatrick's student, has indeed allowed for conjecture in Mark 1:1, marking a new departure for rigorous eclectics.

16. To be sure, evangelicals within one camp are sometimes prone to accuse those in another of not being able to hold to inerrancy. This is particularly true of those in the majority text camp—i.e., they tend to accuse other evangelicals of embracing an errant text (see James A. Borland, "Re-examining New Testament Textual-Critical Principles and Practices Used to Negate Inerrancy," *Journal of the Evangelical Theological Society* 25 [1982]: 499–506). Occasionally, even outside the majority text camp one finds an evangelical who claims, "If you don't hold to this textual variant, the Bible is no longer inerrant." Most notably Gordon Fee has argued this in his New International commentary on 1 Corinthians, claiming that if 14:34–35 is authentic, then the apostle Paul is caught in a contradiction: "Of even greater difficulty is the fact that these verses stand in obvious contradiction to 11:2–16" (Gordon D. Fee, *The First Epistle to the Corinthians*, NICNT [Grand Rapids: Eerdmans, 1987], 702). But most evangelicals—indeed, most New Testament scholars—have not been persuaded by Fee's arguments against the authenticity of these verses, and most see little problem harmonizing this text with chapter 11.

17. To be sure, Old Testament textual criticism is a different animal in that conjecture must be applied in some places. Nevertheless, the third condition is still not met, leaving the agnostic argument without merit.

18. A few manuscripts, especially of the Western variety, delete the offensive words in Mark 2:26. But this illustrates my larger point: evangelicals do not tend to run to the text-critical solutions to difficult problems for inerrancy if the text-critical solutions are not on other grounds particularly compelling.

Chapter 44 Why All the Translations?

1. Paul D. Wegner, *The Journey from Texts to Translations: The Origin and Development of the Bible* (Grand Rapids: Baker Academic, 1999), 281–82.

2. Bruce Metzger, *The Bible in Translation: Ancient and Modern Versions* (Grand Rapids: Baker Academic, 2001), 59.

3. Wegner, *The Journey from Texts to Translations*, 289.

4. Ibid., 307.

5. Metzger, *The Bible in Translation*, 175.

6. Leland Ryken, *Choosing a Bible: Understanding Bible Translation Differences* (Wheaton: Crossway, 2005), 13–18.

Chapter 45 Archaeology and the Bible

1. See Suetonius *Claudius* 25.4.

Chapter 47 The New Testament Canon

1. For the full story, consult Paul D. Wegner, *The Journey from Texts to Translations*.

2. A work that deals more with this question of order than most do is William R. Farmer and Denis M. Farkasfalvy, *The Formation of the New Testament Canon* (New York: Paulist, 1983).

3. For the historical developments and factors involved, see especially F. F. Bruce, *The Canon of Scripture* (Downers Grove, IL: InterVarsity, 1988), 117–269. A fourth criterion was certainly the witness of the Holy Spirit, but because of the more subjective nature of this criterion, competing claims of reliance on the Spirit yielding contradictory conclusions have always required more objective criteria by which to test them.

4. For a complete presentation of the known lists of books for inclusion or exclusion from the New Testament in the early centuries of Christian history, see Lee M. McDonald and James A. Sanders, eds., *The Canon Debate* (Peabody, MA: Hendrickson, 2002), 591–97.

Chapter 48 What Should We Think About the Coptic *Gospel of Thomas*?

1. Elaine Pagels, *Beyond Belief: The Secret Gospel of Thomas* (New York: Vintage, 2003).

2. All quotations come from James M. Robinson, ed., *The Nag Hammadi Library in English*, rev. ed. (San Francisco: HarperSanFrancisco, 1997).

3. Nicholas Perrin, *Thomas and Tatian* (Atlanta: Society of Biblical Literature, 2002).

4. See especially Michael Fieger, *Das Thomasevangelium* (Münster: Aschendorff, 1991). See also Christopher Tuckett, "Thomas and the Synoptics," *Novum Testamentum* 30 (1988): 132–57; and Darrell L. Bock, *The Missing Gospels: Unearthing the Truth Behind Alternative Christianities* (Nashville: Thomas Nelson, 2006).

Chapter 49 What Should We Think About the *Gospel of Peter*?

1. Eusebius of Caesarea *Ecclesiastical History* 6.12.3–6.

2. Origen *Commentary on Matthew* 10.17.

3. Paul A. Mirecki, "Gospel of Peter," in *The Anchor Biblė Dictionary*, ed. David N. Freedman (New York: Doubleday, 1992), 5:278–81, esp. 280.

4. Robert H. Gundry, *Matthew: A Commentary on His Handbook for a Mixed Church Under Persecution*, 2nd ed. (Grand Rapids: Eerdmans, 1994), 584.

5. John P. Meier, *The Roots of the Problem and the Person*, vol. 1 of *A Marginal Jew: Rethinking the Historical Jesus* (New Haven: Yale University Press, 1991), 117.

6. For a more detailed discussion, see Charles L. Quarles, "The Gospel of Peter: Does It Contain a Pre-canonical Resurrection Narrative?" in *The Resurrection of Jesus: John Dominic Crossan and N. T. Wright in Dialogue*, ed. Robert Stewart (Minneapolis: Fortress, 2005), 106–20.

Chapter 50 What Should We Think About the *Gospel of Judas*?

1. Coptic is the language of Egypt which, after Alexander's fourth-century-BC conquest of the Middle East, came to adopt the Greek alphabet (along with a few additional letters). The Nag Hammadi books are also written in Coptic.

2. The convoluted and fascinating history of the codex, now called Codex Tchacos, is narrated by Herb Krosney in his richly documented and insightful book *The Lost Gospel: The Quest for the Gospel of Judas Iscariot* (Washington, DC: The National Geographic Society, 2006). The story is also featured in Andrew Cockburn, "The Judas Gospel," *National Geographic* 209, no. 9 (May 2006): 78–95.

3. Rodolphe Kasser, Marvin Meyer, and Gregor Wurst, eds. and trans., *The Gospel of Judas*, with additional commentary by Bart D. Ehrman (Washington, DC: The National Geographic Society, 2006). The English translation and photographs of the Coptic text are available on National Geographic's website.

4. The translations are based on Kasser, Meyer, and Wurst, *The Gospel of Judas*.

5. Irenaeus *Against Heresies* 1.31.1. Translation adapted from Alexander Roberts and James Donaldson, eds., *The Ante-Nicene Fathers*, 10 vols. (Edinburgh: T&T Clark, 1898; repr. Grand Rapids: Eerdmans, 1989), 1:358.

6. On this interesting hypothesis, see C. B. Smith II, *No Longer Jews: The Search for Gnostic Origins* (Peabody, MA: Hendrickson, 2004).

7. I need to offer a correction to what otherwise I think is a fine piece of journalism. In "The Judas Gospel," Andrew Cockburn summarizes my assessment of the *Gospel of Judas* in these words: "This tale is meaningless fiction" (91). No, it is not meaningless fiction; far from it. The *Gospel of Judas* is loaded with meaning, especially for second-century mystics and Gnostics, who understood the world and mission of Jesus in very different terms.

8. L. Painchaud, "À Propos de la (re)découverte de l'*Évangile de Judas*," *Laval théologique et philosophique* 62 (2006): 553–68; B. A. Pearson, "Judas Iscariot among the Gnostics: What the Gospel of Judas *Really* Says," *Biblical Archaeology Review* 34, no. 3 (2008): 52–57; J. D. Turner, "The Place of the *Gospel of Judas* in Sethian Tradition," in M. Scopello, ed., *The Gospel of Judas in Context* (Leiden: Brill, 2008).

9. A. D. DeConick, *The Thirteenth Apostle: What the Gospel of Judas Really Says* (New York: T&T Clark, 2007).

Contributors

David Beck has been teaching philosophy for over thirty years at Liberty University, where he has also directed graduate studies since 1989. His principal research and writing interests have included the arguments for God's existence, especially the Cosmological Argument, and the nature of Christian university and worldview integration. He holds the PhD in philosophy from Boston University, where his dissertation was on the relationship between philosophy and theology in process philosophy. He also teaches regularly at Tyndale Theological Seminary in Amsterdam, the Greek Bible College in Athens, and at Southern Evangelical Seminary. Dr. Beck is a member of the American Philosophical Association, the Society of Christian Philosophers, and the Evangelical Philosophical Association.

Craig L. Blomberg is distinguished professor of New Testament at Denver Seminary in Littleton, Colorado. He holds the PhD from the University of Aberdeen, Scotland. Craig is the author of twelve books and has coauthored or coedited seven more, along with dozens of journal articles and chapters in multi-author works. His books include three on the historical reliability and interpretation of the Gospels (one specializing on John); two on interpreting and preaching the parables; three commentaries (on Matthew, 1 Corinthians, and James); a textbook on Jesus and the Gospels and another on Acts through Revelation; and two books on material possessions in the Bible.

Darrell Bock is research professor of New Testament studies, Dallas Theological Seminary. He is the author of several books, including commentaries on Mark, Luke, and Acts. He has done advisory work with several translations and is an editor-at-large for *Christianity Today*. He has served as a resource on Christianity and culture on many national television programs.

Raymond G. Bohlin is president of Probe Ministries (http://www.probe.org). He is a graduate of the University of Illinois (BS, zoology), North Texas State University (MS, population genetics), and the University of Texas at Dallas (MS, PhD, molecular biology). He is the coauthor of *The Natural Limits to Biological Change* and *Basic Questions on Genetics, Stem Cell Research and Cloning* (from the Center for Bioethics and Human Dignity), served as general editor of *Creation, Evolution and Modern Science*, and has published several journal and magazine articles. Dr. Bohlin is a fellow of the Discovery Institute's Center for Science and Culture.

Walter Bradley, formerly professor and head of the Department of Mechanical Engineering at Texas A&M University, is distinguished professor of engineering at Baylor University. He received his PhD in material science from the University of Texas at Austin. In addition to publishing over one hundred and fifty technical articles in refereed journals and conference proceedings on material science and engineering, he has coauthored several seminal works on the origin of life, including an article in *Debating Design: From Darwin to DNA* (edited by William Dembski and Michael Ruse) and the book *The Mystery of Life's Origin.*

Denny Burk is the dean of Boyce College and associate professor of New Testament at the Southern Baptist Theological Seminary in Louisville, Kentucky. He is the author of the book *Articular Infinitives in the Greek of the New Testament* and a contributor to *Mounce's Complete Expository Dictionary of Old and New Testament Words*. He is a fellow of the Institute for Biblical Research and holds memberships in the Society of Biblical Literature and the Evangelical Theological Society. Dr. Burk's website is http://www.dennyburk.com.

L. Russ Bush III (PhD, Southwestern Baptist Theological Seminary) was a noted philosopher, Christian apologist, and widely published author. He was the distinguished professor of philosophy of religion at Southeastern Baptist Theological Seminary. His book *Baptists and the Bible*, coauthored with Tom Nettles, is considered by many to have been foundational in the conservative resurgence of the Southern Baptist Convention during the 1980s. He was a humble man who was loved by thousands of students who sat under his instruction. In January 2008, Professor Bush died following a two-year battle with cancer.

Paul Copan (PhD, Marquette University) is professor and Pledger Family Chair of Philosophy and Ethics at Palm Beach Atlantic University. He is author of *True for You, But Not for Me*, *That's Just Your Interpretation*, *How Do You Know You're Not Wrong?*, *When God Goes to Starbucks: A Guide to Everyday Apologetics*, and *Loving Wisdom: Christian Philosophy of Religion*. He has coedited three books on the historical Jesus and three other books on the philosophy of religion in addition to books in Christian apologetics. He is the current president of the Evangelical Philosophical Society. He and his wife Jacqueline live with their five children in West Palm Beach, Florida.

Tal Davis is the interfaith coordinator at the North American Mission Board of the Southern Baptist Convention and has more than thirty years of experience in the field of interfaith studies. He is a graduate of Florida State University and Southwestern Baptist Theological Seminary, and has a DMin degree from New Orleans Baptist Theological Seminary, where he focused his research on the effects of cult involvement on families. Tal was a contributing writer to *Mormonism Unmasked*, by R. Philip Roberts with Tal Davis and Sandra Tanner, *Faith Discipleship: FAITH Reaching Out to Cults*, *Faith Discipleship: FAITH Reaching Out to World Religions*, and *Meeting the World: Ministering Cross-Culturally*. He served as interfaith consultant for two documentary videos and has written extensively for various publications.

William A. Dembski holds doctorates in mathematics (University of Chicago) and in philosophy (University of Illinois at Chicago). He is research professor in philosophy at Southwestern Baptist Theological Seminary in Fort Worth, Texas, and senior fellow with Discovery Institute's Center for Science and Culture. He has authored and edited more than twenty books, including the first book on intelligent design to be published with a major university press, *The Design Inference*. He lectures around the globe on intelligent design and has appeared on numerous radio and television programs, including ABC's *Nightline* and Jon Stewart's *The Daily Show*.

Craig A. Evans is the Payzant Distinguished Professor of New Testament at Acadia Divinity College in Nova Scotia, Canada. He is the author and editor of more than fifty books, including *Jesus and His Contemporaries*, *Fabricating Jesus: How Modern Scholars Distort the Gospels*, and, with N. T. Wright, *Jesus, the Final Days*. Professor Evans has lectured at Cambridge, Durham, Oxford, Yale, and other universities, colleges, and seminaries around the world. He has also appeared in a number of television documentaries.

Joe W. Francis is a professor of biology at the Master's College, where he teaches and supervises an undergraduate research program in microbiology, invertebrate biology, and cellular immunology. He also serves as an adjunct professor with Liberty University's distance learning program. He has developed and taught several online courses in the biological sciences. Dr. Francis has published numerous articles in the area of cellular immunology and theoretical microbiology. He is a member of the American Association for the Advancement of Science and an editor of the Occasional Papers of the BSG. He is also a board member of the BSG (A Creation Biology Study Group).

Guillermo Gonzalez is associate professor of physics at Grove City College. He received his PhD in astronomy from the University of Washington in 1993, and he has done postdoctoral work at the University of Texas at Austin and the University of Washington. He is the author of over sixty peer-reviewed scientific papers. In 2004 he coauthored, with Jay W. Richards, *The Privileged Planet: How Our Place in the Cosmos Is Designed for Discovery*. His most recent book, with D. Scott Birney and David Oesper, is the second edition of the undergraduate textbook *Observational Astronomy*.

Bill Gordon serves as research consultant for the People Group/Interfaith Evangelism Team of the North American Mission Board. He received a ThD in systematic theology from New Orleans Baptist Theological Seminary in 1987. He is a contributor to *Faith Discipleship: FAITH Reaching Out to Cults* and *Faith Discipleship: FAITH Reaching Out to World Religions*. He is a member of the Evangelical Theological Society.

Bruce L. Gordon is senior fellow at the Seattle-based Discovery Institute, where he is research director of Discovery Institute's Center for Science and Culture. He is an historian and philosopher of physics who earned his PhD at Northwestern University, as well as degrees in applied mathematics from the University of Calgary and in systematic theology from Westminster Theological Seminary. Dr. Gordon's scholarly work focuses on interpretive questions at the intersection of quantum theory, cosmology, analytic metaphysics, and philosophical theology, along with fine-tuning issues in physics and biology. He coedited an anthology titled *The Nature of Nature: Examining the Role of Naturalism in Science*. He is currently working on a series of articles that will lead to a book relating quantum physics to theistic metaphysics.

Gary R. Habermas (PhD, Michigan State University) is the distinguished research professor and chair of the Department of Philosophy and Theology at Liberty University. He has published thirty-six books (eighteen on the subject of Jesus's resurrection), most recently *Did the Resurrection Happen?* with Antony Flew and David Baggett. He has also published more than sixty chapters or articles in other books, plus more than one hundred articles in journals and other periodicals. During the past ten years or so, he has been a visiting or adjunct professor, teaching dozens of courses at fifteen different graduate schools and seminaries in the U.S. and abroad. See his website at http://www.garyhabermas.com.

Phillip E. Johnson is the Jefferson Peyser Emeritus Professor of Law at the University of California at Berkeley. Professor Johnson is a well-known speaker and writer on the philosophical significance of Darwinism. His books on this topic include *Darwin on Trial*, *Reason in the Balance*, *Defeating Darwinism by Opening Minds*, *The Wedge of Truth*, and *Asking the Right Questions*.

He taught law for over thirty years at the University of California at Berkeley. He entered the evolution controversy because he found the books defending Darwinism dogmatic and unconvincing. Professor Johnson is an advisor to Discovery Institute's Center for Science and Culture.

Robert Kaita is a physicist with Princeton University's Plasma Physics Laboratory, where he heads a major facility for fusion energy research. He has supervised the research of almost two dozen graduate students in the program in plasma physics in Princeton's Department of Astrophysical Sciences. His work has been presented in lectures around the world, and recorded in nearly three hundred publications. Dr. Kaita is a member of the American Association for the Advancement of Science, a fellow of the American Physical Society, and a past president of the Princeton Chapter of Sigma Xi, the scientific research society.

Michael Newton Keas is professor emeritus at the University of Memphis. He has twice served as president of the Association for the Rhetoric of Science. Professor Keas earned a PhD in the history of science in 1992 from the University of Oklahoma. He experienced some of the last historic moments behind the Berlin Wall as a Fulbright scholar in East Germany. He has contributed articles to several scholarly anthologies and journals. As a senior fellow of Discovery Institute, he coauthors high school and college science curriculum. He also leads workshops for science teachers on how to teach about controversial subjects such as Darwinism.

Andreas J. Köstenberger is professor of New Testament and biblical theology and director of PhD studies at Southeastern Baptist Theological Seminary in Wake Forest, North Carolina. He is also the founder and president of Biblical Foundations®, a ministry dedicated to helping restore the biblical foundations for the home, the church, and society (http://www.biblicalfoundations.org). Dr. Köstenberger is the author, editor, or translator of over twenty books, including *God, Marriage, and Family*; *The Cradle, the Cross, and the Crown*; *Salvation to the Ends of the Earth*; *Encountering John*; *Women in the Church*; and *The Heresy of Orthodoxy*. He also serves as the editor of the *Journal of the Evangelical Theological Society* and is married to Dr. Margaret Elizabeth Köstenberger, author of *Jesus and the Feminists*.

Michael R. Licona received his PhD in New Testament Studies from the University of Pretoria, which he completed "with distinction." His dissertation on the historicity of the resurrection of Jesus received the highest academic mark. He is the apologetics coordinator at the North American Mission Board. He is the author of *Paul Meets Muhammad* and the award-winning *The Case for the Resurrection of Jesus*, coauthored with Gary Habermas. Licona was one of the scholars interviewed by Lee Strobel in *The Case for the Real Jesus*. He has appeared on numerous radio and television interviews and has lectured on more than forty college campuses.

Bruce A. Little received his PhD in philosophy of religion from Southeastern Baptist Theological Seminary in Wake Forest, North Carolina, and a DMin from Columbia Biblical Seminary. He is professor of philosophy at Southeastern Baptist Theological Seminary, where he also serves as the director of the L. Russ Bush Center for Faith and Culture. Since 1995 he has lectured in numerous state and national universities in Eastern Europe, spoken at academic conferences, and conducted workshops on apologetics. In addition, he has coauthored four books with Russian philosophers from the Tavrichesky National University in Simferopol, Ukraine. He is a regular speaker at the European Leadership Forum, which meets annually in Eger, Hungary, and is a guest lecturer at seminaries in Nigeria, Malaysia, and Austria. He has published in academic journals, is the author of a recent book titled *A Creation-Order Theodicy: God and Gratuitous Evil*, and is the editor of a forthcoming book on the life and work of Francis Schaeffer.

Paul L. Maier is the Russell H. Seibert Professor of Ancient History at Western Michigan University and a widely published author of both scholarly and popular works. His novels include two historical documentaries, *Pontius Pilate* and *The Flames of Rome*, as well as a theological thriller that became a number one national bestseller in religious fiction, *A Skeleton in God's Closet*. A sequel, *More Than a Skeleton*, appeared in 2003. His nonfiction works include *In the Fullness of Time*, a book that correlates secular evidence from the ancient world impinging on Jesus and early Christianity; *Josephus—The Essential Works*, a new translation of and commentary on the writings of the first-century Jewish historian Josephus; and *Eusebius—The Church History*, a similar book on one of the first Christian historians. More than five million Maier books are now in print in twenty languages, as well as over two hundred and fifty scholarly articles and reviews in professional journals. Dr. Maier lectures widely, appears frequently in national radio, television, and newspaper interviews, and has received numerous awards. He has also penned four children's books and produced three four-hour video series dealing with Jesus, Paul, and the early church.

Robert J. Marks II is distinguished professor of engineering and graduate director in the Department of Engineering at Baylor University. He is fellow of both the Institute of Electrical and Electronics Engineers (IEEE) and the Optical Society of America. Professor Marks has received the IEEE Centennial Medal and has served as distinguished lecturer for the IEEE Neural Networks Society and the IEEE Computational Intelligence Society. Dr.

Marks served as the first president of the IEEE Neural Networks Council (now a society). He has over three hundred publications, and eight of his papers have been reproduced in volumes of collections of outstanding papers. He has three U.S. patents in the field of artificial neural networks and signal processing.

John McRay is professor emeritus of New Testament and archaeology at Wheaton College in Wheaton, Illinois. He taught at four colleges during his academic career from 1956–2002—Harding University, Lipscomb University, Middle Tennessee State University, and Wheaton College. He worked on archaeological excavations at Sepphoris and Herodium in Israel and supervised excavating teams for several years in Caesarea Maritima, Israel. He has lectured widely on archaeology and the Bible at various colleges, universities, professional society meetings, and churches in the United States, Greece, Israel, Australia, Russia, and Germany. He has published numerous articles in professional journals, and his books include *Archaeology and the New Testament*, *Paul: His Life and Teaching*, and *Bible Archaeology*.

Angus Menuge is professor of philosophy at Concordia University, Wisconsin, and associate director of the Cranach Institute (http://www.cranach.org). His BA is from the University of Warwick, and his PhD is from the University of Wisconsin, Madison. Menuge has written articles on intelligent design, philosophy of mind, and apologetics. He is the author of *Agents Under Fire: Materialism and the Rationality of Science* and the editor of *C. S. Lewis: Lightbearer in the Shadowlands*, *Christ and Culture in Dialogue*, and *Reading God's World: The Vocation of Scientist*.

Nancy Pearcey is the Francis A. Schaeffer scholar at the World Journalism Institute. Having studied under Schaeffer at L'Abri in the 1970s, Pearcey earned an MA from Covenant Theological Seminary, followed by further graduate work in philosophy at the Institute for Christian Studies in Toronto. She has authored or contributed to several works, including *The Soul of Science* and *How Now Shall We Live?* Her book *Total Truth: Liberating Christianity from Its Cultural Captivity* won an Award of Merit in the Christianity Today 2005 Book Awards and the ECPA Gold Medallion Award for best book of the year in the Christianity and Society category.

Charles L. Quarles is the vice president for Integration of Faith and Learning and the William Peterson Carver Jr. Research Professor of New Testament and Greek at Louisiana College. He received the PhD in New Testament studies from Mid-America Baptist Theological Seminary and was recognized as "Outstanding Research Professor of the Year" at New Orleans Baptist Theological Seminary. Professor Quarles is published in both academic and popular literature, where he has written, coauthored, and edited numerous books and articles.

Jay W. Richards is research fellow and director of institutional relations at the Acton Institute in Grand Rapids, Michigan. He has a PhD in philosophy and theology from Princeton Theological Seminary, where he was formerly a teaching fellow. He is the author of many scholarly and popular articles, as well as several books. His most recent books are *The Untamed God: A Philosophical Exploration of Divine Perfection, Immutability, and Simplicity* and *The Privileged Planet: How Our Place in the Cosmos Is Designed for Discovery*, with Guillermo Gonzalez.

Edward Sisson earned a BS in architecture from MIT in 1977 and graduated magna cum laude from the Georgetown University Law Center in 1991. In 2004 he contributed an essay to the book *Uncommon Dissent: Intellectuals Who Find Darwinism Unconvincing*. In 2005 he participated on the side of the "Darwin doubters" in the Kansas "evolution hearings," spoke at the "Uncommon Dissent" conference in Greenville, South Carolina, and appeared at Boston University's "Great Debate" on the intelligent design controversy. As legal counsel he represented Professor Caroline Crocker to defend her right to teach college science students some of the flaws in Darwinism. In 2006 he became executive director of a new nonprofit, the Iowa Institute, whose aim is to carry out scientific experiments relevant to the theory of intelligent design.

Richard Spencer is professor of electrical and computer engineering at the University of California, Davis, and an active consultant to the electronics industry. He received his PhD from Stanford University in 1987. Prior to graduate school he was employed as a circuit designer in Silicon Valley. He has published numerous technical papers and is the main author of an electronics textbook. He is a Fellow of the Institute of Electrical and Electronics Engineers and has won the undergraduate teaching award in his department four times.

Daniel B. Wallace (PhD, Dallas Theological Seminary) is professor of New Testament Studies at Dallas Theological Seminary and executive director of the Center for the Study of New Testament Manuscripts (http://www.csntm.org). He has done postdoctoral studies at Tyndale House, Cambridge; the Institut für neutestamentliche Textforschung, Münster, Germany; and Universität Tübingen, Germany. He is a member of *Studiorum Novi Testamenti Societas*, Institute for Biblical Research, Society of Biblical Literature, and the Evangelical Theological Society. He has published dozens of articles in academic theological journals and has authored, coauthored, edited, or contributed to more than twenty books, including *Greek Grammar beyond* *the Basics: An Exegetical Syntax of the New Testament*; *Granville Sharp's Canon and Its Kin: Semantics and Significance*; *Reinventing Jesus: How Contemporary Skeptics Miss the Real Jesus and Mislead Popular Culture* (coauthor); *Dethroning Jesus: Exposing Popular Culture's Quest to Unseat the Biblical Christ* (coauthor); *Who's Afraid of the Holy Spirit?* (coeditor, author); *New English Translation/Novum Testamentum Graece*; and *Revisiting the Corruption of the New Testament: Manuscript, Patristic, and Apocryphal Evidence*, volume 1 of *Text and Canon of the New Testament* (editor, coauthor).

Bill Wilberforce is the pen name of a young molecular biologist. He has been trained at one of the world's top institutions and is beginning to publish his own research ideas in leading journals.

Ben Witherington III is Amos Professor of New Testament for Doctoral Studies at Asbury Theological Seminary, Wilmore, Kentucky, and is on the doctoral faculty of St. Mary's College, St. Andrews University, Scotland. Dr. Witherington is an ordained elder in the United Methodist Church and a John Wesley Fellow. His most recent books are the highly acclaimed archaeological novels, titled *The Lazarus Effect* and *Roman Numerals*, as well as his textbook *New Testament Rhetoric*. The first volume of his major study on New Testament theology and ethics, *The Indelible Image*, was released in 2009.

Richard Weikart is professor of history at California State University, Stanislaus. He is the author of four books, including most recently *Hitler's Ethic: The Nazi Pursuit of Evolutionary Progress* and *From Darwin to Hitler: Evolutionary Ethics, Eugenics, and Racism in Germany*. With an extensive background in modern German and modern European intellectual history, he has published numerous scholarly articles in journals such as *Isis*, *Journal of the History of Ideas*, *German Studies Review*, *History of European Ideas*, *European Legacy*, and *Fides et Historia*. His research has focused on social Darwinism, evolutionary ethics, and eugenics, especially as practiced in Germany.

Jonathan Witt, senior fellow with Discovery Institute, is coauthor with Benjamin Wiker of *A Meaningful World: How the Arts and Sciences Reveal the Genius of Nature*. Witt earned his PhD in English from the University of Kansas, where his dissertation on aesthetics received highest academic honors and led to articles in *Literature and Theology* and *The Princeton Theological Review*. Witt's essays have appeared in such places as *The Seattle Times*, *The Kansas City Star*, *Touchstone*, and *Philosophia Christi*. His book in progress, *Darwin vs. Shakespeare*, explores how Darwinists employ widely discredited and contradictory aesthetic presuppositions in their arguments against a creator.

David Wood is a teaching fellow in philosophy at Fordham University, where his doctoral work focused on the problem of evil. A former atheist, he became a Christian after investigating the historical evidence for Jesus's resurrection. He is codirector of Acts 17 Apologetics Ministries, has been in more than two dozen public debates with Muslims and atheists, and is a member of the Society of Christian Philosophers. David lives in the Bronx, New York, with his wife, Marie, and their sons, Lucian, Blaise, and Reid.